Agricultural Policy and the Environment

The Political Economy Forum

Sponsored by the Political Economy Research Center (PERC)
Series Editor: Terry L. Anderson

Agricultural Policy and the Environment

Edited by
Roger E. Meiners and Bruce Yandle

ROWMAN & LITTLEFIELD PUBLISHERS, INC.
Lanham • Boulder • New York • Oxford

ROWMAN & LITTLEFIELD PUBLISHERS, INC.

Published in the United States of America
by Rowman & Littlefield Publishers, Inc.
A Member of the Rowman & Littlefield Publishing Group
4501 Forbes Boulevard, Ste. 200, Lanham, MD 20706
www.rowmanlittlefield.com

PO Box 317
Oxford
OX2 9RU, UK

British Library Cataloguing in Publication Information Available

Library of Congress Cataloging-in-Publication Data

Agricultural policy and the environment / Edited by Roger E. Meiners
and Bruce Yandle.
    p. cm.
    ISBN 0-7425-2768-9 (cloth : alk. paper) — ISBN 0-7425-2769-7 (pbk. :
alk. paper)
    1. Agriculture and state—United States. 2. Environmental
policy—United States. 3. Agriculture—Environmental aspects—United
States. I. Meiners, Roger E. II. Yandle, Bruce.
    HD1761 .A62185 2003
    363.7'00973—dc21
                        2002015225

Printed in the United States of America

♾™ The paper used in this publication meets the minimum requirements of
American National Standard for Information Sciences—Permanence of Paper
for Printed Library Materials, ANSI/NISO Z39.48-1992.

Contents

Tables and Figures

TABLES

FIGURES

Acknowledgments

The Political Economy Forum is always a bigger undertaking than the final volume reflects. First, it takes a commitment from idea entrepreneurs who invest in PERC people and programs. Though the funding helps compensate the authors and forum participants, it is never sufficient to cover their full opportunity costs. Therefore we are appreciative of the authors' willingness to donate some of their time and energy to these papers, and their patience with our editing; we hope the reader reaps a return from it. Forum participants take their compensation in the form of intellectual stimulation, but given the quality of the discussion, we know that they gave more than they received.

Also, we can never thank the PERC staff enough. Colleen Lane and Monica Guenther always make sure the forum comes off without a hitch, and Michelle Johnson and Sheila Spain see to the details of communication and word processing. Dianna Rienhart is central to the final preparation of papers and publication of the edited collection. She maintains the quality standard for all PERC volumes. Dianna's name should be listed on the cover as the third editor.

On behalf of all who participated, we, the editors, express our deeply felt appreciation for being able to conduct research and hold an intellectual discussion in an open and unconstrained setting. This, after all, is a rare and cherished human experience.

Introduction

Agricultural Policy and the Environment: Problems, Prospects, and Prosperity

Roger E. Meiners and Bruce Yandle

U.S. agriculture entered the twenty-first century as the international leader in food productivity. As Bruce Beattie (2001) has shown, the real prices of most agricultural commodities have been falling for years and crop output per acre increased by 249 percent between 1945 and 1992; a growing U.S. population has been fed and huge amounts of food have been exported from about the same amount of cropland as was cultivated in 1945. Indeed, in 1999, the United States produced 40 percent of the world's corn, and U.S. corn exports accounted for 67 percent of the world market. Shipments of wheat represented 27.7 percent of the world total (U.S. Department of Commerce [DOC] 2000, 675). All this translates into the fact that Americans spend a diminishing share of income for food. In 1949, roughly 22 percent of income was spent for food (U.S. Department of Agriculture [USDA] 2001, 18). Fifty years later, the share was less than 12 percent. And the food was better!

Although the food production record is astounding, there is another side to the story. U.S. farmers received direct government subsidies and payments that rose to $17.6 billion in 1999 (DOC, 2000, 669). Those giving their political support for the subsidies sometimes pointed to the importance of maintaining the family farm. In the end, the various taxpayer-funded income-support programs were enjoyed more by "corporate agriculture" than family farmers. Yet no matter who enjoyed the political redistribution, the subsidies altered crop production incentives, affected the amount and quality of land cultivated, and in other ways, generated a different environmental footprint.

What about the environment? All things considered, the superficial record is impressive as well. Farmers, ranchers, and forestland owners manage two-thirds of the nation's land (USDA 2001, 72) and are the primary stewards of much of the nation's soil, air, and water. Tillers and managers of land were perhaps the first environmentalists. That is the case not because they were trained to be sensitive about the environment but because they, more than any other people, have long-run incentives to protect and enhance nature's productive features. They own a slice of it. The better its condition, the higher their incomes. Whether it be protecting wildlife habitat, avoiding nutrient runoff from fields, or minimizing the use of agricultural chemicals, left to their own devices, farmers, ranchers, and forestland managers have powerful incentives to do the right thing (Yandle 1997). But government production subsidies and programs can lead to "swampbusting" and excessive use of chemicals (see Meiners and Morriss 2001). These environmental perversions then lead to other government programs developed for the purpose of offsetting some of the ill effects of earlier government programs that usually continue apace.

When all is said and done, the environmental report card for U.S. agriculture has a number of high grades. According to the USDA, wetland losses from agriculture have fallen from almost 593,000 acres per year during 1954–74 to fewer than 27,000 acres per year in 1992–97. Wildlife habitat has been restored and improved by government purchase of easements to sensitive land. In 1999, U.S. taxpayers provided $1.5 billion for the federal Conservation Reserve Program, which funded these contracts (2001, 75). And whereas output has increased, the use of agricultural chemicals has fallen dramatically (Gardner 2001, 89–90).

Most of what is right with U.S. agriculture results from the operation of world market forces. Landowners and managers in agriculture have had little choice but to conserve valuable resources and to minimize the waste of topsoil, chemicals, irrigation systems, and water. At the same time, much of what is wrong in agriculture results from an absence of market forces or their distortion by government programs.

Meeting the environmental challenges of twenty-first-century agriculture calls for a reassessment of incentives and a rigorous application of free market environmentalism to the sector's pressing problems. And what might some of those challenges be? High on the list are the control of chemicals, wildlife habitat, wetlands, and nonpoint source pollution. There is also a growing demand for water and the matter of water for irrigation and how it will be allocated. There is talk about energy scarcity and encouragement of ethanol production. Then there is climate change and agriculture's role in providing carbon offsets. There is international trade and the effect of subsidy programs and monetary policy on production decisions and their environmental impact. To cap it all off, there is the precautionary principle and how its application could lead to an expansion of environmental regulations affecting agriculture.

It was for the purpose of discussing these and other issues that PERC assembled a small group of scholars at Pray, Montana, in December 2001. Over the course of three days, the discussion generated far more potential content than found in the original papers. Seeking to capture the essence of the conference discussion, each of the authors reworked their papers and included new material. The edited papers are now chapters in this book. The chapters can be read selectively or the book, from cover to cover.

The book begins with a chapter by Peter J. Hill discussing a fundamental question about agriculture that is both economic and philosophical. Are farms and farmers special in some fundamental way? Put differently, why have people across time and space always provided special treatment to the problems and challenges of agriculture? Because these problems may at times pale in comparison to those in other sectors and industries, the answer to the question must rest on some deeply held social value. Peter J. Hill, grandson of a Montana homesteader, explores this challenging question and offers a theoretical model that provides insight. His chapter lays a foundation for the remaining papers in the volume.

The next two chapters have a common theme. They each relate to institutional approaches taken to address property rights problems. Roger E. Meiners and Andrew P. Morriss examine a range of problems that relate to farm animal diseases and then discuss the significantly different approaches taken at different times and places to limit these diseases. By focusing on transaction costs, legal constraints chosen for unrelated reasons, and special interest favor seeking, Meiners and Morriss provide a framework that helps to explain our present institutional choice. In doing so, they travel some distance in explaining why, in some cases, only limited property rights and market approaches have come to dominate.

In a companion to the Meiners-Morriss chapter, Bruce Yandle and Sean Blacklocke address one critical current issue—managing the environmental stress that comes with large-scale integrated animal production. Their chapter is also about institutional choice and the associated opportunities for special interest favor seeking. In their detailed review of proposed federal rules for regulating confined animal feeding operations, Yandle and Blacklocke consider competing explanations that range from the rules being the result of a search for efficient solutions to the problem to the rules being a basis for cartelizing and making the industry more profitable. In the end, the authors leave the suggestion that environmental regulation must be cartel-forming if it is to be politically successful.

Nationwide, agriculture accounts for nearly 80 percent of all water consumption, and three-fourths of all cropland west of the Mississippi is irrigated (USDA 2001, 76). Water is a critical agricultural input, but the same can be said about water and growing cities and expanding industry. The competition for water supply has reached a critical stage in many western U.S. locations, critical because of institutional rigidities that limit the transfer of water through water markets. The chapter by B. Delworth Gardner addresses this property rights problem by examining experiences in Utah. His discussion of Utah regulation and case law lays a foundation for identifying the legal bottlenecks that limit gains from trade in water rights. Having found the critical elements, Gardner then comes forward with recommended changes that will assist the birth of markets and the expansion of gains from trade.

U.S. farmers produce about 1 percent of the nation's gross domestic product (GDP), but use some 2 percent of the energy consumed in the United States (USDA 2001, 77). But, whereas the sector is an energy user, it is argued that agriculture could evolve to become one of the nation's more effective energy producers. Alcohol produced from corn can be blended with gasoline to provide a major new source of renewable energy—one that is cleaner and protective of the nation's search for energy independence. At least this is how support is often stated when the federal government's ethanol program is promoted. Gary Libecap tells the ethanol story, one of a host of the federal regulatory schemes in agriculture often publicly justified for reasons other than more money for producers. Libecap explains ethanol's regulatory history and summarizes the fundamental studies that have been conducted to assess the economic and energy efficiency of ethanol production. He considers key arguments offered to support the program and concludes that although subsidized ethanol production may be good for the corn economy, it is not good for the environment, for the energy sector, or for the economy in general.

In the next chapter, Indur M. Goklany takes up the precautionary principle, one of the touchstones of modern environmentalism, explains it, develops a framework for evaluating it, and then applies the framework to technology change in agriculture. Citing impressive data on world agricultural production and the green revolution that enabled some countries to feed themselves for the first time in decades, Goklany asks if application of the precautionary principle would have limited the reduction in hunger and the spread of agricultural production worldwide. He provides a five-part criterion for assessing technology change and the precautionary principle that includes immediate needs, uncertainty, relative costs, adaptation, and irreversibility. Goklany reviews the data, applies the principle, and concludes that a definition of the precautionary principle that can be applied in practice will not impose undesirable social costs.

If every major producer of agricultural commodities worldwide allowed market forces to determine production choices, Adam Smith's prediction of specialization and division of labor would lead to the production of more food and fiber at a lower cost with lower environmental impact. This statement forms the basis of the next chapter by Alex Avery and Dennis Avery. Taking a global perspective, the authors explain how free markets in international agricultural commodity trade might work. Barring major catastrophe, world population will rise by 50 percent in the next fifty years. As rising incomes allow poor people to eat more and better food, world agriculture output must double over that time. The authors explain that various government programs, at home and abroad, that are asserted to protect the environment, may not only not provide local environmental benefits but, by reducing agricultural output, also impose costs on some of the world's most sensitive environment by forcing less productive land into agricultural use. Trade liberalization offers the best hope to feed people at the lowest cost economically and environmentally. Peter J. Hill's chapter sheds light on the political difficulties faced in bringing about such changes.

Since the highly publicized 1997 Kyoto conference on climate change, political expressions of concern about global warming have maintained a regular place in international news. More often than not, the relative positions of the industrial nations of the world are evaluated on the basis of how much carbon dioxide they produce and emit to the upper atmosphere. High production of carbon dioxide leads to a low evaluation of the producer-nation's moral commitment to environmental protection. The United States, as world leader in carbon dioxide production, is often castigated for being the top carbon producer. But few scholars have rigorously questioned the matter of net emissions, instead of gross emissions. If a nation both emits and sequesters (captures) carbon, shouldn't the concern be with the net result? This question motivates the research reported in the chapter by Joshua A. Utt, W. Walker Hunter, and Robert E. McCormick. Representing the results of a massive gathering of data, the chapter builds and reports findings for a series of statistical models that reach to measure net U.S. carbon dioxide emissions. Although it is impossible to track each and every component of sequestration, the major elements reported in the chapter leave a sheen of optimism on the matter of net emissions. Utt, Walker, and McCormick make it clear that there is a distinct possibility that, in spite of producing huge amounts of carbon emissions, because of offsetting carbon capture, the United States may be one of the cleaner members of the world carbon emission club.

If it were possible to follow on a daily basis the development of environmental and other policies affecting U.S. agriculture, and to do so for thirty years, what conclusions would one draw? Perhaps no one is better equipped to fulfill this assumption and answer the question than John K. Hosemann, the author of the book's final chapter. As chief economist for the American Farm Bureau Federation, who, as such, confronted and addressed every major policy issue that faced the agricultural sector, Hosemann considers how environmental and other politically determined constraints affected U.S. agricultural production. Indeed, Hosemann's analysis shows how U.S. macroeconomic forces that affected agriculture may have had a deeper effect on agricultural policy, and thereby the environment, than did federal environmental policy aimed at agricultural issues. This somewhat surprising conclusion underlines the important linkage between free market agriculture and environmental enhancement. When markets are allowed to communicate all costs and to do so continually, then farmers and landowners will take environmental consequences into account as they make production decisions.

In the final analysis, the world of agriculture and its environmental interaction is too complex to be subjected to top-down, detailed, political decision making. Wealth-enhancing environmental improvement will continue to be made in agriculture as property rights are defined and protected and real costs and benefits are communicated through unregulated markets.

REFERENCES

Beattie, Bruce. 2001. The Disappearance of Agricultural Land: Fact or Fiction? In *Agriculture and the Environment*, ed. Terry L. Anderson and Bruce Yandle. Stanford, CA: Hoover Institution Press, 1–23.

Gardner, B. Delworth. 2001. Some Issues Surrounding Land and Chemical Use in Agriculture. In *Agriculture and the Environment*, ed. Terry L. Anderson and Bruce Yandle. Stanford, CA: Hoover Institution Press, 81–103.

Meiners, Roger E., and Andrew P. Morriss. 2001. Pesticides and Property Rights. *PERC Policy Series*, PS-22. Bozeman, MT: PERC.

U.S. Department of Agriculture. 2001. *Food and Agriculture Policy: Taking Stock for a New Century*. Washington, DC.

U.S. Department of Commerce. 2000. *Statistical Abstract of the United States, 2000*. Washington, DC.

Yandle, Bruce. 1997. *Common Sense and Common Law for the Environment*. Lanham, MD: Rowman & Littlefield Publishers, Inc.

1

What's So Special about the Farm?

Peter J. Hill

The chapters in this volume deal with competing claims by those in agriculture and environmentalists. Both groups of claimants value resources such as land, open space, water, and air and believe that their values should determine the highest and best use for these resources.

In a market economy, competing claims are resolved through bids and offers between owners and potential owners. Individuals who believe they have a better use for a resource can gain control of that resource by offering to pay more than its opportunity cost. But politics has replaced markets and property rights as the allocation mechanism for many resources that have value for the production of both agricultural and environmental amenities. The noted historian, Arthur Schlesinger (1984, 8), captures well the relationship between government and agriculture: "No sector of the economy has received more systematic government attention, more technical assistance, more subsidy for research and development, more public investment in education, and energy supply, and in infrastructure, more price stabilization, more export promotion, more credit and mortgage relief."

In other words, property rights have been dramatically attenuated in the agricultural sector. Prior to large-scale government intervention in agriculture, the social coordination mechanism of private property rights and prices, underlain with the rule of law and the common law, did a reasonably good job of accounting for costs and benefits. This system was also dynamic in that it accommodated changing demands for agricultural inputs and environmental amenities. It would have allowed land and other resources to be bid away from agriculture as environmental amenities became more valuable, would have done an adequate job of accounting for most spillovers, and would have accommodated an increased recognition of certain environmental costs of agricultural production.

Instead the regime of regulations and subsidies has allocated inputs to inefficient uses and has encouraged overproduction at the cost of environmental quality. Most important, government intervention in agriculture has allowed people to ignore the opportunity cost of their actions, and in many cases those opportunity costs have occurred in the form of environmental degradation. Sugar subsidies have resulted in pollution of the Everglades (Thurman 1995, 33–38), the Bureau of Reclamation has dammed many free-flowing streams, and its rules plus state laws have kept water from moving to higher-valued uses outside of agriculture (Anderson and Snyder 1997; Gardner 2003), government spraying of DDT caused significant environmental damage because of its exemption from common lawsuits (Meiners and Morriss 2001), and crop support programs have encouraged excessive use of pesticides and fertilizers (Thurman 1995, 15–29). And now that political allocation governs many of the resources used in agriculture, environmentalists have learned to compete in that arena (Avery and Avery 2003; Goklany 2003; Hosemann 2003; Yandle and Blacklocke 2003). They also have been able to secure control of certain resources without paying the true opportunity costs. The overall result of political control has been the misallocation of resources and a process characterized by acrimonious debate and conflict.

Why has this occurred? What are the basic forces that have made agriculture a prime target of government intervention, and why has social engineering been more dominant in this sector than in any other part of the economy? The rest of this chapter takes up that issue.

BOOTLEGGERS, BAPTISTS, AND PUBLIC CHOICE

Bruce Yandle's bootleggers and Baptists model of regulation (Yandle 1983, 1999) and insights from public choice theory are useful tools for understanding government intervention in the economy. Yandle argues that intervention on the behalf of particular interest groups is most likely to happen when two groups can coalesce; rent seekers who can gain from a particular regulation or subsidy joining with those who believe there is a moral case for the intervention. In Yandle's explanation of dry laws or Sunday closing regulations in communities, the Baptists argue for the laws because they want to reduce alcohol consumption and the bootleggers favor the rules because the closing of legal establishments increases their business. The bootleggers and Baptists model has powerful explanatory power in terms of agriculture because the ideal of the yeoman farmer is an important part of American ideology, and farmers, because of their relatively poor income position, have been able to make plausible arguments in the public square as to why they should receive special favors from government.

However, unlike the original bootleggers and Baptists explanation, in this case, there is not an identifiable group like the Baptists who take the moral high ground and reap benefits from government intervention. Instead, the general appeal of agriculture as a superior way of life has provided the same moral cover for rent-seeking farmers that the Baptists did for bootleggers.

The public choice paradigm argues that political choices are heavily influenced by the incidence of the benefits and costs facing decision makers. Hence, an understanding of who is making decisions about the role of government in agriculture, who benefits, and who bears the costs of those decisions is useful in understanding policy outcomes.

Agricultural Fundamentalists—The Baptists of Farming

Agriculture has long had an exalted place in the thinking of the American public (Douglas 1969), and this agrarianism or agricultural fundamentalism is summarized by the agricultural economist Don Paarlberg (1964, 3).

1. Farmers are good citizens, and a high percentage of our population should be on farms.
2. Farming is not only a business but also a way of life.
3. Farming should be a family enterprise.
4. The land should be owned by the man who tills it.
5. It is good to make two blades of grass grow where only one grew before.
6. Anyone who wants to farm should be free to do so.
7. A farmer should be his own boss.

The Physiocrats, a group of eighteenth-century French philosophers, were the intellectual progenitors of agricultural fundamentalism. Led by François Quesnay, the Physiocrats believed that all wealth comes from the physical production of goods and the soil is the ultimate source of that production. Therefore, agriculture is the most deserving of moral approval and is the most important sector of any economy (Landreth and Colander 1994, 50–57). Thomas Jefferson (Foner 1944, 161–62) was the leading advocate of the Physiocrat position in early America.

Those who labor in the earth are the chosen people of God, if ever He had a chosen people, whose breasts He has made His peculiar deposit for substantial and genuine virtue. It is the focus in which he keeps alive that sacred fire, which otherwise might escape from the face of the earth. Corruption of morals in the mass cultivators is a phenomenon of which no age nor nation has furnished an example. . . . Generally speaking the proportion which the aggregate of the other classes of citizens bears in any State to that of its husbandman, is the proportion of its unsound to its healthy parts, and is a good enough barometer whereby to measure its degree of corruption. While we have land to labor then; let us never wish to see our citizens occupied at a work bench, or twirling a distaff. . . . For the general operations of manufacture, let our work-shops remain in Europe. It is better to carry provisions and materials to work-men there, than to bring them to the provisions and materials, and with them their manners and principles. . . . The mobs of great cities add just so much to the support of pure government, as sores do to the strength of human body.

The Jeffersonian ideal of the family farm and the moral superiority of agriculture as a way of life has been a continual part of American culture and ideology. No other sector of the economy has been able to marshal moral arguments in its defense to the extent that agriculture has. The claim that farming is a way of life rather than simply another sector of the economy resonates with most citizens, and politicians of every stripe laud the family farm as something worth preserving.[1]

Agricultural Bootleggers

For the past 200 years, agriculture has struggled relative to other sectors of the economy and that struggle has strengthened the case for government intervention on its behalf. The low incomes have been the result of the market process signaling to farmers that many of them need to move out of that sector, and many have responded to that signal. In 1800, 75 percent of the labor force was in agriculture (Margo 2000, 213). Today it is less than 2 percent (Myers and Kent 2001, 48). Up until 1910, the agricultural labor force grew in absolute terms, although it was falling as a percentage of the total labor force. After that point, there was actually a physical movement of people out of agriculture, an even more painful adjustment (North, Anderson, and Hill 1983, 28). The mechanism of communication has been low incomes for farmers relative to other parts of the economy. Table 1.1 reports the percentage of the labor force in agriculture, the percentage of national income generated by agriculture, and the ratio of two to one. This gives an estimate of the relative income of agriculture to the other sectors of the economy.[2] The average of column 3 is 57.1 percent. Don Paarlberg reaches a similar conclusion using a slightly different data set. "As conventionally computed, per capita farm incomes run a little over half the nonfarm level, rising during wars and inflation, falling during depression, otherwise showing no marked trend" (1964, 57).

Recent work by Caselli and Coleman (2001) also shows agriculture wages lagging behind wages in the rest of the economy, although their data do show an improvement over time. They find agricultural wages as a percentage of nonfarm wages rising from 20 percent in 1880 to 69 percent in 1980. The measure of farm incomes used by the U.S. Department of Agriculture (USDA) in-

Table 1.1. Agricultural Employment and Income

Years	Agricultural Labor Force	Agricultural Income	Relative Income Position
1869	48.3	22.2	46.0
1879	48.9	19.0	38.9
1889	41.6	14.2	34.1
1899	36.9	18.2	49.3
1909	30.4	19.4	63.8
1919	24.6	18.9	76.8
1929–37	21.3	9.3	43.7
1937–44	15.1	8.4	55.6
1944–48	11.8	9.2	78.0
1948–53	10.6	7.2	67.9
1953–57	8.8	4.8	54.5
1957–60	7.6	4.3	56.5
1960–69	5.8	3.6	62.1
1970	4.3	3.1	72.1

Notes: Agricultural labor force refers to people engaged in agricultural production as a percentage of total employment. Agricultural income is represented as a percentage of national income. Relative income position is the ratio of agricultural income to agricultural labor force × 100. Agricultural income data for 1899 based on 1899–1903; for 1909, based on 1907–10; for 1919, based on 1918–20.
Source: Calculated from U.S. Department of Commerce (1975, Series F251).

dicates that farm income was below nonfarm income through most of the twentieth century, but it also shows relative agricultural incomes rising after 1960 and reaching parity with nonfarm income by the early 1970s, although trending downward since then (Olmstead and Rhode 2000, fig. 12.5).

There are two basic reasons for the need to transfer resources out of agriculture. First, rapid technological change has increased labor productivity and the supply of agricultural commodities. The increase in total factor productivity in U.S. agriculture from 1800 to 1900 was approximately 0.5 percent per year, which meant the same quantity of labor, land, and capital produced about two-thirds more output in 1900 than it produced in 1800 (Atack, Bateman, and Parker 2000a, 258).

Labor productivity in agriculture also has grown rapidly in both the nineteenth and twentieth centuries. For instance, from 1840–60 to 1900–10, the man-hours necessary to produce a bushel of wheat fell from 2.96 to 0.71 (Atack, Bateman, and Parker 2000a, 261). Between 1910–14 and 1980–84 the labor required to produce 100 bushels of wheat fell from 106 to 7 hours. Over that same time the labor necessary for producing 100 pounds of milk declined from 3.8 hours to 12 minutes (Olmstead and Rhode 2000, table 12.2).

The low income elasticity for agricultural products is the second important contributing factor to the need for moving resources out of agriculture.[3] Per capita incomes have risen dramatically in the United States over the past

200 years, but the increase in demand for agricultural products has been less than proportionate. As Americans have become wealthier, they have demanded such things as larger houses, better medical care, and more transportation services, but not much more food or fiber. It is true that there have been significant increases in the demand for prepared foods and for restaurant meals, but those demands do not translate into larger incomes for farmers.

Public Choice

But how have farmers been able to parlay the sympathies of the general population into government interventions on their behalf? Agricultural economists have tested several hypotheses with regard to the agricultural support programs, and the public choice explanation fits the data best (Gardner 1987; Gardner 1995; Pasour 1990). The principle of concentrated benefits and diffuse costs is particularly powerful in that most of the agricultural programs are targeted to a very small group while the costs are borne by taxpayers and consumers as a whole. Therefore Congress or a regulatory agency will feel great pressure from those who stand to benefit from a subsidy while those bearing the cost will find it difficult to organize and hardly worth their time to oppose the subsidy. As an example, in 1988, sugar quotas raised the incomes of each farm operator producing sugar beets or sugar cane by $76,000 (Gardner 1995, 152). In this case, the costs were not only diffused but hidden because they came through higher prices for consumers rather than through direct payments from the government's budget. Sugar is not atypical; for almost all agricultural commodities, well-informed organized producer groups provide a powerful lobbying force.

The self-interest of those in government provides a further public choice explanation of agricultural programs. The USDA was created in 1862 and moved to cabinet status in 1889. It has grown to more than 100,000 employees (U.S. Census Bureau 2001, 319), and the self-interest of the department bureaucrats is on the side of program maintenance and expansion.

Farmers, through their producer organizations, have been able to make common cause with politicians who find agrarian fundamentalism useful rhetoric. Saving the family farm, maintaining a way of life, and other moral exhortations provide ready cover for rent seekers who wish to gain from government intervention.[4]

Because agricultural employment has declined rapidly in the twentieth century, one might expect the political clout of the sector to have decreased rapidly also. But the costs of organizing producer groups have fallen with the decrease in numbers of farmers, and the increase in farm size has meant that benefits of agricultural programs are even more concentrated than in the past. Also many congressional districts and several states still have substantial agricultural populations whose representatives and senators have a strong interest in maintaining subsidies.

GOVERNMENT AND AGRICULTURE—A BRIEF HISTORY

Farm discontent is nothing new in American history. In 1786, Daniel Shay led an armed insurrection in Massachusetts in an effort to prevent bankruptcy proceedings against farmers who were struggling because of a drop in agricultural prices. He agitated for legislation that would release farmers from their mortgage contracts. But many of the leading political theorists of the time saw such a move as a serious threat to contract enforcement and private property rights. Shay's Rebellion was one of the forces that led the authors of the Constitution, adopted just three years later, to specifically include protection of property rights in that document. The desire to create stability of expectations and to avoid the rewriting of contracts was a strong motive behind the creation of the new constitutional contract.[5] James Madison, in *Federalist Paper* 62, said:

> Great injury results from unstable government. The want of confidence in the public councils damps every useful undertaking, the success and profit of which may depend on a continuance of existing arrangements. What prudent merchant will hazard his fortunes in any new branch of commerce when he knows not but that his plans may be rendered unlawful before they can be executed? What farmer or manufacturer will lay himself out for the encouragement given to any particular cultivation or establishment, when he can have no assurance that his preparatory labors and advances will not render him a victim to an inconstant government? (Hamilton, Madison, and Jay [1788] 1961, 381–82)

Several parts of the Constitution sanctified property rights and made either private or public violation of those rights less likely. Three sections were of particular importance: (1) Article 1, Section 10, the contract clause, which provides: "No State shall . . . pass any Bill of Attainder, ex post facto law or law impairing the Obligation of Contracts"; (2) Article 1, Section 8, the commerce clause, which gives Congress the power "to regulate Commerce with foreign nations and among the several States and with the Indian Tribes"; and (3) the Fifth Amendment (and later the Fourteenth), which provides that no person shall "be deprived of life, liberty, or property without due process of law."

Each of these clauses was an important contributor to the sanctity of property rights. Freedom of contract was an important part of constitutional interpretation throughout the nineteenth century, although two bankruptcy cases in 1819 (*Sturges v. Crowninshield*) and 1827 (*Ogden v. Saunders*) began the gradual erosion of contractual freedom. Nevertheless, the courts generally assumed holders of property rights were free to contract with other owners and that government interference with contracts should only be allowed in a limited number of areas.

Although the commerce clause would seem to have given substantial power to the federal government, most efforts to intervene in markets came at the state level. For the first 100 years of constitutional interpretation, the commerce clause was primarily used to negate attempts by the various state legislatures to interfere with commerce through restrictions on entry into a particular industry or through direct subsidies. For instance, in 1824 the Court ruled that New York could not grant monopoly privileges to a steamship company (*Gibbons v. Ogden*) and in 1827 it denied Maryland the right to impose taxes on goods imported from other states (*Brown v. Maryland*).

The due process amendments provided specific protection against government takings of private property. The requirement to pay compensation placed a budget constraint on government attempts to take property, and, after the Civil War, several court cases strengthened due process by interpreting the original amendments as granting substantive as well as procedural protection to property rights (Anderson and Hill 1980, 65). In these cases the Supreme Court ruled that following procedural rules such as paying just compensation didn't necessarily mean property rights were adequately protected.

As a result of these clauses and their interpretation, for the first seventy-five years of the nineteenth century, the Constitution provided a formidable bulwark against rent seeking.[6] This applied to agriculture as well as to the rest of the economy. Tariffs and subsidies for transportation were the two exceptions, and in this area agriculture had some success in securing favors. But the basic tenor of constitutional interpretation was such that agricultural rent seekers were largely unsuccessful in securing government intervention on their behalf.

The one area in which the Jeffersonian ideal of the yeoman farmer did play a substantial role was in land policy. The federal government was responsible for disposing of a huge amount of land, and it continually wrestled with the best way to accomplish this. Until the Progressive era after the turn of the century, there was a general commitment to transferring the land to private hands, but the ideal of the family farm and the dislike of speculation in land created inefficiencies in land policy.[7]

The desire to create small family farms culminated in the 1862 Homestead Act, which limited a claim to 160 acres and required five years of continuous residence before ownership was complete. This was followed in 1873 by the Timber Culture Act, which encouraged the planting of trees; the Desert Land Act of 1877, which made landownership contingent upon irrigation; the 1878

Timber and Stone Act; the 1909 Enlarged Homestead Act, which expanded the minimum homestead size to 320 acres; and the 1916 Stock Raising Homestead Act, which further expanded the maximum size to 640 acres.

Each of these acts was predicated upon the belief that family farms were the desirable mode of operation for agriculture and that large-scale landownership was inimical to a healthy society. However, as settlers moved across the West, the homestead acts proved unsuitable for the arid regions, and enormous hardship and suffering resulted (Anderson and Hill 2000). Failure rates were high in many localities, reaching 80 percent of original entries in parts of Montana (Fletcher 1960, 146). Another historian found that by 1922 about 88 percent of those who homesteaded in Montana between 1909 and 1918 had given up and left (Fulton 1982, 66). Gates (1968, 505) records that of the 88,687 homestead entries in Wyoming filed between 1910 and 1934, less than half were completed.

Agriculture received further support from the 1862 Morrill Act, which created the land-grant public universities with the goal of underwriting "such branches of learning as are related to agriculture and the mechanic arts" (quoted in Atack, Bateman, and Parker 2000b, 302). However, more significant pressure for government intervention came after the Civil War. Although farm incomes have been continually lower than nonfarm incomes throughout U.S. history, during the last quarter of the nineteenth century, hardship in agriculture seemed to loom particularly large. The farmers felt that their terms of trade had gone against them, believing that agricultural prices had fallen more than the prices of their inputs. They also decried what they perceived as monopolistic practices of railroads and grain elevators, and they believed that credit markets were structured so that they were being taken advantage of by lenders.[8]

The most important changes in rent-seeking opportunities during this period came through constitutional interpretation. The agrarian unrest during the post–Civil War period led several midwestern states to pass laws aimed at regulating the rates of railroads and other large-scale enterprises, in particular grain elevators. The constitutionality of such price regulation on the behalf of agriculture came before the U.S. Supreme Court in *Munn v. Illinois* in 1877. Such blatant attempts to regulate prices would have been declared unconstitutional under earlier court interpretations, but in this case, the court broke new ground. Chief Justice Morrison Waite spoke for the majority.

> Property does become clothed with a public interest when used in a manner to make it a public consequence, and affect the community at large. When, therefore, one devotes his property to a use in which the public has an interest, he, in effect, grants to the public an interest in that use and must submit to be controlled by the public for the common good to the extent of the interest he has thus created. (*Munn v. Illinois* 1877, 126)

The public interest doctrine, as it came to be known, provided substantial reason for agriculture to increase its rent-seeking activities. It argued repeatedly that railroads, elevators, and farm mortgage companies were using their property in the public interest and hence were subject to public regulation. This doctrine was expanded further with the development of the concept of "reasonable regulation" in other court cases that followed. The ambiguity inherent in the doctrine of reasonable regulation became apparent in the next few decades. In *Muller v. Oregon* in 1908 the Supreme Court ruled on a 1903 Oregon statute that regulated the working hours of women. Lawyer Louis Brandeis, in arguing for the constitutionality of the law, submitted a famous brief (the Brandeis brief) that consisted of only two pages of constitutional arguments and more than 100 pages detailing social conditions.

And finally, in *McCray v. United States* in 1904, the court upheld a statute that regulated margarine production by placing a tax of ten cents per pound on artificially colored margarine, but only one-quarter cent per pound on the uncolored product. Previously, taxes had to have a direct relationship to raising revenue but after *McCray v. United States,* another avenue for agricultural rent seeking through discriminatory taxation became available.

Other rent-seeking opportunities came in the U.S. Congress. In 1902, the Bureau of Reclamation was established with the agricultural creed of "making two blades of grass grow where one had grown before" the major impetus. Although the original legislation supposedly set up a means for self-financing for bureau projects,[9] repayment provisions were either extended or forgiven during times of agricultural hardship and the implicit subsidy for the projects grew large indeed. The subsidy implicit in the repayments required from farmers varied from 48 percent to 96 percent of the original costs (Wahl 1989, table 2.1).

Other interventions in the first part of the twentieth century came through the Smith-Lever Act of 1914, which created the agricultural extension service, and the Federal Farm Board of 1929, which was designed to raise the prices of agricultural output through government purchase and storage (Pasour 1990, 71–72).

With the onset of the Great Depression, the agricultural sector had even more reason to go to the government to seek favors. All parts of the economy suffered economic hardship, but the effect on the farm sector was more severe than on other sectors (Higgs 1987, 162). Output prices for agriculture declined by more than 50 percent, whereas input prices fell only slightly. The collapse of the banking sector was particularly hard on small towns and the rural economy, and many farms were faced with foreclosure. Between 1932 and 1934, twenty-five states passed legislation delaying farm foreclosures (Alston 1983). Robert Higgs (1987, 160) has argued that "the institutional revolution of the 1930s depended crucially on the existence of national emergency, a condition that was partly real, partly contrived, enormously exploited for political purposes."

Higgs's thesis certainly comports with the evidence for agriculture. The dramatic fall in farm incomes and the loss of property by thousands of farmers gave agriculture good reason to demand government intervention. Economic conditions had not been propitious for farmers in the 1920s, and five bills were introduced from 1924 to 1928 to institute the McNary-Haugen Two-Price Plan, which sought to use export subsidies to raise farm product prices above world prices (Pasour 1990, 71). None of these bills passed, but with the deepening crisis of the 1930s, Congress responded. The Agricultural Adjustment Act of 1933 gave broad powers to the secretary of agriculture to intervene in agricultural markets through production and acreage controls and the regulation of buyers and sellers of agricultural products. Restrictive marketing agreements were exempt from antitrust laws as well.

In 1936, the Supreme Court declared most of the provisions of the Agricultural Adjustment Act unconstitutional, but the limitations on government intervention in the agricultural economy were short lived. Later in 1936, Congress passed the Soil Conservation and Domestic Allotment Act and, in 1938, a new Agricultural Adjustment Act. This legislation withstood court review and reinstituted almost all the provisions of the original 1933 Agricultural Adjustment Act.

Earlier, in 1934, the Supreme Court had decided another case that had important implications for freedom of contract and private property rights. In *Nebbia v. New York,* the Court upheld a New York law giving a state milk control board the power to set maximum and minimum prices for milk. The Court used the public interest doctrine of *Munn v. Illinois* in deciding the case. Justice Roberts, writing for the majority said, "There is no closed class or category of businesses affected with the public interest." Therefore, "a state is free to adopt whatever economic policy may reasonably be deemed to promote the public welfare." The decision was five to four, and the dissenting minority foresaw well the rent-seeking possibilities created by the approval of the statute: "If here we have an emergency sufficient to empower the Legislature to fix sales prices, then whenever there is too much or too little of an essential thing—whether of milk or grain or pork or coal or shoes or clothes—constitutional provisions may be declared inoperative" (as quoted in Siegan 1980, 140–41).

Thus by the end of the Great Depression the agricultural sector was well able to use its special interest power in conjunction with the Jeffersonian ideal of the yeoman farmer to secure government subsidies, regulations, and tariffs in its favor. Many of the interventions had negative effects for the environment because of increased agricultural output due to subsidies, the damming of rivers through the Bureau of Reclamation projects, and the overuse of inputs because of acreage limitations. However, there was still one more shoe waiting to drop.

There were still significant limitations on agriculture activity when it had a direct impact on the property rights of others. Common law doctrines of nuisance and trespass served to protect both farmers and nonfarmers from direct expropriation of portions of their property rights through agricultural activities. Throughout the nineteenth century, common law had taken on more of an instrumental purpose in that it was seen as appropriate to use it to further economic development (Horwitz 1977). However, common law remained an important bulwark for protection of both farmers and the environment through protection of individual property rights. For instance, in 1899, a federal court ruled that the city of Texarkana, Arkansas, was liable for damages; it also issued an injunction against the city because its sewage polluted the farm of the Carmichaels, a family that lived just across the state line in Texas. Likewise, in 1913 a New York court ruled that Whalen, a farmer downstream from a new pulp mill could collect damages and that the mill had a year to end pollution or shut down (Meiners and Yandle 1998, 4–6).

After 1970, with the advent of the Environmental Protection Agency and the rise of environmental legislation, statute law came to trump common law. But statute law is much more amenable to special interest pleadings and rent-seeking efforts than is common law (Meiners and Morriss 2000). For example, many states have passed legislation that has exempted certain agricultural operations, in particular large hog farms, from common lawsuits (Yandle and Blacklocke 2003). Under the trespass and nuisance doctrines of common law, hog operations that cause air and water pollution would face liability for their actions.

The permitting process of both state and federal agencies has provided a shield for polluters because court rulings have held that once a permit is granted it may not be challenged on common law grounds (Meiners and Yandle 1998, 20). The regulatory process is both too stringent in some cases, in which actions that do not produce demonstrable harm are illegal, and too lenient in others, in which harmful actions are allowed, because once permits are granted, proof of invasion of another's property becomes irrelevant.

CONCLUSION

The conjunction of the Jeffersonian ethic of the moral superiority of farming with the low incomes necessary to move resources out of agriculture has given ample opportunity for government intervention in farming. The history of agriculture in the United States is a prime example of what can happen when special interest pleading is combined with moral approbation. Although the Constitution and its interpretations set clear limits on interference with property rights, those constitutional provisions gradually deteriorated. Over time, the state and federal governments gained the power to intervene in numerous ways in the agricultural economy. Common law doctrine was also replaced with statute law, which further gave power to rent seekers.

Most important, the interventions described in this paper have attenuated property rights. Such attenuation of rights has made it possible for politicians, farmers, and environmentalists to ignore the full opportunity costs of their actions. Instead of bidding for control of resources through the marketplace, interested individuals and groups must bid in the political arena. But resource control in that arena is tenuous at best. Resource rents, including the flow of income from commodity production and the amenity rents desired by environmentalists, are continually up for grabs. Under such a system competing claimants face an incentive structure that encourages them to attempt to have property rights redefined in their favor. And the threat of a redefinition that takes rights away from an existing holder means politicians can engage in an ongoing process of selling protection (McChesney 1997).

The desire to engage in social engineering, that is to promote social goals through a top-down approach, has lurked just below the surface throughout much of U.S. history. The past 125 years have seen the social engineering mind-set played out in agriculture. Building dams to make the desert bloom, supporting the prices of agricultural commodities, and giving special voice to farmers in the political arena have been deleterious to environmental quality.

As incomes have risen and science has discovered new relationships between human activity and ecological integrity, there has been an increased demand for environmental amenities. In a sense, agriculture has been its own worst enemy because now that property rights can be altered at will, the next wave will probably involve the taking of rights from farmers. Already such provisions as the Wetlands Conservation Act and the Endangered Species Act have served as vehicles for the destruction of farmers' rights. Pigouvian interventions are likely to dominate Coasean contracting (Yandle 1997), with negative effects for environmentalists as well as farmers.

Unfortunately, the desire to engage in social engineering that has driven much of the agricultural program is not likely to decline. For instance, the Campaign for Sustainable Agriculture, a group of 200 organizations supporting environmental agricultural policy change (Thurman 1995, 57), is likely to provide additional opportunities for the moral fervor of Jeffersonians and rent seekers of all stripes to achieve their goals. Sustainable agriculture is a messy concept on which there is little substantive agreement (Ruttan 1994, 3–18), but it offers both the normative appeal and the special interest advantages of the old agricultural programs. Further attenuation of property rights is likely to occur, and agriculture and the environment will continue to be at odds with each other.

NOTES

1. A March 9, 2002, search of the *Congressional Record* of the 2001–02 U.S. Congress for the term "family farm" finds it is used 202 times in congressional speeches or in legislation. A sampling of those 202 uses indicates that politicians use the term either to give moral weight to themselves, as in "I was raised on a family farm," or justify a wide range of legislation (everything from energy policy to tax reforms), in which the operative phrase is "to preserve the family farm."

2. Income for agriculture is the sum of employee compensation, proprietors' income, rental income, corporate profits, and net interest (U.S. Department of Commerce 1975, 222). Because the labor force data are people engaged in production, the ratio shown in table 1.1 is not a measure of relative returns to labor across sectors, but instead represents the total income per person engaged in agriculture. To the extent that some of the factors of production used in agriculture are owned by people not working in the sector, the ratio of column three is not a completely accurate representation of agricultural income relative to nonagricultural income.

3. Bunkers and Cochrane (1957, 217) estimate the income elasticity of demand as 0.279 for the on-farm component of food and 1.322 for the off-farm component.

4. All of this is not to say that there is no truth in the claims of agricultural fundamentalism. It may well be that farming does represent a morally superior way of life to alternative employments, but for the purposes of this paper, the interesting issue is how that claim has influenced government involvement in agriculture.

5. For a more specific discussion of the ideology underlying the Constitution, see Anderson and Hill (1980, 22–27).

6. See Siegan (2001) for a discussion of the protection provided property rights through decisions of the federal and state courts.

7. For a more complete discussion of these inefficiencies, see Anderson and Hill (1983).

8. Each of these complaints has been examined by economic historians and found to be wanting. For a discussion of the evidence, see North, Anderson, and Hill (1983, 127–33). Probably the greatest source of low and fluctuating incomes was the integration of a world market for grains and the commercialization of agriculture, both of which meant that farmers were more subject to the impersonal forces of the market than previously. Whatever the reasons, the farmers' perception was that they were doing very poorly during this period of time and consequently raised their voices in protest.

9. The first financing was to come through the sale of public lands in western states and because those revenues would have gone into the federal treasury, the general taxpayers were supporting all reclamation projects from the beginning.

REFERENCES

Alston, Lee J. 1983. Farm Foreclosures in the United States during the Interwar Period. *Journal of Economic History* 43(4): 885–903.

Anderson, Terry L., and Peter J. Hill. 1980. *The Birth of a Transfer Society*. Stanford, CA: Hoover Institution Press.

———. 1983. Privatizing the Commons: An Improvement? *Southern Economic Journal* 50(2): 438–50.

———. 2000. *The Not So Wild, Wild West: Property Rights Entrepreneurs on the Frontier.*

Anderson, Terry L., and Pamela S. Snyder. 1997. *Water Markets: Priming the Invisible Pump.* Washington, DC: Cato Institute.

Atack, Jeremy, Fred Bateman, and William N. Parker. 2000a. The Farm, the Farmer, and the Market. In *The Cambridge Economic History of the United States.* Vol. II, *The Long Nineteenth Century,* ed. Stanley L. Engerman and Robert E. Gallman. Cambridge, UK: Cambridge University Press, 245–84.

———. 2000b. Northern Agriculture and the Westward Movement. In *The Cambridge Economic History of the United States.* Vol. II, *The Long Nineteenth Century,* ed. Stanley L. Engerman and Robert E. Gallman. Cambridge, UK: Cambridge University Press, 285–328.

Avery, Alex, and Dennis Avery. 2003. High Yield Conservation: More Food and Environmental Quality through Intensive Agriculture. This volume.

Bunkers, E. W., and Willard W. Cochrane. 1957. On the Income Elasticity of Food Services. *Review of Economics and Statistics* 30: 210–17.

Caselli, Francesco, and Wilbur John Coleman II. 2001. The U.S. Structural Transformation and Regional Convergence: A Reinterpretation. *Journal of Political Economy* 109(3): 584–616.

Douglas, Louis H. 1969. *Agrarianism in American History.* Lexington, MA: D. C. Heath and Company.

Fletcher, Robert H. 1960. *Free Grass to Fences: The Montana Cattle Range Story.* New York: University Publishers, Inc.

Foner, Philip S., ed. 1944. *Basic Writings of Thomas Jefferson.* New York: Wiley Book Company.

Fulton, Dan. 1982. *Failure on the Plains: A Rancher's View of the Public Lands Problem.* Bozeman, MT: Big Sky Books, Montana State University.

Gardner, B. Delworth. 1995. *Plowing Ground in Washington: The Political Economy of U.S. Agriculture.* San Francisco: Pacific Research Institute for Public Policy.

———. 2003. Legal Impediments to Transferring Agricultural Water to Other Uses. This volume.

Gardner, Bruce L. 1987. *The Economics of Agricultural Policies.* New York: Macmillan Publishing Company.

Gates, Paul W. 1968. *History of Public Land Law Development.* Washington, DC: Public Land Law Review Commission.

Goklany, Indur M. 2003. Agricultural Technology and the Precautionary Principle. This volume.

Hamilton, Alexander, James Madison, and John Jay. 1788. *The Federalist Papers.* Reprint, New York: New American Library, 1961.

Higgs, Robert. 1987. *Crisis and Leviathan: Critical Episodes in the Growth of American Government.* New York: Oxford University Press.

Horwitz, Morton J. 1977. *The Transformation of American Law, 1780–1860.* Cambridge, MA: Harvard University Press.

Hosemann, John K. 2003. Agriculture and the Environment: A Thirty-Year Retrospective. This volume.

Landreth, Harry, and David C. Colander. 1994. *History of Economic Thought*. Boston: Houghton Mifflin.

Margo, Robert A. 2000. The Labor Force in the Nineteenth Century. In *The Cambridge Economic History of the United States*. Vol. II, *The Long Nineteenth Century*, ed. Stanley L. Engerman and Robert E. Gallman. Cambridge, UK: Cambridge University Press, 207–43.

McChesney, Fred S. 1997. *Money for Nothing: Politicians, Rent Extraction and Political Extortion*. Cambridge, MA: Harvard University Press.

Meiners, Roger E., and Andrew P. Morriss. 2000. *The Common Law and the Environment*. Lanham, MD: Rowman & Littlefield Publishers, Inc.

———. 2001. Pesticides and Property Rights. *PERC Policy Series*, PS–22. Bozeman, MT: PERC, May.

Meiners, Roger, and Bruce Yandle. 1998. The Common Law: How It Protects the Environment. *PERC Policy Series*, PS–13. Bozeman, MT: PERC, May.

Myers, Norman, and Jennifer Kent. 2001. *Perverse Subsidies: How Tax Dollars Can Undercut the Environment and the Economy*. Washington, DC: Island Press.

North, Douglass C., Terry L. Anderson, and Peter J. Hill. 1983. *Growth & Welfare in the American Past: A New Economic History*, 3rd ed. Englewood Cliffs, NJ: Prentice-Hall.

Olmstead, Alan L., and Paul W. Rhode. 2000. The Transformation of Northern Agriculture, 1910–1990. In *The Cambridge Economic History of the United States*. Vol. III, *The Twentieth Century*, ed. Stanley L. Engerman and Robert E. Gallman. Cambridge, UK: Cambridge University Press, 693–742.

Paarlberg, Don. 1964. *American Farm Policy: A Case Study of Centralized Decision-Making*. New York: John Wiley & Sons.

Pasour, E. C., Jr. 1990. *Agriculture and the State: Market Processes and Bureaucracy*. New York: Holmes & Meier Publishers, Inc.

Ruttan, Vernon W., ed. 1994. *Agriculture, Environment, and Health: Sustainable Development in the 21st Century*. Minneapolis: University of Minnesota Press.

Schlesinger, Arthur, Jr. 1984. The Political Galbraith. *Journal of Post-Keynesian Economics* 7(Fall): 7–17.

Siegan, Bernard H. 1980. *Economic Liberties and the Constitution*. Chicago: University of Chicago Press.

———. 2001. *Property Rights: From Magna Carta to the Fourteenth Amendment*. New Brunswick: Transaction Publishers.

Thurman, Walter N. 1995. *Assessing the Environmental Impact of Farm Policies*. Washington, DC: AEI Press.

U.S. Census Bureau. 2001. *Statistical Abstract of the United States*, 121st ed. Washington, DC.

U.S. Department of Commerce. 1975. *Historical Statistics of the United States, Colonial Times to 1970*. Bicentennial Edition, Series F251. Washington, DC: U.S. Census Bureau.

Wahl, Richard W. 1989. *Markets for Federal Water: Subsidies, Property Rights, and the Bureau of Reclamation*. Washington, DC: Resources for the Future.

Yandle, Bruce. 1983. Bootleggers and Baptists: The Education of a Regulatory Economist. *Regulation* May/June: 12–16.

———. 1997. *Common Sense and Common Law for the Environment.* Lanham, MD: Rowman & Littlefield Publishers, Inc.

———. 1999. Bootleggers and Baptists in Retrospect. *Regulation* 22(3): 5–7.

Yandle, Bruce, and Sean Blacklocke. 2003. Regulating Concentrated Animal Feeding Operations: Internalization or Cartelization? This volume.

CASES CITED

Brown v. Maryland, 12 Wheaton 419 (1827).
Gibbons v. Ogden, 9 Wheaton 1 (1824).
McCray v. United States, 195 U.S. 27 (1904).
Muller v. Oregon, 208 U.S. 113 (1908).
Munn v. Illinois, 94 U.S. 126 (1877).
Nebbia v. New York, 291 U.S. 502 (1934).
Ogden v. Saunders, 12 Wheaton 213 (1827).
Sturges v. Crowninshield, 4 Wheaton 122 (1819).

2

Agricultural Commons Problems and Responses: Sick Hogs at the Trough

Roger E. Meiners and Andrew P. Morriss

Over the centuries, as humans struggle to raise cattle and other domesticated animals, the spread of disease among livestock has been a major threat. Consider the following instances—spread out over many years and in different places—that illustrate the problem.

- Bison leaving Yellowstone National Park in search of food in the winter of 1996–97 are discovered to be carrying brucellosis, a deadly disease that also exists in cattle. Fearing infection of their herds, Montana ranchers bring pressure to bear on the state government. State employees are sent to shoot the bison as they leave the park.
- Ranchers in the Texas panhandle in the 1870s and 1880s confront problems in controlling rustling, improving their stock of cattle, and improving their rangeland. They purchase tracts of land, fence them, and make improvements in all three areas.
- Ranchers in Wyoming in 1885 struggle to control the disease glanders among their horses. The Wyoming Stock Growers Association sends a committee to inspect herds in which the disease is suspected to be present to ensure that control measures are taken.
- Large herds of domesticated animals are slaughtered in 2001 in England and other countries due to foot-and-mouth disease. Government authorities mandate the slaughter to arrest the spread of the highly infectious disease. Farmers are compensated for their losses.

All of these are examples of commons problems that are not uncommon in agriculture. Farmers and ranchers have used a variety of institutions to solve commons problems. What is different about each of the examples is the institution chosen to respond to the commons problem. The brucellosis and foot-and-mouth problems were solved by public sector solutions; the Texas ranchers solved their problems with private property rights; and the Wyoming ranchers solved their problem through nongovernmental collective action. Each of these institutions has advantages and disadvantages for agricultural producers and for society as a whole. In this chapter we survey some of the examples of private and public institutions used to resolve some of the commons problems in agriculture. Much as Bruce Yandle and Sean Blacklocke conclude in their chapter about the current issue of Concentrated Animal Feeding Operations (CAFOs), we conclude that a range of creative collective private solutions to commons problems was derailed more than a century ago, forcing agricultural decision makers into the more restrictive world of individual private or public solutions.

THE COMMONS IN AGRICULTURE

Garrett Hardin's (1968) classic statement of the commons problem used the example of the English medieval commons to frame the problem. Medieval peasants held a portion of a community's land in common for use as pasture. Hardin noted that without a mechanism for restricting access to the commons, rational peasants would overstock the commons, depleting the resource. Medieval peasants did not, in fact, persistently overstock the commons. Instead they developed a complex set of property rights tied to their other land holdings to allocate rights to the commons (Ridley 1996, 232). Thus, the classic commons problem, which could have produced ruin, was solved by the evolution of a system of functional private property rights.

The history of agriculture indicates a persistent need to address problems arising from the commons. Cattlemen running cows on the open range faced commons problems in preventing disease from spreading among their herds, improving the range, ensuring quality breeding stock, and preventing overstocking (Morriss 1998). Cattle drives of the nineteenth century were feared by many communities along their routes because the cattle might bring disease with them (Whitaker 1975, 59–62). Such problems still persist. Farmers fear that pests from their neighbors' fields and orchards will overrun their own crops (Morriss 1997, 138). Hunters fear that game ranches will introduce diseases into wild game stock (Geist 2000).

Such commons problems can be addressed through several basic organizational means. First, individual agricultural producers may take steps on their own to prevent problems. Second, farmers and ranchers may band together in private organizations to battle common pests and diseases. Third, farmers and ranchers may resort to public mechanisms to address common threats.

Although individuals choose among institutions with a variety of characteristics, we argue that transaction costs are central to determining which institutions thrive and which do not. Some commons problems are solved by privatizing the commons—that is, they are solved by replacing common property rights with individual property rights, as happened in the Texas panhandle. Some commons problems are solved by using voluntary groups to address them, as happened with the glanders control program in Wyoming. Individual action could not solve the problem because the disease did not respect private property boundaries. Cattlemen used a private organization to address the problem. Some commons problems are solved by reliance on state action—as with the Yellowstone bison and the British foot-and-mouth disease. The state offered the lowest-cost means of controlling diseased animals because it could compel action.

Each of these mechanisms has costs and benefits. Individual private action requires no investment in coordination mechanisms with others who face the same afflictions or benefits, but also offers little opportunity to share fixed costs or to avoid free riding by others. Private cooperation requires individuals to bear organizational and production costs, which can be significant, but avoids the public choice problems faced by public solutions. Public mechanisms eliminate free riding on the service provided, but are subject to the regulatory capture and subsidy schemes predicted by public choice theory.

Rather than considering the alternative institutional solutions possible when faced with a commons problem, as John Hosemann (2003) notes, the debate over agricultural policy tends to focus immediately on how to structure government interventions. Due to pervasive government involvement in agriculture for more than a century, we have become used to thinking of agricultural problems as things that justify a variety of public interventions.

Despite the heavy degree of government intervention, we know agriculture generally to be a highly competitive industry. Indeed, it is often used as a classic example of perfect competition in principles of economics. There are so many wheat farmers and so many wheat buyers that no one buyer or seller can affect wheat prices. The atomistic nature of the industry eliminates problems that are alleged to arise from small numbers, such as oligopoly, and is evidence of how well markets work with strong property rights in place. The prevalence of subsidy schemes and federal market orders in many agricultural markets means that the prices that emerge are not free market prices. Numerous public choice issues arise involving rent seeking

(McChesney 1997). Politicians cater to agricultural interests (Libecap 2003). Those in the industry come to rely on a system of government controls and subsidies that some producers rely on to survive and that others have come to believe are needed to survive.

Direct crop subsidies are generally easily identified as destructive of consumer welfare through the perverse incentives caused by price distortions. Our focus is not on intervention such as price supports, but on forms of intervention that draw fewer critiques. When commons problems exist, it has come to be accepted that government action is necessary.

For example, pest infestation appears to be an instance in which private action is unlikely to be successful. If insects blight a huge area, individual actions, such as farmers spraying their own fields, may not be as effective as large-scale spraying, which ensures that more insects are eliminated because bigger areas are sprayed. The practicality of such spraying is coupled with the need to reduce the problem of free riding. That is, some farmers might choose not to spray as long as their neighbors spray, so the nonsprayers may get most of the benefits of the spray without bearing the costs. Similarly, foot-and-mouth disease in cattle, in which the spread is quite rapid, or mad cow disease, in which the consequences to innocent purchasers of the product are severe, are also areas in which public action is presumed to be necessary to avoid catastrophic losses.

RANGES OF ORGANIZATIONAL CHOICE

A purpose of this chapter is to question the assumption of the need for government intervention to solve commons problems in agriculture. Intervention is often justified on the basis of organizational problems that are presumed to be insurmountable. Whereas there are significant transaction cost issues in the evolution of effective private solutions to real problems, it may also be that private organizational problems are used as polite justifications for federal subsidies. Public health and welfare has long been a catchall justification for myriad public sector programs that ultimately have little to do with that rationale. The possibility of collective private action may often be overlooked because of public programs that have evolved and eviscerate the need for voluntary action to help resolve problems.

The Role of Individual Action

Solutions to commons problems are most likely to evolve when there are well-defined property rights. In practice, these are most likely to exist when transaction costs are low relative to the gains from private action. Thus, for example, in the Texas panhandle in the 1870s and 1880s, privatization required merely the application of a well-established body of land law to public lands and the transfer of those lands to private ownership. Because the state of Texas was a willing seller, as it sought revenues from the sale of state land, and because the mechanism of private ownership of land was already well established in Texas, privatizing the panhandle area was straightforward. Once land was purchased, individuals could, and did, take steps to secure their property rights.

Privatization is more costly when new types of property rights must be developed to resolve the problem. Thus when protecting instream flows is necessary to preserve fish stocks in a river, but existing statutory water rights require use of the water and do not allow retention of rights where water is left instream, solving the fish problem requires amending the water rights statutes to provide for instream flow rights (Gardner 2003).

Privatization also works well when the commons problems can be contained within resources controlled by a single individual. Again, the problems of overgrazing and rustling in the Texas panhandle provide a clear example. By fencing their property, panhandle ranchers were able to control access and prevent overgrazing. By contrast, ranchers on the northern Great Plains could not control access because federal land policy prevented them from acquiring sufficient land for economically viable cattle operations (Morriss 1998, 2001).

The costs of privatization are higher, and so privatization is relatively less attractive when the commons problem cannot be contained within the boundaries of a single unit of property. Where many landowners' property sits atop a common aquifer, for example, a rush to exploit the water may develop because no one landowner can reap the benefits of conservation of the resource.

Private Collective Action

As James Buchanan has noted, a large amount of activity takes place in membership organizations or clubs (Buchanan 1965). When we classify goods as either private or public, we ignore a huge range of activity in between. Eating food, wearing clothes, or getting a haircut are all private activities—the benefits primarily accrue to the consumer. Others may enjoy watching another person eat, observing the clothing, or the stylish haircut, but most benefits are private. With a public good, such as national defense, many receive much the same benefits, desired or not, and all may be required to help pay for its provision. But many goods or services have elements of publicness that make purely private provision infeasible for most people, but yet do not rise to the level of publicness that is used to justify mandatory contribution for governmental provision.

For example, most people cannot afford a personal golf course, so golfers join in a membership organization called a golf club to obtain golfing services. Membership includes payment of fees and a requirement that rules be followed. Members have an incentive to follow these rules and pay dues because if they do not, their membership may be terminated. Clubs are used in the production of environmental amenities, as we observe from membership organizations such as The Nature Conservancy that people join to help provide protection for desired land and species by contributing to an action that few could afford individually. All who contribute can share in the joy of having saved something they believe to be worthwhile.

Of course, those of us who do not contribute to The Nature Conservancy, but enjoy its work, can free ride on the contributions of those who make the club a success, so a critical issue is if the free-rider effect will swamp the willingness of people to contribute. That problem will not be as significant if there is an ability to exclude people from enjoying the benefits of the club. Golf clubs have little difficulty enforcing rules against course use by nonmembers; The Nature Conservancy can do little to exclude nondonors from the pleasure of knowing about protected bits of the environment.

Clubs have a long history of solving problems in agriculture. For example, local, regional, breed, and animal-specific associations promoted improvements in agriculture and animal husbandry throughout the United States as early as the mid-nineteenth century (Whitaker 1975, 91–102). Groups sponsored journals, fairs, competitions, and speakers on a variety of topics.

If a club provides a service that has limited publicness, that is, can be enjoyed only by a certain number of people before the benefits diminish, then a limit on the number of club members will be desired, such as a fixed number of golf club members. More members may reduce the average cost of membership, but at some point the benefit of lower cost is swamped by the congestion of club facilities because of too many members clogging up the course. The fact that clubs call themselves "exclusive" is thus not an indication of snobbishness, regardless of the image they may wish to project, but a reflection of the fact that membership must be limited for the club to be useful.

Elinor Ostrom elaborates that point in *Governing the Commons*. She shows that common resources may be subject to exploitation by multiple "appropriators" who have arrangements to contribute to maintaining the valuable resource and to exclude others from using the resource to prevent overexploitation (1990, 31). Ostrom provides case studies of collective management arrangements, some of which worked, some of which failed. As she explains, and as Anderson and Leal (1995) have explained, state intrusion into collective solutions often results in a new set of institutional arrangements, some of which are economically and environmentally destructive.

The Role of Governments

Governments offer a third set of institutions for solving commons problems. Public action is often seen as effective because of its ability to overcome the free-rider problem that can prevent club solutions from working. Because preexisting force (e.g., police, courts) can be brought to bear on noncomplying individuals, preventing free riding is relatively cheap and does not depend on providing values that individuals voluntarily agree to support. But simply because government can compel obedience does not mean that government provides the most effective solution to a commons problem.

Because the public choice literature on the costs of government action is well known and extensive, we mention only three points. First, the cost of government coercion is so low that society must guard against "buying" too much. Thus government structures are often deliberately inefficient precisely to raise the cost of government action (e.g., separation of powers). Second, governments must be monitored to ensure that they restrict their actions to public purposes—in other words, that they are not captured by special interests. Because the prize of cheap coercion control is so attractive, special interests will invest in gaining that prize. Third, once the machinery of government is in place, a special interest—the bureaucracy—is born that will lobby for continuation of programs beyond their useful life.

All these costs, moreover, are not borne wholly by those initiating government action. Indeed, government action is itself a commons problem of sorts—because the costs of the government are borne by all citizens, whereas the benefits of solving particular commons problems may be reaped largely by a few. These costs require that we give careful consideration to the actual costs of government solutions before choosing them as the low-cost solution. In the case of agriculture, this consideration has been lacking in all too many instances, as agricultural interests assume that individual and collective private actions solutions are inadequate and so lobby for governmental solutions, perhaps without comparing the relative institutional costs.

APPLYING CHOICES TO PROBLEM SOLVING IN AGRICULTURE

Next we turn to a consideration of the mix of actions possible in the handling of problems that have been observed in agriculture and look at the kinds of arrangements used to help resolve the problem. Although we note various private and public solutions to problems, our focus will be on private collective arrangements used and that may be possible to solve problems now classified as public. We then turn to a consideration of barriers to further development of private collective action to solve problems that afflict agriculture.

Individual Solutions to Problems in Agriculture

In the 1870s and 1880s, ranchers in Texas undertook extensive private action to solve commons problems. Charles Goodnight, a pioneer panhandle rancher, purchased more than 1.3 million acres; the XIT Ranch grew out of a 3-million-acre land grant obtained in exchange for building Texas a $3 million state capitol (Morriss 2001, 569).

Large private-range cattle operations traditionally faced problems of keeping livestock under control. Texas ranchers invested in private solutions to the commons problems (Anderson and Hill 1975). Barbed wire enabled ranchers to fence their land to exclude outsiders and control their roaming cattle, allowing the owners to internalize the benefits of their investments. That it was worth doing so is evident from the scale of their investments: The XIT spent more than $180,000 on building an external fence that ran almost 800 miles and used more than 300 carloads of materials (Haley 1953, 87–88).

Equally important, the Texas ranches also used fencing to divide their holdings internally:

> By the late [1890s] cross fences cut the XIT into ninety-four pastures, making a total of about 1,500 miles of fence, which, in single strand, would have stretched for over 6,000 miles. Besides the wire, over 100,000 posts, five carloads of wire staves, and one car of staples were required. So many gates were necessary in the corrals and along the fences that the first general manager just ordered a carload of gate hinges. (Haley 1953, 88)

Internal fencing allowed the ranchers to solve the "commons problems"[1] of their own land: Stock could be rotated to rest pastures, unimproved cattle kept away from improved breeding stock, and experiments conducted with different breeds of cattle (Haley 1953, 187–88).

Private, individual action requires the ability to exclude at least enough others from the land to allow the actor to capture the benefits of the investment in solving the problem. Barbed wire enabled ranchers to exclude others; Texas law enabled ranchers there to acquire sufficient property rights to be able to solve the commons problems with fence. Cattlemen on the northern plains were not so fortunate, as public land holdings and parcel size restrictions in the homestead laws blocked private ownership of large, contiguous tracts (Morriss 2001, 573–75). Similarly today, many agricultural operations have grown in size to internalize the benefits of investments in expensive agricultural machinery and other capital investments.

Private action solutions have limits, of course. Once a problem spills over boundaries, individuals must confront free-rider problems if neighbors refuse to carry their share of common burdens or the spillover effects of their own actions. Our neighbor's planting of a crop that a particular pest finds attractive can draw that pest to our land as well; his spraying of chemical controls may cause some of the chemicals to drift onto our land, with the potential to harm our crops.

For some of these problems the courts offer a solution. The drift of a harmful chemical onto my land from a neighbor's spray program can be corrected with a suit for damages (Meiners and Morriss 2001); a neighbor who refuses to carry his share of the burden necessary for common efforts may face a variety of social and other sanctions (Ellickson 1991).

Not all commons problems, in agriculture or elsewhere, can be solved through individual action. For example, those with diseased animals may attempt to sell them despite their disease. In the sale of individual animals, buyers can often spot diseased or injured animals and refuse to buy. In mass sales, however, flaws may go undetected and be difficult to trace back to a particular seller. A federal Senate investigation in 1889, for example, found cattle owners sometimes sold diseased or injured animals to slaughterhouses: "The temptation to sell animals suffering from lumpy jaw, and from bruises received on crowded cars, or rendered feverish from thirst or hunger, is irresistible to the mercenary and avaricious" (Select Committee on the Transportation and Sale of Meat Products 1890, 26). To solve some commons problems, individuals turn to private clubs and public entities.

Private Collective Action to Solve Agricultural Problems

Private coordination can solve commons problems by bringing together at least some of those facing a problem into an organization that provides a mechanism for addressing the problem. Open-range cattlemen, for example, faced the commons problem of providing sufficient breeding stock of sufficient quality to ensure that their cattle reproduced. Anyone who invested in a high-quality bull that was loose on the range was effectively donating that breeding capacity to others with cattle on the same range. At the same time, any individual with female breeding cattle risked having them impregnated by his neighbor's lower-quality bulls. Quality breeding stock was thus a commons problem. Considering that a high-quality Hereford bull might cost more than $2,000 on the western range (Sullivan 1968, 159), this was not a trivial problem. By banding together into a private association, the open-range stockmen were able to allocate the responsibility to provide quality breeding stock.[2] That the solution worked can be seen from Wyoming stockmen's investment of more than $200,000 in thoroughbred bulls in 1883 alone (Osgood 1929, 94). Similarly, cattlemen banded together in 1834 in the Ohio Company for Importing English Cattle to sell ninety-two subscriptions at $100 each to purchase and import English purebred cattle. Two years later the company disbanded and paid an amazing dividend of $280 per share (Thompson 1942, 130).

Another example of private coordination to resolve an agricultural commons problem was the response of the Wyoming Stock Growers Association (WSGA) to the appearance of glanders among horses in Wyoming Territory in the 1880s. Glanders is a usually fatal disease of horses caused by bacteria. "Glanders is one of the oldest diseases known and once was prevalent throughout the world. It has now been eradicated or effectively controlled in many countries, including the USA" (Merck & Co., Inc. 1986, 307). Its appearance was a cause for serious concern.

The WSGA was a powerful organization; its members included virtually all significant cattle operations in the territory. Membership carried with it important benefits, such as the ability to participate in the association's roundups. Without the assistance of other ranchers in the roundups, an individual rancher would find it difficult to locate and secure his cattle on the vast open range (Webb 1959, 230). Members had strong incentives to comply with the association's rules. To fund its activities, the WSGA assessed its members a fee based on the number of cattle they held. The executive committee determined the association's expenses and then voted an assessment that yielded the necessary revenue. In 1889, for example, the fee was $0.0125 per head listed on each member's 1888 property tax return.

Because glanders was a significant threat to horses, and because horses were vital to a functioning cattle outfit, the WSGA required its members to act promptly to control the disease when glanders was discovered in their herds. When a member was suspected of having infected horses and not taking steps to prevent the spread of the disease, the association appointed a committee to investigate. In June 1885, for example, a committee accompanied a veterinarian "to the Douglas-Willan Sartoris Co.'s horse ranch, and other horse ranches in that neighborhood, to ascertain whether neglect had been shown in not reporting to the vet the existence of suspicious disease at the above mentioned ranches" (WSGA 1885b, 2). The committee observed the inspection of the horses, questioned the owner and his men about when symptoms in affected horses were first observed, and examined ranch records on livestock. After reviewing the evidence, the committee concluded that the rancher "was not neglectful in reporting the existence of disease at his ranch" and that once it had been discovered the rancher "used all due precaution to prevent the spread of the disease" (WSGA 1885b, 6).

The nonprivate part of the program came from the fact that the state paid an indemnity for horses with glanders that had to be destroyed, so long as they could be shown not to have already been infected when brought into the state. As the territorial veterinarian reported, that law was "very popular with the people, and its beneficial effects have done much to control and prevent the spread of glanders" (Hopkins 1887, 11).

The mix of private and public action was also exemplified by the WSGA's provision of a quarantine stockyard for use with imported cattle suspected of infection. When, in 1885, the territorial veterinarian sought to quarantine eight herds passing through Cheyenne from infected states, there was no safe place to keep the cattle.

> In this emergency, I [the Territorial Veterinarian] applied to the Executive Committee of the Wyoming Stock Growers' Association, who supplied the means to build the present Territorial quarantine yards, about one mile east of Cheyenne; these yards cover an area of about thirty acres; it is divided into nine corrals, with sheds and fence six feet high; each corral is furnished with an unlimited supply of water from the City water works and the whole yard is surrounded by a substantial wire fence—through the kindness of the Union Pacific railroad, these quarantine yards are connected with the main line by a switch and cattle can be unloaded directly into the different corrals. (Hopkins 1887, 8)

The territorial veterinarian claimed that, together with the legal ability to quarantine animals, Wyoming's possession of these yards played a significant role in preventing "unscrupulous individuals from forwarding to our Territory, cattle from infected localities; in other words, it made them 'respect the Governor's proclamation' when he scheduled a state . . . it compelled the buyer of breeding cattle to make his purchase in states where contagious disease was unknown" (Hopkins 1887, 9).

Private coordination has costs. People must join associations, attend meetings, pay dues, and live up to the obligations the associations impose. For private reputational sanctions to work, people must find their reputations sufficiently valuable to be worth protecting. At times the state can offer a less expensive solution—less expensive because the state can shift the cost of providing the solution to the taxpayers and because the state has a competitive advantage in using coercive means to resolve conflicts. Public solutions have their own costs, however, as discussed below.

Public Mechanisms to Solve Agricultural Problems

Sometimes farmers and ranchers turn to the state to solve free-rider problems with commons solutions. Apple growers in Washington State sought legislative assistance in the early 1900s to ensure that all growers in the area used pesticides on their orchards to control pests (Wharton 1974, 72). The logic was clear: If Farmer Smith and Farmer Jones both sprayed their orchards, but Farmer Thomas did not, the insects on Farmer Thomas's trees could migrate onto Farmer Smith's and Farmer Jones's trees despite their efforts to eradicate the pests. In addition, Farmer Thomas would have a competitive advantage over Farmer Smith and Farmer Jones because he would reap some of the rewards of their spraying (fewer bugs in general) but not incur spraying costs. The resulting law mandated spraying of apple orchards.

Similarly, in the 1950s and 1960s the U.S. Department of Agriculture (USDA) launched massive spraying programs to control various pests, from fire ants to gypsy moths, that were attacking valuable crops and trees across the United States. These programs were carried out despite objections (including lawsuits) from affected landowners, some of whom included organic farmers; courts upheld the USDA's actions as justified by the public good provided by the spray programs (Meiners and Morriss 2001, 6, 9–10).

This demonstrates a problem with public solutions—their "one-size-fits-all" nature does not lend itself to competing uses or innovation. When a problem has more than one dimension, public solutions involve forced tradeoffs between those who value one dimension and those who value another. For those who loved oak trees on Long Island, for example, the USDA spraying programs to control the gypsy moths were an effective solution to a commons problem (gypsy moths).[3] Without the USDA's involvement, too little spraying would occur. For organic farmers, however, the USDA's program threatened their livelihoods by contaminating their crops and land. They were willing to accept more gypsy moths and fewer oak trees than their neighbors because they valued pesticide-free food production more highly than did their neighbors. Similarly, bird lovers objected to the spray program because of its presumed effect on the bird population.

As long as the problem was simply a free-rider problem, as it was with the Washington apple growers at the turn of the twentieth century, the public solution's advantages might outweigh its disadvantages (especially if the growers paid the cost of the program). Once the problem involved tradeoffs among competing values, however, the winner-take-all nature of the public solution was a significant problem.

Freeing the solution from the discipline of the market was also problematic. Public sector solutions overcome the free-rider problem but lose the benefits of market discipline. Private associations must motivate their members to participate by delivering real benefits. Public-sector organizations need not. The first attempts by the federal government to disseminate agricultural information, through the U.S. Patent Office in the first half of the nineteenth century, focused on promoting ideas from British research that was impractical for American farmers—and some of which the USDA's first reports in the 1870s determined were inadvisable (Whitaker 1975, 106–107).

The most important general advantage of public solutions is their ability to resolve free-rider problems. Because the state may legitimately use force, it can credibly threaten to do so to enforce rules. The most important general disadvantage of public solutions is their breaking of the links between costs and benefits and the subsequent lack of appropriate incentives for decision makers. By shifting a commons problem to the public sector, particular interests can obtain solutions paid for by taxpayers in general, not just by those who benefit from the solution. The standard public choice story of concentrated benefits and dispersed costs applies. In addition, the public officials and employees who administer the solution lack the proper incentives because they do not receive the benefits or bear the costs of their actions.

INSTITUTIONAL CHOICE

Why do farmers and ranchers choose private individual actions in some cases, private coordinated actions in others, and state action in still others? What costs and benefits do they compare across institutions? If their choices consider the full range of costs and benefits that different institutions impose on society as a whole, then, although interesting as an academic question, their choices are of little social concern. If, however, their choices are based only on a subset of social costs and benefits, these choices may be inconsistent with the efficient social solution and thus an appropriate subject of concern for society as a whole.

A second important question is whether agricultural commons problems are different from commons problems generally. Agriculture is often claimed to be "special"—particularly by politicians campaigning in the Iowa presidential caucuses. Consumers tolerate costly agricultural protectionism to an extent that seems difficult to imagine in other sectors of the economy. The European Union's Common Agricultural Policy costs union citizens €2.25 billion per year on olives alone, and more than €40 billion overall (*Economist* 2001); the Organisation for Economic Co-operation and Development (OECD) countries generally spent more than $360 billion in agricultural subsidies and support programs in 1998 (*Economist* 2000). Does this "specialness" mean that agricultural commons problems are different from commons problems generally? It is more likely determined by the large number of farmers in a large number of jurisdictions, who, tending to have most capital tied up in their operations, are less mobile than urban workers, and so invest more in politicians who maintain the mishmash of programs (Hosemann 2003).

Agriculture has long had one of the most extensive sets of subsidies and controls of any industry. Depending on the crop or critter, there are federal quotas on production, price supports, special fees (taxes), research support, peculiar tax rules, and a multiplicity of inspection programs for sanitation and other purposes. Ignoring subsidies and production restrictions, which are generally recognized for what they are, we focus on the rationale for government inspection for sanitation and government intervention for the purpose of dealing with animal health problems, which are the oldest parts of public policy toward agriculture in the United States, and probably the least controversial.

Restrictions on Private Collective Enforcement

Meat sanitation arose as a major political issue in the 1880s with the growth of the Chicago meatpacking houses, which affected the structure of the meat industry from ranching to retailing. Disease in cattle was used as the excuse for state inspection programs, quarantines on shipments, and anti-trust laws designed to attack the Chicago packing houses that were forcing large changes in the structure of the industry, to the disadvantage of some states' cattle interests. The issue went from the state to the national level, re-sulting in extensive congressional hearings and, eventually, the Meat In-spection Act of 1891, the first federal food quality assurance statute that put meat inspection under the secretary of agriculture. The existence of the packing houses also played a significant role in the passage of the Sherman Antitrust Act of 1890 (Libecap 1992, 252–53, 255–58).

These statutes illustrate how public interference with private sector devel-opments may retard innovations that could solve collective problems. Dis-ease in livestock is a serious issue. The concern that individual growers had (and still have)—that they are at the mercy of large packing houses—may be little more than a reflection of market reality, or it may reflect the conse-quence of antitrust laws preventing cattlemen from banding to solve the is-sues of animal health and marketing. That path has not changed in more than a century, locked in by regulations, subsidies, and restrictions on vol-untary contracting.

In the absence of federal inspection and standards, agricultural producers would devote more resources to quality assurance of their products. Not only do producers have strong incentives to protect their brand capital (Klein and Leffler 1981), but, in the case of disease, they wish to protect themselves from loss of stock and from liability that could arise from selling a diseased product. Meatpacking plants such as Swift and Armour have par-ticularly strong incentives to protect their brand names. Individual cattle growers offering cattle to the market have little brand name to protect, and, if their cattle are mixed at market with many others, they may have less in-centive to be concerned about diseases than if there were clear liability. Those incentives, and market structure, could have been quite different un-der a regime of private collective action to provide assurances to customers of quality control.

In the absence of federal agricultural inspection programs, producers and retailers would develop standards to ensure customers of the safety of their products.[4] To make standards work, there must be enforcement mecha-nisms. Some hints of how those might have developed are discussed when we examine some historical incidents, but first we must consider how an-titrust law has been a barrier to voluntary contractual arrangements that would have allowed agricultural producers to ensure product quality and safety. The antitrust laws that farm-state legislators thought would discipline the large packing houses serve instead to prevent growers from coming together to promote their interests.

For producers to be able to join to produce a common good, such as health standards and product quality standards that would apply to all of their output, they would have to belong to an organization that would set standards that must be followed by all members. Standards would provide information to buyers, much as Underwriters Laboratories and other quality assurance organizations do. Members would have to abide by quality standards or be subject to sanction, including boycotts by buyers who help enforce the quality standards. Similarly, buyers who refuse to abide by quality and safety standards would be subject to boycott by sellers' organizations. Without boycotts, enforcement of standards would be very difficult. Antitrust law makes the use of boycotts almost impossible.

Cooperative voluntary ventures, whereby parties agree to meet certain rules to preserve valuable assets, are much more effective if there is some ability to inflict monetary damage on noncooperating parties by refusing to deal with such parties. No coercion need be used, only a willingness to abide by an agreement. Such voluntary agreements are generally stricken under antitrust law. Sullivan gives the example of a group of manufacturers agreeing not to sell output to retailers who buy output from manufacturers who refuse to comply with industry purity standards; such a boycott would be a per se violation of the law (Sullivan 1977, 231–65). The standard may exist, but private enforcement is discouraged. The result of the fact that this arrangement is unavailable has increased demand for government controls as a substitute.

A classic boycott case is *Fashion Originators' Guild of America v. FTC* (1941). In that case, designers and producers of quality original-design clothing and other textiles agreed, as part of guild membership, not to sell to retailers who stocked products that copied designs of guild members. Fashion designers have long had problems with knock-off clothing that imitates materials and designs, making it difficult to capture the gains from design efforts. The Supreme Court, observing that guild members had 60 percent of high-priced women's garment sales, struck down the arrangement as a boycott in violation of the Sherman Antitrust and Clayton Acts. The Court noted that the guild served as "an extra-governmental agency, which prescribes rules for the regulation . . . of interstate commerce, and provides extrajudicial tribunals for determination and punishment of violators," thereby invading "the powers of the national legislature" (*Fashion Originators' Guild v. FTC* 1941, 465).

The alternative to this voluntary agreement is for the fashion originators to lobby for stronger copyright and trademark statutes and assistance from law enforcement agencies in seizing copied designs. It is not clear that voluntary extragovernmental agencies may not be better than the alternative of all or nothing: governmental protection and controls or little right to protect assets. With few rights, there is less incentive to invest in assets, so they are more likely to be left in the commons.

Boycotts in agriculture have fared little better than the fashion originators. In a case in which dairy farmers in a cooperative agreed to boycott milk producers that did not deal exclusively with their cooperative, the Court found a violation of the Sherman Antitrust Act (*Otto Milk Company* 1967). As the Court noted, the Capper-Volstead Act provides no protection for such cooperative activities.[5] Agricultural cooperatives receive no exemptions for activities called monopolistic under the Sherman act (Anderson 1982). Other cases have confirmed that agricultural cooperatives may be subject to triple damages for monopolizing activities (*April* 1958; *North Texas Producers* 1965).

Yandle (1997) has discussed the fact that antitrust law prevents the evolution of voluntary arrangements that could protect resources. As Yandle notes, efforts by oystermen and shrimpers to protect natural resources along the Gulf Coast from overexploitation due to open access rules was stricken by the courts as anticompetitive. The rules used by the fishers were indeed restrictive, but restrictions on valuable property are essential to preserving property for productive use over time. Fortunately, antitrust laws do not prevent all restrictive contracts and voluntary arrangements from existing, or there would be few incentives to amass and protect resources.

In agriculture, as in other sectors, there have been few restrictions on vertical integration, so that large processors such as ADM and Cargill can, within the firm, handle a wide range of activities. However, individual growers are denied the benefits of limited horizontal integration by which they would join together for certain purposes, such as to protect their crops and herds from diseases. This limitation has made the evolution of federal health and safety regulations the only viable alternative. As a result, the USDA, an agency that suffers from the same incentive problems as any other government agency, dominates the provision of such services. This need not have been the world we live in, as we examine next in considering bits of evidence from alternative arrangements that growers tried before being cut short in the late nineteenth century from further experimentation in the evolution of collective private solutions.

Evidence of Private Collective Action

Institutional choice is not an all-or-nothing proposition. The same people may sometimes choose private action, sometimes choose private associations, and sometimes choose to act through the state. As the secretary of the Wyoming Stock Growers Association wrote his members in 1888, "[t]he

Board of Live Stock Commissioners, the Special Inspection Fund Comm. and the Executive Comm. of the Association are working harmoniously together. These various bodies have one common end in view—and it is earnestly hoped that the united support of the stockmen in the Territory may be given them without hesitation" (WSGA 1888c, 2).

We identify five factors that affect whether private institutional choices are a matter of concern. These are (1) barriers to entry, (2) differential impacts, (3) cost shifting, (4) type of sanctions, and (5) speed of response.

Economic advantage may accrue from using public institutions and public health concerns to block competition. For example, in the 1880s, northern plains cattlemen vigorously opposed attempts by southern plains cattlemen to continue bringing southern cattle north onto the open range. A congressional investigation into this resistance concluded that

> [i]t appears to be a fact beyond all controversy that a very large number of the present occupants of the northern ranges, constituting probably more than a majority of their total number, is openly and earnestly opposed to the driving of Texas cattle to the northern ranges upon considerations of a purely commercial and economic nature. First, they do not wish to be confronted by the competition of the Texas cattle in their midst. Second, they find that the Texas cattle in very many places "eat out" the grasses upon ranges which for years past they have regarded, as by prescriptive right, their own. Third, the contact of their herds with the Texas herds tends to depreciate the breed of their cattle, owing to the fact that the Texas herds usually contain a certain proportion of Texas bulls. Cows and bulls usually intermingle freely on the ranges. This, of course, interferes with the efforts of the northern herdsmen to improve the breed of their cattle by importing at considerable expense high-grade bulls. But the fact that the herdsmen of Texas are also making strenuous efforts to improve the breed of their cattle promises in the future to meet that objection. (WSGA 1885a, 2)

The congressional investigators' conclusion was bolstered by comments made by a Wyoming stockman at the National Cattlemen's Convention in St. Louis in November 1884:

> We came from Wyoming objecting to the idea of a [national cattle] trail. Our objection has to some extent, been misunderstood. We did not object to it on the ground of the liability of infection, or of cattle disease, because cattle driven from the south have never hurt us so far north, and we are not afraid of them. We have objected to the trail simply on the ground of safety of our investment. We have believed that if Government made an appropriation whereby a public highway for cattle was to be established, over which the immense herds of surplus cattle from Texas were to be invited to come and overwhelm us, we were in danger of obliteration and extinction. (WSGA 1885a, 3)

The Wyoming cattlemen's objection to measures facilitating trade of cattle between the northern plains and Texas thus rested on their determination to avoid competition with the Texas herds, although the public discussion was frequently couched in public health terms. Similarly, a coalition of interests resisted the introduction of dressed beef in the 1890s on sanitary grounds to protect their financial interests in the existing live cattle trade. Although consumers were suspicious of dressed beef, it was "sufficiently cheaper than local butcher stock that people were willing to try it" (Whitaker 1975, 47–48). Similar arguments are often advanced today in favor of various forms of phytosanitary restrictions on trade in agricultural products and livestock. The *Economist* (2000, 82) magazine concluded a survey of agricultural markets and trade by noting that "there is a fine line between protection and protectionism, and it is tempting for local producers to keep out foreign competition by invoking food safety or environmental concerns."

The shoe was on the other foot, however, when the Wyoming cattlemen confronted similar public health arguments from European governments seeking to ban Wyoming cattle exports. Wyoming cattleman and British subject Morton Frewen, uncle by marriage to young Winston Churchill (Smith 1966, 16), wrote the British government seeking to export his cattle to Britain through Canada, to avoid disease-based restrictions on shipment from American ports. The British Agriculture Department refused permission, stating that the Canadian government, "after the fullest consideration of the subject," had "decided that they could not assume the responsibility of allowing cattle to be exported from the United States through Canada, as they consider the risk of introducing disease in this way to be too great" (Frewen 1884, 1–2). The political calculus for the Canadian and British officials was straightforward—American cattlemen were competition for their domestic constituents. Any risk of disease was enough to support a finding against the interest of their competitors and in favor of their constituents. Indeed, a Senate investigation noted in 1890 that "it is in the interest of some British stock raisers and dealers to foster and enlarge this impression [that American cattle are diseased] . . . (Select Committee on the Transportation and Sale of Meat Products 1890, 30). Similarly, a WSGA correspondent in England lamented recent reports of "Texas fever" near Wyoming in a telegram to the association, noting: "I know every Irishman in the House of Commons & every hostile paper will use this outbreak so near our own ranges as a means of continuing the restrictions that are depressing our business" (WSGA 1888a). The quarantine line in the midwestern states became "a political football," as those dependent on the cattle trade and those who benefited from excluding competition battled over its location (Miner 1982, 64).

During the same period, American cattlemen were dealing with the threat of "lung fever" or pleuropneumonia. This disease came from Europe through a diseased cow imported in 1843 from Great Britain into New Jersey (Committee on Agriculture 1881, 2). The disease spread slowly into other eastern states over the next thirty years, with its progress west limited by the small numbers of cattle being traded east to west, compared with the large numbers being traded west to east.

Massachusetts was one of the first states to take action against the disease. Pleuropneumonia first appeared in Massachusetts in 1859. By 1866, the disease was eradicated in the state. The state quickly established a commission to eliminate the disease, empowering it to condemn and kill all cattle determined to be infected; 1,164 cattle were slaughtered by orders of the state commission (additional cattle were destroyed by local officials) and the cost of the eradication program was just over $77,000 over the six-year period (Committee on Agriculture 1881, 4–5).

What distinguishes the Massachusetts response from the efforts of the Wyoming cattlemen? One clear difference is that Massachusetts was required to pay for the cattle it destroyed. Cattle owners were thus compensated for their loss of property. The cost of advancing the greater good fell on the taxpayers generally rather than on the individual cattle owner. The Wyoming cattlemen, on the other hand, used sanitation and disease arguments to attempt to avoid competition. The costs of their actions fell upon the consuming public and on the Texas cattlemen. Because the Wyoming cattlemen did not have to compensate either, they were free to advance such arguments even when they were not justified.

Public solutions carried the risk of capture of the regulators. As concerns about "Texas fever" increased calls for legislation, northern plains cattlemen found that who was doing the regulating made an enormous difference. One group of ranchers, with holdings along northern New Mexico and southern Colorado, protested Colorado's attempts to quarantine with a petition, giving one of the grievances as "[t]hat we earnestly protest against the appointment of such men as are known to be the heaviest bidders for Texas cattle, as members of the live stock sanitary veterinary board of the state of Colorado" (Owen et al. n.d.). Indeed, many of the Texas cattlemen saw protectionism behind the quarantine legislation (Whitaker 1975, 62).

The same group also noted another effect of the public solution: differential impact. By creating a regulatory haven, the Colorado quarantine law would draw cattle into the area defined as free. This would "cause complete destruction to the grass." Yet, they also concluded, "[w]e have no just reasons to believe that there would be no attempt made on the part of the Texas men to drive their cattle on to our ranges, was it not for the inducements offered under said Colorado quarantine law, together with the assurance on the part of some of those north of us who are desirous of purchasing Texas cattle, that said law can be evaded" (Owen et al. n.d.). Similarly, Illinois's 1869 restriction of imports of cattle to those that had wintered in Kansas, Nebraska,

Missouri, Iowa, or Wisconsin led to Kansas county clerks issuing certificates of wintering "liberally" (Whitaker 1975, 62).

Another factor affecting institutional choice is the desire to shift costs from the private association to the public purse. The WSGA, for example, sought to shift the cost of the quarantine yards and other services it provided to its members to the public by having the state take over responsibility for various services. Thus at the March 31, 1890, executive committee meeting of the WSGA, the minutes include notations of discussions of "[a]n informal agreement" under which the state would assume the cost of the horses provided to association brand inspectors, horses the association valued at $315. When the entire cost could not be shifted, part was—the WSGA paid a supplemental salary to the official veterinarian in a number of years, for example (WSGA 1911, 91–92).

Another factor relates to the sanctions and means of sanctioning available. Private associations can limit their members' behavior only through sanctions ultimately based on refusal to associate.[6] Thus a cattlemen's association could refuse to allow a noncooperator to participate in a joint roundup—a costly penalty, but short of the sanctions based on force available to the state. Such associational sanctions can be extremely powerful. Lisa Bernstein (1992), for example, has explained how Hasidic diamond merchants abide by industry norms because expulsion from the industry group would effectively end any individual's business.

Force-backed sanctions available to the state also carry a price. To invoke the sanctions requires the state to follow procedures aimed at avoiding mistakes. In criminal cases, for example, the state must prove guilt beyond a reasonable doubt to a jury. Even in civil cases, and even in the nineteenth century, due process concerns limited state action. Thus private groups sometimes have greater ability to act (and a greater ability to make mistakes, of course). This is illustrated nicely by the response to a cattleman's complaint by the WSGA. The cattleman complained that he was being unfairly labeled as a thief of unbranded calves (mavericks) by his neighbors. After investigating, the secretary of the WSGA wrote back:

> I have talked with some of the stockmen whose cattle run on the same range as yours, and from all sides I get the same unfavorable report as to your reputation. These men know, as well as you do, that it would be almost impossible to prove anything against you, under the rules of evidence in a court of law, or even in any investigation that might be made at your request, by the Executive Committee of this Association, but yet the fact remains that they all believe that you have on several instances, violated the "Maverick Law." It seems strange to me that there should be such a strong, and such a general prejudice against you, in view of the fact that you have never done anything to deserve it. If your own neighbors will not work with you, I do not see how any one else can help you out of your difficulties. If there was simply *one* outfit down on you, the matter

would be different, and might be adjusted, but I can assure you that more than one man believes you guilty of rustling. . . . For reasons of which must appear sufficient to many of the stockmen in your part of the country, you have been debarred from the privileges of cooperating with the round-ups. This is unfortunate, and may be unjust, but it is a matter over which the outfits directly interested have entire control, and nothing I could say would have the slightest effect one way or the other. Besides this, I am bound to believe that the parties who have taken a stand against you are acting in a way which they deem just and proper under the circumstances. They are men who know how to protect their own interests without any suggestions from me. (WSGA 1888a, 490–91)

A final factor relates to the speed with which institutions can react. Private institutions can often react more quickly than governments—with good reason; governments must comply with numerous safeguards to protect the public purse. An activity may be started with private funds, where the need is urgent, but ultimately shifted to the public purse if the beneficiaries can arrange to do so. For example, the Wyoming Stock Growers Association responded to a cash shortfall at the territorial Live Stock Commission in 1888 by seeking to temporarily raise funds privately to keep the commission functioning. As the WSGA secretary wrote to cattleman John B. Thomas, the shortfall meant that "[i]t is very evident that the expense incurred must either be paid by the Association under assessment, or be special tax upon the live stock interests of the Territory, under sanction of the Legislature." If Thomas's operation would contribute "two or three hundred dollars . . . in the *form of a loan* to the Live Stock Commissioners," the loan would be repaid "at the earliest possible moment" when the legislature could appropriate the funds to do so (WSGA 1888b, 1–2).

CONCLUSION

A large part of the property rights work pioneered by PERC researchers has been to document that a lack of property rights often means lack of protection for valuable resources. Although some people do not like what other people do with their property, there is general agreement that strong property rights gives incentives to exploit and protect resources over time. Public control of resources means political decision making that tends to be more shortsighted, due to the time horizons of elected politicians, is subject to special interest interference, and suffers from problems of mismanagement due to incentive problems of government managers.

Getting the institutions "right" (or at least better) may be assisted greatly by technology, as in the case of barbed wire, or may be due to the evolution of organizations that asset owners come to discover are advantageous. There are limits to how much a property owner can do alone, regardless of how strong rights are for individual property owners, especially if there are limits placed on collective private action. If such limits exist, such as antitrust restrictions on boycotts and other voluntary enforcement mechanisms that private organizations might use, the second-best alternative often becomes collective public action. Private resource owners, including agricultural property owners, have natural incentives to seek benefits from the public trough. The incentive to go to that trough is stronger when there are limits placed on the creation of voluntary alternatives. After a while, it becomes second nature—just the way things are.

Moreover, reliance on government action offers opportunities to shift cost to others through moving expenses from the private to the public purse. Government's transaction cost advantage—cheap coercion to solve free riding—makes it an attractive solution even when private or club solutions are more effective. That same cost advantage also offers opportunities for rent seeking, as activities that could be done privately or through clubs are added to the government mandate.

Agriculture in the United States suffers from political domination. Whereas individual farmers and ranchers have rather strong ownership rights over their property, their ability to come together in private organizations to promote their common interests and to help solve their common problems has been restricted. As a result, they turn to government for solutions. It may be that even problems of diseases, which are generally presumed to be a proper role for government action, may in fact be issues that could be resolved by organizational entrepreneurs who devise private collectives. That path has not been taken, and our agricultural sector is much poorer for it.

NOTES

1. Because the ranch was owned by a single entity, it technically did not have a commons problem; we use this as shorthand for the class of problems that would exist if the land had been held in common.

2. Range cattlemen generally adopted rules that required each member to provide quality bulls based on the number of cows each owned on that range.

3. Some spray program opponents asserted that there was scientific backing for doing nothing—that the pests would dissipate on their own. But public solutions tend to settle on one view of science.

4. Private producers have higher sanitation standards than the USDA imposes, at least for certain issues. Because disease can wipe out an entire herd, many growers have strict controls on livestock movement that goes beyond federal requirements.

5. 7 U.S.C. §291.

6. Nonstate groups can, of course, resort to force, but doing so carries with it the risk of incurring serious penalties. Nonstate groups have resorted to force successfully, without incurring sanctions for doing so on a number of occasions. See Morriss (1998) for further discussion.

REFERENCES

Anderson, Alan M. 1982. The Agricultural Cooperative Antitrust Exemption— *Fairdale Farms, Inc. v. Yankee Milk, Inc. Cornell Law Review* 67(January): 396–414.

Anderson, Terry L., and P. J. Hill. 1975. The Evolution of Property Rights: A Study of the American West. *Journal of Law & Economics* 18(1): 163–79.

Anderson, Terry L., and Donald Leal. 1995. Fishing for Property Rights. In *Taking the Environment Seriously,* ed. Roger E. Meiners and Bruce Yandle. Lanham, MD: Rowman & Littlefield Publishers, Inc., 161–84.

Bernstein, Lisa. 1992. Opting Out of the Legal System: Extralegal Contractual Relations in the Diamond Industry. *Journal of Legal Studies* 21: 115–58.

Buchanan, James M. 1965. An Economic Theory of Clubs. *Economica* February: 1–14.

Committee on Agriculture. 1881. Pleuro-Pneumonia among Cattle. Report No. 344, U.S. House of Representatives, 46th Congress, 3rd sess. Washington, DC.

Economist. 2000. A Not-So-Perfect Market. May 23.

———. 2001. Glut, Fraud and Eco-Damage. June 28.

Ellickson, Robert. 1991. *Order without Law.* Cambridge, MA: Harvard University Press.

Frewen, Morton. 1884. Letter from Agriculture Department, Privy Council Office, September 3, 1884. Wyoming Stock Growers Association Collection, Accession Number 14, Box 224, Folder 1. American Heritage Center, Laramie, WY.

Gardner, B. Delworth. 2003. Legal Impediments to Transferring Agricultural Water to Other Uses. This volume.

Geist, Valerius. 2000. Public Elk, Private Profit: The Perils of Selling Wildlife. Montanans against the Domestication and Commercialization of Wildlife. Online: www.macow.org/articles/geist1.htm (cited: March 11, 2001).

Haley, J. Evetts. 1953. *The XIT Ranch of Texas and the Early Days of the Llano Estacado.* Norman: Oklahoma University Press.

Hardin, Garrett. 1968. The Tragedy of the Commons. *Science* 162: 1243–48.

Hopkins, James D. 1887. Sixth Annual Report of James D. Hopkins, Territorial Veterinarian to Hon. Thomas Moonlight, Governor of Wyoming Territory. Cheyenne, WY: Cheyenne Leader Book and Job Print.

Hosemann, John. K. 2003. Agriculture and the Environment: A Thirty-Year Retrospective. This volume.

Klein, Ben, and Keith Leffler. 1981. The Role of Market Forces in Assuring Contractual Performance. *Journal of Political Economy* 89(3): 615–42.

Libecap, Gary D. 1992. The Rise of the Chicago Packers and the Origins of Meat Inspection and Antitrust. *Economic Inquiry* 30(April): 242–62.

———. 2003. Agricultural Programs with Dubious Environmental Benefits: The Political Economy of Ethanol. This volume.

McChesney, Fred S. 1997. *Money for Nothing: Politicians, Rent Extraction, and Political Extortion.* Cambridge, MA: Harvard University Press.

Meiners, Roger E., and Andrew P. Morriss. 2001. Pesticides and Property Rights. *PERC Policy Series,* PS-22. Bozeman, MT: PERC, May.

Merck & Co., Inc. 1986. *Merck Veterinary Manual,* 6th ed. Rahway, NJ: Merck & Co., Inc.

Miner, H. Craig. 1982. *Wichita: The Early Years 1865–80*. Lincoln: University of Nebraska Press.

Morriss, Andrew P. 1997. Pesticides and Environmental Federalism: An Empirical and Qualitative Analysis of §24(c) Registrations. In *Environmental Federalism,* ed. Terry L. Anderson and Peter J. Hill. Lanham, MD: Rowman & Littlefield Publishers, Inc., 133–74.

———. 1998. Miners, Vigilantes, and Cattlemen: Overcoming Free Rider Problems in the Private Provision of Law. *Land & Water Law Review* 33: 581–696.

———. 2001. Returning Justice to Its Private Roots. *University of Chicago Law Review* 68: 551–78.

Osgood, Ernest Staples. 1929. *The Day of the Cattleman*. Minneapolis: University of Minnesota Press.

Ostrom, Elinor. 1990. *Governing the Commons: The Evolution of Institutions for Collective Action*. Cambridge, UK: Cambridge University Press.

Owen, T. E., et al. n.d. Petition "To Cattlemen." Wyoming Stock Growers Association Collection, Accession Number 14, Box 224, Folder 3. American Heritage Center, Laramie, WY.

Ridley, Matt. 1996. *The Origins of Virtue*. New York: Viking, Penguin Group.

Select Committee on the Transportation and Sale of Meat Products. 1890. Report to Accompany S. 3717, 3718, 3719 and Senate Joint Resolution 78. U.S. Senate, Report No. 829, 51st Congress, 1st sess.

Smith, Helen Huntington. 1966. The War on Powder River. Lincoln: University of Nebraska Press.

Sullivan, Dulcie. 1968. *The LS Brand: The Story of a Texas Panhandle Ranch*. Austin: University of Texas Press.

Sullivan, Lawrence A. 1977. *Handbook of the Law of Antitrust*. St. Paul, MN: West Publishing.

Thompson, James Westfall. 1942. *A History of Livestock Raising in the United States, 1607–1860*. Washington, DC: U.S. Department of Agriculture.

Webb, Walter Prescott. 1959. *The Great Plains*. Lincoln: University of Nebraska Press.

Wharton, James. 1974. *Before Silent Spring: Pesticides and Public Policy in Pre-DDT America*. Princeton, NJ: Princeton University Press.

Whitaker, James W. 1975. *Feedlot Empire: Beef Cattle Feeding in Illinois and Iowa, 1840–1900*. Ames: Iowa State University Press.

Wyoming Stock Growers Association. 1885a. Typescript of portions of House Executive Documents, 48th Congress, 2nd sess., 1884–1885, vol. 29. Wyoming Stock Growers Association Collection, Accession Number 14, Box 224, Folder 1. American Heritage Center, Laramie, WY.

———. 1885b. Report of the Committee Appointed to Accompany Dr. Hopkins to the Douglas-Willan Sartoris Co.'s Ranch on Glanders, June 27, 1885. Wyoming Stock Growers Association Collection, Accession Number 14, Box 224, Folder 3. American Heritage Center, Laramie, WY.

———. 1888a. Letters, Volume 10, 1888. Wyoming Stock Growers Association Collection, Accession Number 14, Box 3, bound volume. American Heritage Center, Laramie, WY.

———. 1888b. Letter from Thomas B. Adams, June 28, 1888. John B. Thomas Collection, Accession Number 141, Box 17, Folder 2. American Heritage Center, Laramie, WY.

————. 1888c. Letter from Thomas B. Adams, November 20, 1888. John B. Thomas Collection, Accession Number 141, Box 17, Folder 2. American Heritage Center, Laramie, WY.

————. 1911. Executive Committee, July 14, 1885–April 5, 1911. Wyoming Stock Growers Association Collection, Accession Number 14, Box 45, bound volume. American Heritage Center, Laramie, WY.

Yandle, Bruce. 1997. *Antitrust and the Commons: Cooperation or Collusion?* Washington, DC: Competitive Enterprise Institute.

CASES CITED

April v. National Cranberry Association, 168 F. Supp. 919 (D. Mass., 1958)

Fashion Originators' Guild of America v. FTC. 312 U.S. 457 (S. Ct., 1941).

North Texas Producers Association v. Metzger Dairies, Inc., 348 F.2d 189 (5th Cir., 1965).

Otto Milk Company v. United Dairy Farmers Cooperative Association, 388 F.2d 789 (3rd Cir., 1967).

3

Regulating Concentrated Animal Feeding Operations: Internalization or Cartelization?

Bruce Yandle and Sean Blacklocke

On May 27, 1935, in *A.L.A. Schechter Corp. et al. v. United States,* the U.S. Supreme Court ruled the National Industrial Recovery Act (NIRA) unconstitutional. In doing so, the Court struck down the federal government's national price-fixing scheme that rewarded colluding firms and dismantled one of the key elements in President Roosevelt's Depression recovery program. The Court's decision also returned thousands of independent grocers and other retailers to a competitive jungle with expanding chain stores that had no difficulty selling at rock-bottom prices (Calvani and Breidenbach 1990). Prior to *Schechter,* the retail trade associations and their lobbyists had celebrated the sheltering price codes embodied in the NIRA. *Schechter* sent the lobbyists back to the drawing board.

It was not a long trip. Fifteen days after the *Schechter* decision was announced, Congressman Wright Patman of Texas introduced antiprice-cutting legislation. The 1936 Robinson-Patman Act, drafted by the Wholesale Grocers Association, was designed to protect small retailers from ravaging chain store price competition. Still on the books, the 1936 statute enjoys paradoxical enforcement by the Federal Trade Commission. By far the majority of the Robinson-Patman actions are taken against smaller firms. And by far the majority of the complaints come not from consumers, but from competitors. Robinson-Patman has been shown to be cartel-forming legislation (Faith, Leavens, and Tollison 1982; Mackay, Miller, and Yandle 1987).

What does this short story about a New York slaughterhouse taken from antitrust history have to do with the current Environmental Protection Agency (EPA) proposals for regulating concentrated animal feed operations (EPA 2001)? If we start with the notion that legal institutions evolve endogenously in a competitive environment, then destruction of an existing equilibrium institution will lead inevitably to a replacement. Any institutional vacuum will be filled. In this sense, Robinson-Patman replaced the NIRA.

Now to the task at hand. On September 28, 1998, the Iowa Supreme Court ruled unconstitutional a part of the Iowa Right-to-Farm law that shielded agricultural activities from common lawsuits. The statute at issue said: "A farm or farm operations located in an agricultural area shall not be found to be a nuisance regardless of the established date of operation or expansion of the agricultural activities of the farm or farm operation."[1] In the ruling, the court stated that when the Iowa legislature passed the statute, that action constituted a taking of private property for public use without the payment of just compensation; the benighted statute was in violation of federal and state constitutions.

The court's decision cast doubt on the validity of right-to-farm laws that existed in various forms nationwide. Every state had statutes that in some way shielded farms, and in some cases hog farms specifically, from common lawsuit. The common law shields were valuable; the Iowa decision was challenged. On June 2, 2001, the U.S. Supreme Court chose not to hear the appeal. The Court's decision let stand the lower court ruling and left the now uncertain right-to-farm laws in legal limbo.

If there had been a state of institutional equilibrium prior to the Court's action, the destruction of the common law shield disturbed that equilibrium and left a vacuum to be filled in the political economy of large farm operations. Just as Robinson-Patman replaced the NIRA codes, the EPA's recently proposed concentrated animal feeding operations (CAFO) regulations must be viewed as part of an institutional bundle replacing the court-destroyed common law shield that was a part of a previous regulatory regime protecting large CAFOs from common law threats.

But of course, there is a competing hypothesis to consider. The new and far-reaching CAFO regulations have nothing whatsoever to do with large firm privilege, cartels, rules of liability, and common law shields. The fact that rigorous CAFO regulation began to emerge with vigor in March 1999 is purely coincidental.[2] CAFO is about the formation and enforcement of public property rights to clean water. This is about the eternal search for efficiency. It is about internalizing externalities; it is not about cartelization.

To make matters even more complex, there is a third possible explanation for CAFO regulation, which may be thought of as a footnote to the first explanation. CAFO regulations, like all federal attempts to improve environmental quality, must yield a profit-making cartel. There is no other choice in the matter. Otherwise, the political interests necessary for final action will not lend their support. In other words, cartelization goes with government attempts to define regulatory property rights (Weiner 1999).

This chapter explores these three possibilities.

ARE CAFO RULES ABOUT
INTERNALIZING EXTERNALITIES?

In recent years the mode and location of farm animal production has changed. For example, there are now fewer dairy farms in the United States, but with more cattle per farm. In 1988, the average dairy had 44 cows; by 1998, the average had risen to 70. In 1999, the U.S. Department of Agriculture (USDA) reported that 33 percent of the nation's milk production came from dairies with more than 500 cows (Keith, Jones, and Johnson 2000, 7). The USDA also reports that the number of CAFOs (dairy, beef, swine, and poultry) with more than 1,000 animals has grown from 6,600 in 1992 to more than 10,000 in 1999.

There can be little doubt that concentrated feed operations generate large amounts of animal waste, odors, unpleasant sounds, and other effects that are at best uncelebrated and at worst despised by occupants of newly constructed gated communities. Indeed, even seasoned neighboring farm operators, presumably with well-conditioned noses, have been known to register concern about news of expanding hog operations in their neighborhood.[3] Recognition of such concerns has long been found in the common law of nuisance, which, although less than perfect, seems ideally suited for dealing with unwanted harms generated by neighbors.

It was a common lawsuit from antiquity about hogs that addressed just this set of circumstances and helped to establish the common rule for the law of nuisance. In *William Aldred's Case* (1610), the plaintiff asked for and received injunctive relief from the smell and fumes that emerged from a neighbor's pigsty. The court agreed that homeowners and occupants held property rights to a reasonable level of wholesome air and surroundings and that operators of hog operations had a duty to act in ways that would not impose unwanted costs on downwind and downstream parties. In short, unless contracted away, the folks downstream held environmental rights.

A similar set of facts is found in a multitude of modern nuisance suits brought against feedlot operators in the United States. Indeed, in a survey of right-to-farm law and statutory limits on nuisance suits, Grossman and Fischer (1983) found that almost all the reported agricultural nuisance cases involve feedlots. Almost without exception, if an owner or occupier of land showed evidence of harm from unreasonable operation of an animal feedlot, courts have granted a remedy of either damages or injunction, unless, of course, the farm operation was protected by statute. As with *Aldred,* most of the private nuisance actions surveyed by Grossman and Fischer related to odor problems.

When Common Law Is Set Aside, Regulation May Be Necessary

The common law of nuisance seems to work reasonably well when it is allowed to operate. But if after years of statute and regulation writing, political bodies set aside common law protections, as in the case of right-to-farm and feedlot statutes, or if for other reasons common law remedies and property rights are not allowed to function, it goes without saying that a concentrated animal feeding operation could impose uncompensated costs on downstream parties.[4] But for this to be justification for federal regulatory action, one would expect the EPA at least to provide evidence that CAFOs degrade the quality of the national waters of the United States. Systematically demonstrated water quality degradation could proxy for uncompensated damages imposed on downstream holders of property rights. Of course, while water quality per se may matter, even in the absence of human life or economic value, economists— the high priests of efficiency—would feel better if the EPA's documentation of water quality deterioration were to show that CAFOs impose unwanted costs on people and their property, and that these costs could be cost-beneficially controlled. With extensive evidence of biological and chemical deterioration, combined with some evidence of net economic harm, the body politic might reasonably support a proposal to impose stricter federal, as opposed to state or local, regulation on concentrated animal feeding operations.[5]

EPA's Evidence of Harmful Effects

In the EPA's analysis of the stricter CAFO rules proposed in 2001, the agency attempted to provide just such evidence. The EPA reports that "agricultural operations, including CAFOs, are considered a significant source of water pollution in the United States" (EPA 2001, 2972). But of course, the agency could not make this assessment on the basis of its own permitting and monitoring operations because only 2,000 of the estimated 10,000 CAFOs have obtained EPA-issued discharge permits (Keith, Jones, and Johnson 2000, 9). Instead, the EPA based its conclusion on reports from the states indicating that the agricultural sector is the leading cause of water quality impairment in the U.S. rivers, streams, and lakes that have been assessed. Using the state data, the agency estimated that water pollutants from agriculture account for 59 percent of water quality impairments to state-assessed rivers and streams. In addition, the agency estimated that 31 percent of assessed lakes might be impaired by agricultural sources. The EPA's interpretation of the state data suggests that the agricultural sector is the fifth leading cause of water-quality impairment in estuaries (EPA 1998).[6]

The EPA also reported that incidences of illness and even death have been traced to CAFO pollutants in drinking water in the Midwest. The panoply of harms continues. Between 1987 and 1997, forty-seven fish kills in the United States were attributed to CAFO water pollutants originating at hog farms. Feedlots were also identified as the source of contamination of 3 percent of shellfish grounds in twenty-one coastal states. And one California community was identified as anticipating the expenditure of $1 million a year to remove CAFO-generated nitrates from their potable water supplies (EPA 2001, 2981–83).

How reliable are these conclusions? Every two years, the EPA's Office of Water reports on the quality of U.S. surface waters to Congress, as required by the Clean Water Act. Regional EPA offices, the U.S. Geological Survey, state pollution control authorities, and a variety of other federal, state, and local organizations contribute to the effort. State waters that do not meet state water quality standards for water uses are designated by states as impaired. State pollution control authorities contribute significantly to the biannual effort by reporting the impairment status of their state surface waters to the EPA. But there is no uniform definition of impairment across states, and the national sampling of surface waters is not scientifically structured. Water quality monitoring in states has historically been done with the intent to identify water pollution control problems, not for the purpose of comprehensively assessing the quality of rivers, streams, lakes, and estuaries. Because of this, inferences cannot be made about the population of surface waters from these samples of U.S. rivers, streams, lakes, and estuaries.

State pollution control authorities also periodically review geographic information system mapping data and watershed-level study findings to assist them in making estimations about the sources of water pollutants that are responsible for water quality impairments. These estimates are also not generated in a scientifically structured process and tend to be predominantly subjective in nature.

Thus, although valuable for identifying specific impaired waters, the state data cannot be aggregated and used to make water-quality inferences for the nation, which is what the EPA has done in justifying the need to regulate CAFOs. As mentioned, the EPA reported that 59 percent of the assessed U.S. rivers and streams and 31 percent of the lakes identified as impaired are in that condition because of agricultural activity (EPA 2001, 2973).

It is noteworthy, however, that only 23 percent of U.S. rivers and streams and only 42 percent of the lakes have actually been assessed. And although it is true that agriculture has been identified by states as the leading cause of impairment in these assessed waters, it is also true that states have only actually assessed and attributed impairments to agriculture in 4.7 percent of U.S. rivers and streams and 5.8 percent of the lakes. Reports by states of water quality impairments due to animal feeding operations indicate that less than 1 percent of rivers, streams, and lakes have actually been identified as impaired by animal feeding operations. Also notable is the fact that estuaries comprise roughly 50 percent of the total surface waters, and states report that the agricultural sector is thought to be only the fifth leading source of impairment to estuaries (EPA 2001, 2973).

Thus, whereas the EPA relies on these state data to suggest that large percentages of water bodies are impaired by agriculture, the actual fraction of water bodies that have been positively identified as being impaired by agriculture is quite small. Overall, only an estimated 3.7 percent of water quality impairment has actually been attributed to agriculture through any objective or even subjective formal reporting process. Only an estimated 0.35 percent of surface water pollution has actually been attributed to animal feeding operations through any reporting process. As table 3.1 illustrates, agriculture, and especially animal feeding operations, has hardly been demonstrated to be a major source of water pollution.

The EPA reports that of the 840,402 miles of rivers and streams in the United States that have been assessed, 170,750 miles have been reported by states to be impaired by agriculture. The twenty-eight states that have differentiated between agricultural sectors in attributing impairment responsibility indicate that 16 percent of agriculture-impaired rivers and streams are thought to be impaired due to animal feeding operations specifically. In other words, 27,320 miles of the total 3,662,255 miles of rivers and streams, or 0.75 percent, have actually been identified by states as impaired by animal feeding operations (EPA 2001, 2973).

The EPA reports that of the 17,400,000 acres of lakes that have been assessed, 2,417,801 acres have been reported by states to be impaired by agriculture. The sixteen states that have differentiated between agricultural sectors in attributing lake impairment responsibility indicate that 4 percent of agriculture-impaired lakes are impaired due to animal feeding operations specifically. This means that 96,712 acres of the total 41,700,000 acres of lakes, or 0.23 percent, have actually been identified by states as impaired by animal feeding operations (EPA 2001, 2973). The EPA indicates that of the 28,687 square miles of estuaries that have been assessed, 1,827 square miles have been reported by states to be impaired by agriculture. The EPA does not report estuary impairment by agricultural sector in the preamble of the proposed new CAFO regulations.

Although the EPA accurately reports that 59 percent of assessed rivers and streams have been reported to be impaired by the agricultural sector, what appears to be the common interpretation of this, that the majority of surface waters are impaired by agricultural sources including and especially CAFOs, is incorrect. Water quality impairments from animal feeding operations are only evidenced in a fraction of 1 percent of total surface

Table 3.1. U.S. Water Quality Impairment by Source and Water Body Type

	Rivers and Streams (miles)	Lakes (acres)	Estuaries (square miles)	U.S. Surface Waters (square miles)
Total	3,662,255	41,600,000	90,465	181,518
Total assessed	840,402	17,400,000	28,687	62,241
	(23.0%)	(42.0%)	(32.0%)	(34.0%)
Total assessed & designated impaired	291,263	7,900,000	12,482	1,827
	(7.9%)	(19.0%)	(14.0%)	(15.0%)
Total assessed & designated impaired by agriculture	170,750	2,417,801	1,827	6,804
	(4.7%)	(5.8%)	(2.0%)	(3.7%)
Total assessed & designated impaired by animal feeding operations	27,320	96,712	292	634
	(0.75%)	(0.23%)	(0.32%)	(0.35%)

Notes: Total estuaries assessed and designated impaired by animal feeding operations is based on the 16 percent estimate of total agriculture impairment attributed to animal feed operations on rivers and streams in twenty-eight states. Assessed U.S. surface waters back-calculated from 181,518 total square miles.
Source: U.S. Census Bureau (1998, 235).

waters. Most important here is the fact that water quality monitoring of surface waters and water pollution source determinations in states prohibit scientifically valid conclusions to be drawn about surface water pollution or polluters.

The data relied on by the EPA to designate CAFOs as major contributors to water pollution do not support the assertion. Put differently, we simply have no way of knowing the extent to which agricultural activities and CAFOs are significant sources of pollutants in the nation's rivers, streams, and lakes. To the extent that CAFOs are a problem, the problem is not national in scope. Even so, those anxious to regulate might still base their case on some estimate of benefits and costs.

What about Benefits and Costs?

Using what we have shown to be a misinterpretation of water quality data, the EPA applied its Water Pollution Control Assessment Model to estimate the value Americans would assign to restored and protected swimming, boating, and fishing opportunities made possible by the proposed CAFO regulation. This benefit component ranged from $108.5 to $127.1 million annually. The agency then estimated the benefits associated with reducing pathogen-laden runoff to shellfish grounds, avoiding CAFO-related fish kills, and preventing CAFO-contaminated groundwater via new CAFO regulations. These estimated benefits range from $0.2 to $2.7 million, $0.2 to $0.4 million, and $35.4 to $53.9 million, respectively (EPA 2001, 3029).

When combined, these quantified benefits and costs yield costs in excess of benefits of between $664.2 and $803.9 million annually. In other words, there is a net social cost associated with the EPA's proposed CAFO regulations even when the most generous estimate of water quality impairment and thus improvement is applied. Obviously, there are potential benefits that were not included in the estimates just given. For example, the EPA considered but did not quantify the air quality benefits expected to accrue to home dwellers in the vicinity of CAFOs. A summary of the cost-benefit analysis is provided in table 3.2 (EPA 2001, 3029).

Table 3.2. Estimated Annual Costs and Benefits of EPA's Proposed CAFO Regulations

Estimated costs	$846.5 million to $949.4 million
Estimated benefits	$145.5 million to $182.3 million
Estimated net social costs	$664.2 million to $803.9 million

Note: Estimates are in 1999 dollars.

WHICH OF THE THREE THEORIES
IS BEST SUPPORTED BY THE FACTS?

The EPA estimates that the proposed CAFO regulations annually will impose net social costs of at least $664 million. The fact that estimated costs are so much larger than estimated benefits could reflect one of two possibilities that relate to our competing hypotheses about the CAFO venture. Those hoping for an efficiency story, which says the regulation is about internalizing externalities, might argue that the rule provides significant benefits that were not quantified and valued, but which, when combined with quantified benefits, would outweigh social costs. Indeed, the agency's preamble to the proposal suggests this is the case, pointing primarily to anticipated air pollution reductions that would contribute environmental benefits that were not accounted for in the cost-benefit analysis.

The second possibility, which would be consistent with our cartel hypothesis, says that the rule indeed imposes more burdens on Americans than benefits, but that this outcome doesn't really matter; the parties seeking to cartelize assign lower priority to environmental outcomes. The EPA's treatment of state water quality data clearly supports this possibility, but there is an even more compelling element to the agency's proposal that supports the cartel story. The problems associated with CAFOs are always confined to particular watersheds. They are never national in scope. In other settings, the EPA has appealed for the use of watershed planning and river-basin association management as a way to account for environmental differences while attempting to improve water quality. In 1996, the agency reported that $611 million to $5.6 billion *cost savings* could be generated if water quality goals in watersheds were pursued under a strategy that promoted effluent trading between permitted wastewater dischargers and unpermitted sources of runoff water pollution, including CAFOs as defined in the regulatory proposal (Luttner 1996). Indeed, the agency's Total Maximum Daily Load regulations are exclusively focused on watersheds and river basins. But an effluent trading strategy, even though explicitly endorsed by the EPA, is not included in the analysis of the proposed new CAFO regulations. In the case of CAFOs, the agency seems to have fallen back into its older command-and-control habits, which are clearly not cost effective. Do we have an anomaly or something else?

Are the CAFO Rules about Cartels?

Theories of regulation leave little room for strong efficiency outcomes, which is to say there is no scientific reason for any person to expect the EPA or any other government body to deliver cost-beneficial rules, assuming a narrow interpretation of these words. Obviously, when all costs and all benefits are considered—political, social, economic, and otherwise—all actions taken by political decision makers are cost-beneficial, at least to the decision makers. In other words, incentives matter.

We should also recognize that even if government were about maximizing net social benefits, this is not what is claimed by the Clean Water Act. The statute plainly states that it is about reducing discharge to national waters. It is only through presidential executive orders and congressional oversight that economic considerations are forced upon the EPA. In spite of the statute's silence on economic efficiency, the agency does have leeway to act cost effectively, if not cost beneficially. Given that the EPA is proposing rules that affect CAFO operations and given that it has flexibility in the choice of instrument to be used in achieving regulatory goals, at least conceptually, why is the EPA proposing old-time technology-based command-and-control regulation accompanied by heavy self-monitoring and reporting requirements? Why not at least allow states to adopt watershed approaches for reducing discharge that focus on ambient standards and outcomes, and going further, why not allow states to regulate by means of strengthened common law if not by specialized environmental courts? Why is the EPA so reluctant to experiment?

A first clue for answering these questions is found in the stimulus for proposed CAFO regulations. Regulatory action was undertaken to satisfy obligations arising from negotiations over the terms of a 1992 consent decree that settled *Natural Resources Defense Council, Inc., et al. v. Reilly* (1992). The agreement commits the EPA to propose and take final regulatory action on nineteen industrial categories of facilities that discharge wastewater to the environment. In addition to requiring regulatory action, the decree stipulates that the agency must use the National Pollution Discharge Elimination System permitting program (command and control). The consent has no provisions for the employment of decentralized, property rights–based strategies, regardless of whether they can be demonstrated to achieve like or better water quality at lower costs. Put simply, the EPA resorted to old-fashioned command-and-control regulation because it had no other choice in the matter. But just saying that the court required a particular regulatory instrument does not tell why the plaintiff, Natural Resources Defense Fund (NRDF) wanted that instrument to be applied.

Citizen Suits and Environmental Cartels

In 1990 Greve (1990) explained why national environmental organizations prefer the citizen suit enforcement features of command-and-control regulation that can be provided only by the central government.[7] Greve pointed out that the citizen suit opportunity provides a means for environmental organizations to earn net revenues from litigation, obtain special court-administered grants for environmental purposes from unlucky defendants, and reward and punish other environmental organizations who might not toe the party line. Buchanan and Tullock (1967) earlier had explained why industry preferred technology-based command-and-control federal regulation to common law or incentive-based pollution control. As they made clear, the one-suit-fits-all aspect of federal command-and-control regulation reduces output across all plants in an industry and limits the entry of new firms. "Polluters' profit" results from a regulator-managed cartel. When Greve is combined with Buchanan and Tullock, we get a double cartel story that finds polluters and purity lovers seeking similar political action, yet another bootlegger and Baptist story (Yandle 1983, 1999). Then, when rational ignorance is added to the political recipe, the combination seems to provide a robust theory of command-and-control dominance.

Prior to the federal government's takeover of the management of environmental resources, the common law of nuisance was a fundamental tool for protecting environmental rights, but it was by no means the only tool. In the vast pre-1970 U.S. federalist system, one searching for environmental property rights protection would have found a rich array of common law, city ordinances, state laws, regional compacts, private trusts, associations, and other forms of action (Ceplo and Yandle 1997). In some cases, the underlying property rights were public, which is to say, a city council managed and allocated the rights. In other cases, the rights were common to particular Indian tribes and community members. In still other cases, the rights were private, and common law controlled their protection. When a combination of social and political forces moved environmental decision making to the federal government level, the institutional structures that had evolved for well over a century were suddenly placed on hold and then reshaped. With environmentalism in full sway, federal politicians took action to redefine rights. The emerging environmental statutes nationalized each element of the natural environment. Although many of the preexisting institutions continued to have some bearing on outcomes, federal law and regulation were destined to be constitutionally dominant, if not by law, surely by practice of law. What the politicians must have seen at the outset was eventually understood by economists and other social scientists. The politicians gave themselves the power to convert private property rights to regulatory property rights and to change state public property to federal public property. Of course, all this was done in the good name of environmental quality.

The common law process had nothing to offer the politicians who sought to reward rent-seeking interest groups. Judge-managed common law actions were slow, unpredictable, and limited in their scope. Actions taken at common law require evidence of harm that has befallen a plaintiff and the results at law apply only to the parties in court; the ruling in a particular case cannot be extended beyond the plaintiff showing harm and the defendant causing the harm. Although lacking political appeal, common law was also unattractive to industrial firms that wanted uniform and predictable rules that they could expect to find anywhere in the nation. Industrialists had little interest in maintaining the common law status quo. Environmentalists of different stripes seeking tough federal controls were also looking for change. Those most focused on regulation for the sake of regulation wanted strict and uniform standards imposed from the top down. Others more dedicated to the religious aspects of environmentalism were on a crusade to impose high cost on polluters, even higher than might be found in common law courts. And of course, the "let's do something about it" attitude found at the center of government fit the approach understood by dedicated bureaucrats. Given the chance, the technocrats would find a comprehensive solution for the problem of water pollution. In short, politicians were not alone in seeking to move from private property to regulatory rights based on command-and-control regulation. Of course, these considerations were compatible with a rent-brokering politician's motivation.

The Cartel Enforcer's Cartel

From the very first, proponents of river basin associations and other decentralized approaches to pollution control have expressed concern about the prospects for monopolization of markets. Any shared constraint that effectively coordinates output decisions of producers in the same market can become the means for achieving monopoly profit (Riggs and Yandle 1997). Even those who claim efficiency for the command-and-control regulation that dominates much of U.S. environmental policy grant that government-enforced output restrictions can result in a regulatory cartel.

This particular cartel story, told many times, hinges on the fact that federal regulation is technology based and is based on input not environmental outcome. The regulation applies across the board to every firm in an industry, no matter where the firm is located, and generally requires more costly controls for new than for old plants (Buchanan and Tullock 1967).[8] In short, once a set of EPA effluent guidelines is made final, all firms in the industry face the same environmental constraint, and new firms systematically face a stricter constraint along with the gatekeeper's closer scrutiny. Clearly the same result cannot obtain where pollution is limited by taxation, fees based on environmental use, and cap-and-trade discharge permits. When it comes to rents induced by regulation, command and control takes the day.

Citizen Suits and Cartel Enforcement

No cartel is better than its enforcement mechanism, and this is where citizen suits enter the story. As outlined here, the polluter cartel story relies on federal regulator gatekeepers, who restrict the entry of new polluters and keep existing polluters in line. In addition, the gatekeeper (cartel manager) must find a way to monitor polluters by the tens of thousands and make certain they are abiding by their restrictive permits. With the output restriction yielding higher prices, there is a natural tendency for cartel members to cheat. The regulator must find low-cost ways to maintain the cartel. In actual fact, the federal government delegates to the states the enforcement of the Clean Water Act. To make matters more difficult for cartel managers, there is compelling empirical evidence of considerable variation in the stringency of enforcement across the states (Helland 1998). Faced with limited resources and variation in enforcement across the states, it is reasonable to expect government to design private enforcement of environmental law of the sort found in Section 505 of the Clean Water Act. But is it equally reasonable to expect that the act would revolve around the potential for technical violations—reporting, testing, and record keeping—more than pollution violations? Of course, the government cartel manager needs enforcement reinforcement and the members of a Buchanan-Tullock cartel require enforcement, too.

But whereas the industry cartel story is now a standard part of regulatory lore, the story of cartelization induced for environmental organizations remains largely uncelebrated. First told by Michael Greve (1990) and then expanded upon by Barnett and Terrell (2001), the prospect for this cartel story relies on command-and-control regulation with a special enforcement feature of U.S. environmental regulation. The Clean Water Act makes private individuals and organizations enforcement deputies by means of provisions for citizen suits. Precluded from making a profit in their enforcement endeavors, private citizens join public agents to enforce the law. Effluent standards of the sort contemplated by CAFO regulations make it easier. The technology-based command-and-control regulation that focuses on inputs, permits, and reporting; environmental organizations; and any other concerns about compliance, can readily examine the individual plant reports filed regularly with state and federal regulators. Private parties can read the required reports and identify firms that have failed to report properly or that have reported pollution excedances and other permit violations. It is interesting that the EPA addressed this very point in responding to environmental organizations' concerns about reporting requirements. The proposed rules must include the usual reporting requirements. With evidence of technical or other violations in hand, private parties can sue the polluter and, if successful, recover the cost of their legal action. Just cost recovery is not on its face all that attractive, of course. To make things more interesting, cost is something that can be negotiated, and is not necessarily the audited cost incurred by the organization bringing suit. At this point, the whole process seems unattractive. After all, the resulting fines levied against the convicted polluter must be paid to the U.S. Treasury. The statutes make it clear that private parties cannot earn a "profit" from their enforcement-related litigation activities. It is also fairly clear that citizen suits cannot be brought against parties who are already being investigated or sued by the EPA. However, as Greve points out, there is another payoff for environmental organizations, and it is this payoff that lays the foundation for the seeds of the environmental cartel. Environmental organizations bringing suit can fully recover litigation costs and obtain for environmental purposes court-ordered credits or grants above and beyond the penalties and fines paid by a convicted polluter. The court-ordered credits cannot redound to the direct benefit of the environmental organizations bringing suit, but can be designed by the plaintiffs so that organizations they favor will obtain the grants.

The prospect of profitable regulation by litigation is made even more attractive by virtue of the fact that most permit violation suits brought by private parties are won by the plaintiffs. When informed that a suit is pending, the affected polluter has a powerful incentive to settle out of court. A well-crafted settlement accomplishes several important cartel-enforcing functions. The polluter's opportunity cost of settling is represented by the expected value of fines, legal costs for both parties, and environmental credits that may be demanded by the judge in the case. Given the fact that most polluters lose, the polluter is likely to settle for some amount close to this full opportunity cost. The settlement payments discipline firms that may have broken the cartel's output constraint, and the environmental organization bringing suit helps to enforce the regulatory cartel. Then, the design of the credit program to be undertaken by the polluter provides a way to reward good environmental organizations and punish bad ones. Organizations that have cooperated in going after violators can obtain court-administered revenues. Those organizations that favored economic incentives, property rights, or some decentralized alternative to federal command-and-control regulation can be omitted from sharing in the litigation largess.[9]

Putting Enforcement to Political Advantage

A combination of private and public enforcement enables command-and-control regulation to become a vehicle for forming and maintaining industry *and* environmental cartels. The resulting barriers to entry generate rents for the cartelized industry, and the payments extracted through settlements and litigation reward environmental organizations that rally to help maintain the industry cartel. Although the resulting rents may be dissipated through the process of getting them, the regulation that yields the rents in the first place becomes capitalized in the resulting social structure. The resulting symbiotic relationship leads to high-cost environmental protection, and thus less of it, and reduced production of goods and services.

Like other biological symbiotic relationships, the double cartel offers little opportunity to either party to exert control over the other. Both parties are rent seekers. Industrial polluters hope to avoid common lawsuits and environmental taxes while using pollution control to wall out competitive entry. The environmental organizations obtain rents while playing an important role in policing members of the cartel that break the output constraint. The environmental litigators, however, cannot perfectly identify the polluter that deliberately breaks the cartel from the firm that experiences an accidental discharge or simply fails to maintain required records. Regulation by litigation is no more precise than any other regulation—all forms are crude.

The Bias and Growth in Citizen Suit Litigation

Unfortunately, the litigation process is both unguided and misguided. The citizen suit litigation introduces a distinct bias to the enforcement process. Environmental organizations seeking litigation-generated revenues will not likely target municipalities, which are the leading sources of water pollution, but will go for deep-pocket, high-profile industrial firms and executives who have a high incentive to settle out of court. Along with this unfortunate bias, as noted by Ashford and Caldart (2001, 113), the crude private litigation process chills the prospects for any experimentation that the EPA and other agency might wish to undertake.[10]

Is there any evidence to suggest that citizen suits were spurred by the federal statutes? A shift in litigation activities in the post-1970 citizen suit world can be seen in data reported by Frank Cross (1999). He gathered data on the number of reported cases in which the plaintiff included a common law nuisance pleading. Going far beyond what might be termed traditional common law actions, these cases included citizen suits as well as actions by regulatory agencies; both would have been filed in federal court. The data in table 3.3 show how federal court action experienced explosive growth after 1970 and the passage of major environmental statutes.

Table 3.3.   Reported Environmental Nuisance Actions

Period	State	Federal
1945–50	145	18
1955–60	207	31
1965–70	228	31
1975–80	378	149
1985–90	447	324
1990–95	610	504

Source: Cross (1999, 970).

To give perspective to the data, consider that real gross domestic product (GDP) grew roughly 4.5-fold from 1945 to 1995, which is more than the growth of state court nuisance cases. Notice that federal court cases grew by 28-fold during the same period. These data may indirectly reflect the opportunity for out-of-court settlements entered into by environmental litigation organizations.

FINAL THOUGHTS: IS CARTELIZATION NECESSARY?

When environmentalists seek federal solutions to environmental problems, does a successful outcome require cartelization of interest groups? Consider two pieces of theoretical work that may help to address this question. In 1981, Robert E. McCormick and Robert D. Tollison published an analysis that explained the occupations represented by elected politicians in state legislatures. Whereas the specialized analysis is itself interesting, the theoretical model they developed is of greater interest for the task at hand.

McCormick and Tollison assumed that legislative bodies are solely involved in redistributing wealth; government does not engage in the production of public goods and services. In their model, all wealth is in the hands of citizens, and to provide a dollar to one interest group requires taking that dollar from another citizen. The resistance encountered when taxing to obtain a dollar is part of the cost that must be paid when politicians move resources from one group to another. And of course, the greater this cost, the more likely the group being taxed will organize to deflect the cost to some other group. In a similar way, those seeking transfers have an incentive to organize as well, provided doing so will reduce transaction costs. In fact, every person and every group in their model is simultaneously organizing to seek payment and resist paying. In the extreme, it is the unorganized, unknowing, and uncaring who will bear the wealth of transfer burden, and it is the well-informed, highly organized, and specialized who stand to gain the most in the transfer game. What does this say about the use of regulation as a transfer mechanism?

In 1983, Nobel laureate Gary Becker (1983) published a theory of regulation in which he argued that elected politicians in a constitutional democracy do their best to regulate efficiently. His theory was not about political efforts to avoid deadweight losses or to apply traditional cost-benefit analysis to proposed regulations. Becker used "efficiency" in a much broader sense. He was describing the behavior of purposeful political agents who use the political machinery to transfer income to favored interest groups. His point, though controversial, was rather simple. If politicians could painlessly order the U.S. Treasury to send checks to the people who keep them in office, they would do so. But such blatant and open redistribution would not be tolerated. In a McCormick-Tollison sense, those paying will resist this method. Instead, the politician must use subsidies, tariffs, tax loopholes, and regulations to achieve redistribution goals. Becker argues that when a more efficient and effective way of making transfers becomes feasible, politicians will adapt their transfer mechanisms.

What about the cartels? The organization theory that springs from this theoretical discussion causes us to realize that the ongoing interest group struggle simultaneously forms organizations of payment seeker/avoiders who hope to come out ahead in the political economy. Alliances among these groups are costly to form and maintain; they face the free- or cheap-rider problem. It is cheaper for groups that share a common interest to organize informally than it is to incorporate as one entity. Environmentalists and agriculturists do not have to form a for-profit firm to enjoy polluter and environmental profits.

In an evolutionary sense, the cartel outcome is unavoidable. Environmental regulations that form output restrictions or that impose differential costs, or that deflect even more costly forms of social regulation, offer the promise of rents. All government efforts to "internalize externalities" by means of regulation will be cartel-forming actions.

This chapter began with the notion that institutions are constantly evolving in response to a host of social forces. The institutions we observe on a daily basis represent some sort of equilibrium outcome. With respect to regulations, the equilibrium represents hard-fought battles where political and economic forces converged to yield an outcome. Any shock to the system that shatters the foundation of a regulation or law will be followed by human efforts to rebuild the institution that has crumbled. If doing so is precluded by the shock that destroyed the original institution, then a substitute will emerge. This is the case so long as the political/economic forces that support the institutional purpose remain intact.

The EPA's treatment of concentrated animal feeding operations has followed a tortuous path since the 1972 passage of the Clean Water Act. During these three decades, major parts of agricultural production and activity have enjoyed protection from the EPA's regulatory authority. When the institutions that form that protection are attacked politically or through the courts, the agricultural community has sought substitute protection by other means.

This chapter put forward the thesis that the EPA's proposed CAFO regulations represent yet one more example of cartelization by regulation. Drawing on cartel theories, the paper has argued that the citizen suit provisions of the Clean Water Act will now serve as an enforcement mechanism for larger CAFOs that have joined environmental organizations in operating a new profit-generating regulatory refuge.

NOTES

The authors express appreciation to Susan Dudley of George Mason University's Mercatus Center for helpful comments on related work. Appreciation is also expressed to the Mercatus Center for permission to draw on a Center Public Interest Comment authored by Sean Blacklocke (2001).

1. Iowa Code, Section 352.2(6).

2. The EPA and U.S. Department of Agriculture announced on March 9, 1999, the final Unified National Strategy for Animal Feeding Operations. The plan's major details emerged when the EPA issued its Draft Guidance Manual and Example NPDES Permit for Concentrated Animal Feeding Operations on August 6, 1999. CAFOs had been subject to government rules before this, but the rules were vague, subject to wide-ranging interpretations, and were not filled with command-and-control detail. (See EPA 1999.)

3. This, of course, was the basis of the Iowa suit that led to the ruling that right-to-farm laws limiting common law liability were unconstitutional.

4. In their review of feedlot and right-to-farm statutes, Grossman and Fischer indicate that some apparently protective statutes attempt mainly to codify "coming to the nuisance" protection for farmers. That is, unchanged agricultural operations that were "there first" are protected from nuisance suits that might be brought by new suburbanites who move to the agricultural fringe and learn to their surprise that farms do not always smell good. However, other such statutes limit nuisance suits from neighboring farmers, and even in situations in which there is no coming to the nuisance problem. As Grossman and Fischer (1983, 7–8) point out, these statutes are there primarily to protect an industry.

5. Federal regulation of the environmental effects of animal feeding operations and other aspects of agricultural animal production has been a fact of life for decades. But the agricultural community has been successful in obtaining special treatment for its nonpoint-source pollution as well as funding to assist in dealing with state-imposed regulations. Part of the relatively relaxed regulation of animal feeding operations was changed by a 1994 citizen suit brought against a large New York cattle operation. The U.S. Court of Appeals for the Second Circuit tightened the definition for CAFOs and ruled that what had been treated as nonpoint-source pollution would be treated as point source. See *Concerned Area Residents for the Environment v. Southview Farm* (1994).

6. The EPA also reports on a variety of studies that correlate high nutrient levels in U.S. watersheds with livestock operations (EPA 2001, 2980).

7. For an elaboration on Greve's insight, see Barnett and Terrell (2001).

8. There seems no end to the number of instances of bootlegger/Baptist examples. A recent example is seen when North Carolina, the nation's number two hog producer, imposed a moratorium on new large-scale hog farms, and other leading hog-producing

states imposed stricter operating requirements. Indicating that he welcomed the restrictions, Joseph W. Luter III, CEO of Smithfield Foods, Inc., North Carolina's and the nation's largest hog producer/processor said: "Nobody can duplicate what we've done" (Kilman 2001). For more examples, see Adler 1996 and Yandle 1999.

9. Greve (1990) reports that a 1983 review of consent orders indicated an amount equal to about 400 percent of the penalties paid to the U.S. Treasury was paid to environmental groups for attorney fees. In addition, the value of the credit projects required of the convicted polluters amounted to millions of dollars and far exceeded the value of fines. His report of an analysis of thirty private enforcement actions brought in Connecticut between 1983 and 1986 shows the cases were settled for payments in excess of $1.5 million. See Greve (1990, 359).

10. There are no good data on out-of-court settlements and private litigation. But the pace of these activities under the various statutes enforced by the EPA can be inferred from the pace of actions taken by the EPA and federal prosecutors. Mark A. Cohen (1992) notes that only twenty-five criminal environmental cases were prosecuted in the entire decade of the 1970s. Then as Mandiberg and Smith (1997, 3) indicate, "from 1982 through April 1995, the agency brought charges against roughly 443 corporations and 1,068 individuals and obtained convictions against roughly 334 organizations and 740 individuals."

REFERENCES

Adler, Jonathan. 1996. Green Politics and Dirty Profits. *Regulation:* 26–34.

Ashford, Nicholas A., and Charles C. Caldart. 2001. Negotiated Environmental and Occupational Health and Safety Agreements in the United States: Lessons for Policy. *Journal of Cleaner Production* 9(April): 99–120.

Barnett, Andy H., and Timothy D. Terrell. 2001. Economic Observations on Citizen-Suit Provisions of Environmental Legislation. *Duke Environmental Law & Policy Forum* 12: 1–30.

Becker, Gary S. 1983. A Theory of Competition among Pressure Groups for Political Influence. *Quarterly Journal of Economics* 98(August): 371–400.

Blacklocke, Sean. 2001. Public Interest Comment on EPA's National Pollution Discharge Elimination Guidelines and Standards for Confined Animal Feeding Operations. George Mason University, Mercatus Center, Regulatory Studies Program.

Buchanan, James M., and Gordon Tullock. 1967. Polluters' "Profit" and Political Response. *American Economic Review* 65: 139–47.

Calvani, Terry, and Gilde Breidenbach. 1990. An Introduction to the Robinson-Patman Act and Its Enforcement by the Government. *Antitrust Law Journal* 59: 765–75.

Ceplo, Karol, and Bruce Yandle. 1997. Western States and Environmental Federalism. In *Environmental Federalism,* ed. Terry L. Anderson and Peter H. Hill. Lanham, MD: Rowman & Littlefield Publishers, Inc., 225–57.

Cohen, Mark A. 1992. Criminal Law: Environmental Crime and Punishment: Legal/Economic Theory and Empirical Evidence on Enforcement of Federal Environmental Statutes. *Journal of Criminal Law & Criminology* 82(Winter): 1054–98.

Cross, Frank B. 1999. Common Law and the Conceit of Modern Environmental Policy. *George Mason Law Review* 7(Summer): 965–82.

Environmental Protection Agency. 1998. *National Water Quality Inventory: 1998 Report to Congress* (EPA 841-R-00-001).Washington, DC.

———. 1999. Memorandum: Draft Guidance Manual and Example NPDES Permit for Concentrated Animal Feeding Operations. Washington, DC: EPA (August 6).

———. 2001. A National Pollutant Discharge Elimination System Permit Regulations and Effluent Limitation Guidelines and Standards for Confined Animal Feeding Operations (CAFO). *Federal Register* (January 12) at 66FR2959.

Faith, Roger L., Donald R. Leavens, and Robert D. Tollison. 1982. Antitrust Pork Barrel. *Journal of Law & Economics* 15(October): 329–42.

Greve, Michael S. 1990. The Private Enforcement of Environmental Law. *Tulane Law Review* 65: 339–82.

Grossman, Margaret Russo, and Thomas G. Fischer. 1983. Protecting the Right to Farm: Statutory Limits on Nuisance Actions against the Farmer. *Wisconsin Law Review* 1983: 95–165.

Helland, Eric. 1998. The Revealed Preference of State EPAs: Stringency, Enforcement, and Substitution. *Journal of Environmental Economics and Management* 35: 242–61.

Keith, Gary, Ron Jones, and Stan Johnson. 2000. Livestock and the Environment: Industry-Led Solutions, PR0004. Stephenville, TX: Texas Institute for Applied Environmental Research, May.

Kilman, Scott. 2001. Smithfield Foods CEO Welcomes Backlash over Its Hog Farms. *Wall Street Journal,* August.

Luttner, Mark. 1996. *President Clinton's Clean Water Act Initiative: Costs and Benefits.* Online: www.epa.gov/docs/epajrnal/summer94/12.txt.html (cited: March 21, 2001).

Mackay, Robert J., James C. Miller III, and Bruce Yandle, eds. 1987. *Public Choice and Regulation: The View from Inside the Federal Trade Commission.* Stanford, CA: Hoover Institution Press.

Mandiberg, Susan F., and Susan L. Smith, 1997. *Crimes against the Environment.* Charlottesville, VA: Michie.

McCormick, Robert E., and Robert D. Tollison. 1981. *Politicians, Legislation, and the Economy: An Inquiry into the Interest-Group Theory of Government.* Boston: Martinus Nijhoff Publishing.

Riggs, David W., and Bruce Yandle. 1997. Environmental Quality, Biological Envelopes and River Basin Markets for Water Quality. In *Water Marketing: The Next Generation,* ed. Terry L. Anderson and Peter J. Hill. Lanham, MD: Rowman & Littlefield Publishers, Inc., 147–66.

U.S. Census Bureau. 1998. *Statistical Abstract of the U.S.* Washington, DC.

Weiner, Jonathan B. 1999. Global Environmental Regulation: Instrument Choice in Legal Context. *Yale Law Journal* 108(January): 677–800.

Yandle, Bruce. 1983. Bootleggers and Baptists: The Education of a Regulatory Economist. *Regulation* (May/June): 12–16.

———. 1999. Bootleggers and Baptists in Retrospect. *Regulation* 22: 5–7.

CASES CITED

A.L.A. Schechter Corp. et al. v. United States (1935), 295 U.S. 723; 55 S. Ct. 651; 79 L. Ed. 1676.

Concerned Area Residents for the Environment v. Southview Farm (1994), 24 ELR 21480.

Natural Resources Defense Council, Inc., et al. v. Reilly (1992), Civ. No. 89-2980 (RCL) (D.D.C.).

William Aldred's Case (1610), 9 Co. Rep 57b Eng. Rep. 816.

4

Legal Impediments to Transferring Agricultural Water to Other Uses

B. Delworth Gardner

Practically all water in the arid western United States has already been appropriated. Increasing and changing water demands resulting primarily from significant population and economic growth, therefore, can be accommodated only by a high degree of water mobility. Transfers of water involve changes in one or more of the following: the ownership of water rights, the location of water use, the type of use, the season of use, and the point of diversion from a water course.

In all states of the region, a high percentage (usually more than 75 percent) of water is consumed by the agricultural sector, especially via crop irrigation. Meeting changing demands means a transfer of water from agricultural to municipal, recreational, and industrial uses in which the value is higher. Unfortunately, these transfers are often impeded, if not prohibited, by institutional policies and legal rulings that prevent the owners of rights from selling water to demanders.

The general public, as well as policy makers and implementers, often underappreciate the importance of property rights in a market economy. "Property refers to the right of the owner, formally acknowledged by public authority, both to exploit assets to the exclusion of everyone else and to dispose of them by sale or otherwise" (Pipes 1999, xv). Terry Anderson (1983, 5) indicates the role of property rights this way: "When property rights are well defined, enforced, and transferable, individuals will reap the benefits and bear the costs of their decisions and actions. Through this connection, property rights guide the invisible hand of the marketplace."

This chapter discusses the importance of durable property rights that will encourage market transfers of water in the western United States from lower-valued irrigation use to higher-valued nonagricultural uses. It is the principal thesis of the paper that a significant weakening of these property rights has occurred in recent years. Even though they are similar in many respects, each western state has developed its own legal and administrative regimes for water allocations. This diversity has merit because comparative analyses of alternative state arrangements might suggest which are more successful than others. What the country does not need is a one-size-fits-all national water policy that would give central control to such a vital resource, thus exposing it to the influence of special interests that is so characteristic of national agricultural policy as described in Hosemann (2003).

Recent legal challenges, however, have been made to these long-established state water-allocation regimes, and in the process have created uncertainty in property rights that is affecting water transfers in a significant way. The Utah situation was selected for analysis in this paper because of the author's familiarity with recent changes made in that state. The shifting institutional structure in Utah can be categorized under three principal rubrics: the impairment rule and changing approval criteria relating to water transfer applications, forfeiture provisions in prior-appropriation law, and uncertainty as to the ownership of irrigation water rights.

THE CHANGING REGULATORY
ENVIRONMENT AFFECTING WATER TRANSFERS

Under the prior-appropriation doctrine, utilized in most western states, a water right specifies the purpose of water use, the quantity of water diverted from the source, the point of diversion, and the season of use. If alterations are proposed in any of these items, a change application must be submitted to and approved by a state regulatory agency (Gardner 2001). The agency assigned this task varies among states; in most it is the office of the state engineer or some comparable agency in a state department of water resources, but in California it is the Water Resources Control Board and in Colorado it is water courts specifically established to regulate transfers.

It has been recognized everywhere that moving water in response to changes in demand might have effects on third parties not directly involved in negotiations for these transfers. The main reason for these third-party effects is that diversions of water are rarely matched by consumptive use. The unused water becomes incorporated into the rights of successive users. Therefore, there was deemed to be a need for a regulatory authority to monitor and authorize proposed transfers to make sure that all water rights were protected. The criterion utilized by most of these state agencies to approve or disapprove water change applications was whether other water rights would be impaired.[1] If so, the impaired party was given legal standing to protest the change application, and the state engineer was required to investigate the merits of the protest. If no significant impairment of other rights were found, the change application would be approved. If there were impairment, however, the application normally would be denied unless the injured party was made whole, either by monetary compensation or by limiting the amount of water transferred so that the quantity available to other rights was not diminished. If the protestor is not satisfied with the decision of the state engineer or the proposed remedy, he can resort to tort law and sue the state engineer and the applicant perpetrating the injury.

Two characteristics of these "impairment" procedures are significant. First, determining impairment of other water rights is principally a hydrologic question, i.e., how the quantity (and perhaps quality) of water available to other rights might be affected by a proposed change. Hence, the state engineer's office employed experts in hydrology to analyze these effects. Second, as the region changed demographically and economically, it became apparent that some parties who were not existing holders of water rights might be affected by water reallocations, but they lacked legal standing to protest change applications. These other "stakeholders" might include instream water users (primarily recreational users); those responsible for protecting fish and wildlife habitat, endangered species, and wetlands; and proximate property landowners who could be affected by the water changes proposed.

Utah law requires any person seeking to appropriate water to file an application with the state engineer describing the proposed appropriation.[2] Information required is similar to that required for a change application: the quantity of water being appropriated, the time during the year when the water would be used, the water source, the place of diversion and use, the diverting works, and a few other facts disclosing the purpose of the proposed appropriation (Jensen 1999).

Utah law also specifies the criteria the state engineer must use in evaluating the appropriation application as well as protests that might be made. Included are unappropriated water must be available, the proposed use must not impair other water rights or interfere with a more beneficial use, the proposed plan must be physically and economically feasible, and it must not be detrimental to the public welfare, public recreation, or the natural stream environment.[3] Just as for change applications, if the state engineer were to reject any protest to a proposed appropriation, that decision may be appealed in district court.

The phrase "not detrimental to the public welfare" is the source of much of the current controversy. What does "public welfare" mean? Is it different from what follows in the statement of the code, namely, "public recreation, or the natural stream environment"? Is private wealth creation included in public welfare, or are they mutually exclusive? The statute is silent on these crucial questions.

The Utah Code further specifies that water may be transferred "by deed in substantially the same manner as real estate."[4] As indicated, however, just as an original appropriation must be approved, so a proposal to change the point of diversion, the place of use, or the purpose of use, must also be approved by the state engineer.[5] And as also indicated earlier, a change application normally will be approved if it does not impair any existing vested water right. But with a change application there is no requirement for considering the public welfare. These procedures for new water appropriations and change applications were followed in Utah, and most other western states, for nearly a century before 1980 (Davis 1989).

Because water allocations have come to affect so many interests, however, it seems inevitable that the "narrow" impairment criterion would be challenged, and indeed it was in Utah. In 1988, a nonowner of a water right, Stanley Bonham, protested a proposed transfer on the basis that his land would be affected. His protest was denied by the state engineer because he lacked legal standing under the impairment rule because he did not have a water right that could be impaired (Gardner 2001). Bonham sued. It was clearly recognized that this would likely turn out to be a landmark case testing state water transfer procedures, so Bonham was joined in the suit by an environmental organization that perceived it had an important stake in water reallocations. Likewise, the irrigation companies seeking approval of the transfer application (and were joint defendants with the state engineer, Robert Morgan) were joined in the suit by other water companies that wished to minimize transfer impediments as conditions might become propitious to sell their own rights.

The suit finally went to the Utah Supreme Court, which ruled that the state engineer must use a public welfare criterion to approve water change applications, just as he was required to do when approving new water appropriations (*Bonham v. Morgan* 1989). It is far from clear at the present time, however, how the state engineer will respond to the court's directive, and even if it is possible to do so (Gardner 2001). Obviously, evaluating changes in public welfare resulting from a water transfer will require a large change in the way the state engineer's office operates, including an expansion in expertise in a wide variety of disciplines. It is not at all clear that this is operationally feasible, given personnel and budgetary constraints and the inherent fuzziness of the public welfare criterion. An implication of all this for efficient water allocations is that as soon as it is realized that almost anyone has legal standing to protest, there will be more protests. Moreover, the approval process for each application will be much more complex, leading to costly delays and probably more disapprovals.

It is interesting that a similar case was heard by the Nevada Supreme Court in the 1990s (Gardner 2001); that court ruled that the state engineer was *not* required to change the criteria for considering water change applications.

That court held that the standard requirements of beneficial use, the financial capability of the proposed users, and "impairment" (all standard requirements in most western states) were perfectly adequate indications of the public interest. It must be noted, however, that two justices wrote a biting dissent. A safe conclusion is that neither the Utah court nor its counterpart in Nevada will be regarded as the last word on the matter, even in those states.

THE LAW OF FORFEITURE

Early legislatures in the prior-appropriation states enacted statutes that required water to be put to actual use or the right could be forfeited. At the time such a requirement would seem to have been desirable for several reasons. The recording of a water right and the requirement that water be put to beneficial use was a way both of legitimizing the right and providing a low-transaction-cost tool for keeping track of the identity of the water users. In addition, it was believed that economic development would be promoted by requiring that water actually be put to use within a specified time rather than hoarded and held for speculation.

The Utah Code[6] specifies that water rights may be forfeited under the following conditions:

> When an appropriator or his successor in interest shall abandon or cease to use water for a period of five years the right shall cease and thereupon such water shall revert to the public, and may be again appropriated as provided in this title, unless before the expiration of such five-year period the appropriator or his successor in interest shall have filed with the State Engineer a verified application for an extension of time, not to exceed five years, within which to resume the use of such water and unless pursuant to such application the time within which such nonuse may continue is extended by the State Engineer as hereinafter provided. . . . Such applications for extension shall be granted by the State Engineer for periods not exceeding five years each, upon a showing of reasonable cause for such nonuse.

An exception is made, however, for municipalities looking toward future growth: "The holding of a water right without use by a municipality . . . to meet the reasonable future requirements of the public, shall constitute reasonable cause for nonuse."[7]

The forfeiture rule has produced results that have turned out to be at variance from those intended by the originators. Forfeiture amounts to a "use it or lose it" rule. For many reasons it may be economically inefficient to require that a fixed water quantity as specified in a right be put to actual use. Consider the problem of water utilization by a typical irrigator. Water needs of crops can be satisfied by precipitation as well as from an irrigation right. If a farmer had complete freedom to use water from the right in profit-maximizing quantities, he would apply it until marginal benefits equaled marginal costs. Irrigating crops involves variable labor and energy costs, even if the capital costs are largely fixed. In the event of high precipitation, the marginal benefits from applying irrigation water would fall, implying that the optimal quantity of water applied from the right would fall. However, if all the water in the right must be used or run the risk of forfeiture, economically excessive water could be applied, resulting in reduced crop yields as well as waterlogged soils and perhaps excessive runoff. Of course, this implies that a record of water use is kept and is available to parties who might be interested in invoking the forfeiture rule.

Perhaps even more important, because the right specifies the purpose and season of water use as well as the point of diversion, the threat of forfeiture may mean that water would be locked into a given use, time, and place when economic efficiency might require short-run or long-run transfers. Short-run transfers generally take the form of annual water rentals without the right changing ownership, whereas long-run transfers involve the outright sale of the right itself. Efficient transfers of water are especially valuable under water shortage or drought conditions because irrigation water may have far less value than water used for municipal and industrial use, including the generation of electricity. This precise situation clearly existed in the summer and fall of 2001 in the northwestern United States and California, where drought conditions made the value of water for generating electricity many times higher than for growing agricultural crops upriver (Hamilton, Whittlesey, and Halverson 1989). A water exchange to accommodate the difference in water value was hindered because of the risk that the forfeiture law could be used to deprive irrigators of their rights (*Economist* 2001).

Another consequence of the forfeiture rule results from the development of irrigation technologies that have sharply increased irrigation efficiency. Less water needs to be diverted per acre for the consumptive use of a farmer's crop. So what is the farmer to do with the water that it is now uneconomic for him to use on appurtenant land? If it might be lost due to the forfeiture law, the farmer may elect to expand his irrigated land base if that option is available. Or, if legally permissible, he may sell or rent the excess water to others without taking cognizance of the effects on other use-dependent water rights (Huffaker, Whittlesey, and Hamiliton 2000). Such actions may or may not be economically efficient when considered from the point of view of an entire water basin, where return flows from irrigation are significant.

Finally, there is the matter of speculation in water rights that at least partially gave rise to the forfeiture law in the first place. Speculation may make good economic sense for the community as well as the holder of the water right, even if water is withheld from use in a given location at a given time and for a given purpose. A water right is an entitlement in perpetuity to the value of an expected annual flow of water. The owner of a right will continue to hold it so long as the anticipated present value of the future flow is higher than it would be if he sold the right to someone else. However, anticipated income flows from future use are highly stochastic, depending on many factors that are variously evaluated by different potential owners of the right. Evaluating this uncertainty is the special province of speculators. And just as land justifiably may be held idle for speculation in a market where factors affecting land values are variously estimated, so a water right might be held for such speculative purposes. Withholding water from current use, especially if it can be stored and used or sold later when its value is higher, may be quite feasible and a good reason for holding on to the right. (This point has already been recognized in law in the case of municipalities looking toward future growth.) But if the right may be forfeited if the water is unused by its owner, the incentive to sell the right is enhanced, even if it made good economic sense to retain it.

Furthermore, is this speculative motive for holding a right necessarily a bad thing from the community's point of view even if the water is not used by the owner of the right? It might be if this nonuse created significant negative third-party technological effects. In fact, however, usually the opposite occurs. If the owner of the right does not use his water, it does not magically disappear from the water supply system. Instead, the probability is high that the water will be used by others. So benefits, rather than costs, accrue to third parties. A good example is provided by use of the water in the Colorado River. At present, some upper basin states, such as Utah, Colorado, and Wyoming, cannot economically use their river entitlements that were negotiated by treaty in the 1920s. So the unused water flows down the river and is ultimately used in Nevada, Arizona, California, and Mexico. Likewise, an irrigator who does not use his water potentially confers benefits on other users along the water supply course. But because the right might be forfeited if the water is unused by its owner, the forfeiture rule could produce premature and inefficient water applications and conversions.

Another problem imposed by the forfeiture rule is more long term. Consider a vested irrigation right on a parcel of land used to grow crops. But then, at a later time, suppose that the land is converted to urban uses. The urban developer might purchase the water right and file an application to change the beneficial use and perhaps the point of diversion. But suppose it would be less costly for the developer to hook on to an existing municipal water system to service his urban customers, and the irrigation right becomes inactive. Then, suppose that at some later time (after five years) the owner of the right wished to sell it. Obviously, the law of forfeiture would come into play, and the state engineer could deny the change application;

the water could then be available for reappropriation. Through forfeiture the owner of the old right would be deprived of the wealth incorporated in the right. The threat of this outcome could induce the owner of the right to use the water in economically wasteful ways in order to circumvent forfeiture, or it might induce him to sell the right, perhaps economically prematurely. In fact, some municipalities have imposed the requirement that developers acquire water rights as a precondition for approval of development plans. Then if the developer hooks onto a municipal water system, the right would be turned over to the municipality. In principle, however, there are no reasons for believing that such requirements generally will be economically efficient.

As with other issues discussed in this paper, precedent court cases have put "teeth" into the law. Such a case on forfeiture was provided in Utah in 1989 (*Nephi City v. Hansen*). Early in the twentieth century, Nephi City in central Utah acquired four water rights on Salt Creek. The city used the water to generate electricity, a beneficial use under the law. In the early 1950s a flood on Salt Creek destroyed the diversion and conveying works. For more than thirty years, therefore, these water rights were not beneficially used by Nephi City. In 1982, however, the city proposed to construct a new hydroelectric facility. Believing that its rights were still valid, the city filed applications with the state engineer to change permanently the points of diversion.

The change applications were protested by the Utah State Division of Wildlife Resources on the basis that a renewal of water use would diminish habitat for wildlife. After a hearing, the state engineer rejected the change applications on the grounds that the water rights had not been used for a period exceeding five years and thus were forfeited. Because there were no subsisting water rights, there could be no change in points of diversion.

Nephi City disagreed with the state engineer's decision and brought an action in district court for a review. The city did not challenge the forfeiture law directly, but instead argued that forfeiture of its water rights was unconstitutional under Article XI, Section 6, of the Utah State Constitution. This article provides that

> no municipal corporation, shall directly or indirectly, lease, sell, alien, or dispose of any waterworks, water rights, or sources of water supply now, or hereafter to be owned or controlled by it; but all such waterworks, water rights and sources of water supply now owned or hereafter to be acquired by any municipal corporation, shall be preserved, maintained and operated by it for supplying its inhabitants with water at reasonable charges; provided, that nothing herein contained shall be construed to prevent any such municipal corporation from exchanging water rights, or sources of water supply, for other water rights or sources of water supply of equal value, and to be devoted in like manner to the public supply of its inhabitants.

In short, Nephi City argued that the constitution prohibited it from disposing of any water rights owned or controlled by it, and therefore it could not forfeit water rights it could not legally dispose of.

The district court granted the motion of the state engineer and the Utah State Division of Wildlife Resources for summary judgment. It held that there were no disputed issues of material fact, and that the state engineer was correct in concluding that the water rights had been forfeited by nonuse. In addition, there was no conflict between Article XI of the constitution and Section 73-1-4 of the code because the constitution only prohibits the voluntary, intentional disposition of water rights, whereas forfeiture under Section 73-1-4 is involuntary. Nephi City appealed to the Utah Supreme Court.

The court held that the question was purely a matter of law, and that there could be no dispute that Section 73-1-4 of the code works a forfeiture of Nephi City's rights because they were unused for thirty years. No extension of rights was sought by or granted to Nephi City. Therefore, under the plain terms of Section 73-1-4 the rights were forfeited for nonuse by operation of law.

But there was also the matter of whether Section 73-1-4 of the code is inconsistent with Article XI of Utah's constitution. As the court saw it, the question was whether the article bars all transfers, voluntary or involuntary, or whether it is limited to voluntary transfers as the state engineer and the district court implicitly held. The court held that Article XI, Section 6, is applicable to voluntary transfers only. It found that involuntary forfeiture of rights has been a basic part of Utah water law since 1880, and the law was in effect when the Utah constitution was adopted in 1896. It must be presumed, therefore, that the framers of the constitution were aware of the forfeiture provision in the then-existing statutory law. The summary judgment thereby upheld the state engineer's decision rejecting Nephi City's applications to change the points of diversion of the four claimed water rights (*Nephi City v. Hansen* 1989).

For Utah, this case seemed to settle the validity of the forfeiture law even when applied to municipalities. What remains unresolved is the effect of the forfeiture rule on whether water is efficiently allocated. By losing the water right, Nephi City had to make other (and presumably more costly) arrangements for providing power to its customers. There do not appear to be provisions in appropriation law that would prohibit the city from applying for a new appropriation, but the application probably would have been protested by the same interests that gained from forfeiture of the right.

All of which raises an important question. Precious little empirical information is known regarding the economic misallocations induced by the forfeiture rule. One issue is what happens to the water that might be legally available for reappropriation as a result of a right forfeiture? In the current environment of tight water supplies, appropriation of available water is not so easy as it once was. The point has already been made that if a right is not exercised for a given period the water simply does not disappear. It will be available to be used by others on the water system, even if they do not have legal rights to it. This will be particularly true for instream uses and wetlands used for wildlife habitat. If a new party attempts to reappropriate the water, those who were benefiting from the previous nonuse of the right will be affected and likely will protest the new appropriation. Recall that the criteria for granting new appropriations are much broader than for change applications, especially before the Bonham challenge. In a post-Bonham world, however, it is far from clear how both the state engineer and the courts will respond to future protests. The legal situation is likely to be murky at best. Such attenuated rights can discourage investments and encourage strategic behavior that attempts to exploit the legal uncertainty.

Another complicating factor is that the status of a water right with respect to forfeiture may not be evident until a change application is filed. The state engineer does not monitor water rights to determine if water is being used according to the law. Only when a change application is filed and protested is a forfeiture allegation likely to arise. Therefore, it is unclear how much water could be potentially affected by the forfeiture rule. What is clear is that urban water delivery is very complex in western states with municipal public utilities, water conservancy districts, and private water companies all vying for customers and all concerned with the acquisition and maintenance of water rights.

WHO OWNS IRRIGATION WATER RIGHTS?

A third major issue affecting market transfers of water to higher-valued uses is the ownership of the water rights, and therefore who controls market exchanges. Because agriculture is the marginal user (the user of lowest value) of water in most areas, especially those experiencing rapid urban development, the most frequent transfers are those from agricultural to urban uses. And because agriculture was the dominant industry in the settlement period of most western states, and is still the dominant consumptive water user, problems with the ownership structure of water rights in this sector could lead to inefficient allocations of water.

The foremost organization distributing water for irrigation in Utah and most other western states was and still is the private mutual irrigation company (or corporation). These companies issue water shares to individual farmers in the company, generally in proportion to the acreage served. But it was usually the company that received and held the appropriative water rights, and the officers of the company, representing the shareholders, naturally assumed the authority to negotiate transfers of these rights. But this authority has been challenged in recent years as conflicts have arisen between individual shareholders and company officers as to who controls the rights. This is an extremely important matter when considered in light of the question raised earlier as to what is a property right. As mentioned, a nonattenuated property right must be clearly defined so that it is evident what can be traded, it must be defendable against possible encroachments, and it must be divestible at the discretion of the owner. If any component is missing, a serious attenuation in the right exists and the market cannot be expected to be efficient in transferring the asset incorporated in the right to its highest-valued use. As with other issues discussed, ownership of water rights has been tested in Utah's courts, but the court ruling does not appear to have settled the question as evidenced by the fact that the issue has been taken up by a recent Utah legislature.

The court battle in Utah (*East Jordan Irrigation Company v. Morgan and Payson City* 1993) is especially instructive because so many factors of interest were present: a proposed transfer from agricultural to urban use, a surface-water ground-water trade, and a change in diversion from a point on the water course to one nearly fifty miles distant.

East Jordan is a nonprofit mutual water company and was established to supply water to its shareholders, principally irrigators. The company owns legal title to water rights in Utah Lake and the Jordan River that connects Utah Lake, in Utah County, to the Great Salt Lake. The company diverts water from the Jordan River to a canal and delivers it to about 650 irrigator shareholders in Salt Lake County. Each of the 10,000 shares entitles a shareholder to receive a pro rata share of the company's canal water (*East Jordan v. Morgan* 311).

Payson City, located about 15 miles south of Utah Lake, bought 38.5 of East Jordan's shares in 1987, representing the delivery of an average of 186.34 acre-feet of water annually (*East Jordan v. Morgan* 311). Following the statute, Payson filed an application with the state engineer to change the point of diversion to a city-owned well near the city that draws water from a basin connecting to Utah Lake. Payson also sought to use this water for year-round municipal purposes.

East Jordan protested the change application on two grounds: (1) the change application should have been filed by East Jordan as owner of the water right, and (2) the proposed change would impair the company's vested water rights in Utah Lake. The state engineer held two hearings and then approved Payson's change application. As for the objections raised by East Jordan, the state engineer concluded first that Payson held a vested water right by virtue of its ownership of East Jordan stock and, therefore, could legitimately file a change application in its own name. And second, the state engineer considered a number of hydrologic factors relating to impairment of other rights: the amount of water consumed by irrigation, the amount of water that would be returned to Utah Lake from municipal use, and the seasonal variation in water use. He ordered that Payson be allowed to divert 144 acre-feet between April 15 and October 31 and 38 acre-feet the rest of the year, and that East Jordan reduce the diversion into its canal by 186.34 acre-feet per year. In addition, the state engineer required that Payson install a meter on its diversion well that would be available for inspection by East Jordan, and that Payson be liable for assessments and any other obligations it may incur as a shareholder in the company (*East Jordan v. Morgan* 311).

This ruling by the state engineer demonstrates how hydrologic factors, including consumptive use and return flows, are taken into account in his decisions. In the ensuing court actions, these determinations by the state engineer were not challenged.

After the state engineer's decision, the parties filed cross-motions in district court for summary judgment on the stipulated issues: first, whether Payson as a shareholder in the corporation had the legal right to file a change application in its own name without the consent of East Jordan. And second, whether the state engineer had jurisdiction to consider such an application. The district court denied East Jordan's motion and granted Payson's. East Jordan then appealed to the Utah Supreme Court.

East Jordan argued that the trial court had erred on both points at issue (*East Jordan v. Morgan* 311). Basically, East Jordan's argument was that because the company was the legal owner of the water rights, only it had the right to change the point of diversion. East Jordan also asserted that allowing shareholders to file change applications in their own names would violate the corporate structure of such companies and make it impossible to manage them. East Jordan further argued that its articles of incorporation and company policies contain a specific restriction preventing a shareholder from filing a change application without the company's consent. Moreover, the company stipulated that the specific change application would impair the vested rights of the company and its other shareholders, and that the state engineer's ruling in effect would wrongfully partition the company's title to its water rights. On the second issue of jurisdiction, East Jordan contended that the state engineer lacked authority to approve a change application in such a complex situation because he fulfills only an administrative function and lacks the authority and training to adjudicate the legal rights of the parties.

Payson City countered that mutual irrigation companies are fundamentally different from other types of corporations because shareholders have direct interests in the water rights held by the companies, and that among these interests is the right to change the point of diversion. Payson also argued that although East Jordan may have legal title to the water rights, it is the shareholders who really have equitable title (*East Jordan v. Morgan* 312).

The Utah Supreme Court first addressed the issue of whether Payson had the legal right to file a change application with the state engineer in its own name without the consent of East Jordan, and held that it had no such right. The court said that it based its decision on the "statutory scheme governing the appropriation of public waters, the principles of corporate law bearing on the function and power of boards of directors to manage corporate affairs in the interest of shareholders as a whole, and the dictates of sound public policy" (*East Jordan v. Morgan* 312).

The court granted that the Utah Code 73-3-3 (2) provides that any person *entitled to* the use of water may petition for changes in the point of diversion, the place of use, and the purpose of use. And, of course, Payson had argued that it had the right to change its point of diversion over East Jordan's objection. But the court held that the code provision must be read in light of the entire statutes, and that Payson had failed to prove that it was entitled to the use of water. The water rights belonged to the company, a point that had been affirmed in previous legal decrees. Hence, Payson's ownership of shares in the company did *not* give it a right conferred by the state to the use of water as contemplated by Code 73-3-3 (2). The court found it necessarily follows that any change in the point of diversion could be initiated only by East Jordan itself because it alone owned the right as an appropriator to the use of public waters.

Further, even though Payson claimed to be the "equitable owner" of its shares of East Jordan's water rights, the court held that its equitable ownership remained subject to the general rule governing corporations that directors, rather than shareholders, control the affairs of the corporation. East Jordan had been organized under the territorial laws in 1878 and was governed by the Utah Nonprofit Corporation and Co-operative Association Act. Section 16-6-34 of that act specifies that "the affairs of a nonprofit corporation shall be managed by a governing board" (*East Jordan v. Morgan* 313). In addition, Article VII of East Jordan's articles of incorporation provided that "the Board of Directors shall have the general supervision, management, direction, and control of all the business and affairs of the company, of whatever kind" (*East Jordan v. Morgan* 313–14).

The Utah Supreme Court reasoned that what Payson gained by its purchase of East Jordan shares was only the right to receive a proportionate share of the water distributed by the company out of its system. Because Payson was seeking a point of diversion, a place of use, and a nature of use that were substantially different from those of the other shareholders, as well as those anticipated in East Jordan's articles of incorporation, the city was asking more than its legal entitlement allowed. Payson wanted to divert its share of the water before it entered East Jordan's delivery system, to transport the water outside the company's service area, and to use it for municipal purposes—all beyond its authority as a single shareholder.

The court's ruling has far-reaching implications for economically efficient transfers of water rights. Indeed, at least part of Payson's proposal is the sine qua non of all rural-to-urban water transfers that are required to accommodate changes in demand. If the court's finding in this suit were to hold in all transfer cases, then it is clear that boards of directors of irrigation companies could block efficient water transfers.

But the court wasn't finished. It held that the agreement between East Jordan and its shareholders imposes the duty on the company to manage its affairs in the interest of the shareholders as a whole, and that this duty must not be infringed by the state engineer. It went even further to suggest that any dispute that might arise between the company and its shareholders should be resolved, not by a state administrative agency, but by a court of competent jurisdiction. The court believed that this was necessary because Payson City had argued that a precedent case in Colorado had settled this issue in its favor. In that case (*Wadsworth Ditch Co. v. Brown* 1907) a Colorado court held that a shareholder had the right to change a point of diversion over the objection of an irrigation company in which the shareholder had shares

However, in response to Payson's argument, the Utah Supreme Court pointed out that unlike Utah law, under the Colorado appropriation scheme the change process is commenced in a court of competent jurisdiction rather than with the state engineer. The Utah court opined that a court is better suited to construe a company's articles of incorporation and bylaws than a state engineer, who merely performs an administrative function. Therefore, the Utah high court found the Colorado case inapposite (*East Jordan v. Morgan* 315).

What may be most significant in the long run about the court's decision is the compelling minority dissent of Justice Christine Durham (*East Jordan v. Morgan* 316–21). Her arguments are so convincing that it would be difficult not to expect them to surface frequently in the future, and indeed, they have in recent legislative action that will be discussed later.

Durham (*East Jordan v. Morgan*, 316) argued that the majority had crucially erred in a number of its findings:

1. Water was improperly treated like an ordinary corporate asset, and mutual water companies were assumed to be the same as other corporations.
2. Long-established Utah case law was ignored, holding that mutual water companies may not interfere with a shareholder's use of his shares of water unless the shareholder's use harms the corporation or other shareholders.
3. The majority's holding was bad policy because it assumed without adequate analysis that allowing shareholders to change their points of diversion would destroy water corporations, and it ignored the need for flexibility and transferability of water rights.

In short, Durham's dissent indicates a more thorough understanding of the nature of water property rights (definable, defendable, and divestible) than was found in the majority opinion. She cited precedent to find that "water rights are pooled in a mutual company for convenience of operation and more efficient distribution of water, and perhaps for more convenient transfer. But the stock certificate is not like the stock certificate in a company operated for profit. It is really a certificate showing an undivided part ownership in a certain water supply" (*East Jordan v. Morgan* 318). She also pointed out that on numerous occasions the court "reiterated the principle that shareholders in a mutual water corporation actually own water rights" (*St. George City v. Kirkland* 1966). In *St. George,* for example, a mutual water company's charter lapsed in 1953 after fifty years of existence, and the company did not reincorporate until four years later. A number of people filed claims to the company's water, arguing that the corporation had forfeited its water claims. The Utah Supreme Court rejected these claims, holding that the shareholders continued to own the water rights, although the company charged with delivering the water was defunct. The court thus held that the company was not the owner of the water rights; it simply provided a method for the shareholders to distribute water among themselves.

In *East Jordan v. Morgan* the majority held that East Jordan was the sole owner of the water rights because it was named as the owner in the water decree. Justice Durham rejected this claim on the grounds that ownership of water is far more complex than ownership of other forms of property, and that the mere existence of legal title did not determine the rights of ownership. Although a water right is considered a "property right," certain legal principles regarding water have developed in the West that differ significantly from those regarding other forms of property. A private person does not really "own" the water itself, the acquired usufructuary right depends on putting the water to beneficial use, and the rights may be forfeited to the state if the water is not used for five years. Durham argued that these differences are crucial in determining the respective rights of mutual water companies and their shareholders. Whereas the water right may be held in the company's name, only the shareholder has the right to use the water and hence must decide whether, how, and where to use it. Furthermore, the mutual company is under a perpetual duty to deliver water to the shareholder, but may not decide that it would rather deliver water to someone else or for some other purpose. So if the company has the right, what does the right allow the company to do? Very little it seems, except block transfers. Moreover, the company cannot even maintain the water rights unless its shareholders use the water, and Justice Durham pointed out that even East Jordan had conceded this point (*East Jordan v. Morgan* 317). Therefore, the correct inference must be that the shareholders owned the water rights, de facto.

To buttress her conclusion, Durham asserted that the majority opinion failed to recognize case law that had developed regarding the relative rights of mutual water companies and their shareholders. Whereas she acknowledged that the court had never explicitly faced the issue of whether a shareholder may change the point of diversion without company consent, it had considered the relationship in a number of other contexts. These cases clearly established that a shareholder has a right to do whatever he wants with his shares of water, and the company may not interfere with this right.

For example, in *Baird v. Upper Canal Irrigation Co.* (1927), the court found that water becomes the shareholder's property once it is delivered to him, and that the shareholder has the right to use it as he wishes as long as it does not interfere with the rights of others. Durham argued that *Baird* was binding here. First, East Jordan complained that Payson's proposed change would result in the removal of water from East Jordan's service area and would thus change from irrigation to municipal use. But *Baird* demonstrated that these are not the valid concerns of the company. Second, *Baird* implied that a shareholder would not need the company's permission to file an application for a change in place and purpose of use. Most important, *Baird* suggested a practical reason to allow a shareholder to change his point of diversion over the company's objection (*East Jordan v. Morgan* 319). Under its own reasoning, East Jordan could not object if Payson took its share of water through the company's canal, and then somehow delivered it to the city through its own facilities. Because Payson had the right to take its water wherever it wanted after the water entered its own pipes and ditches, surely the city should also be allowed to take the water from farther up the natural watercourse.

Justice Durham also argued that earlier cases had established that a shareholder's interest in the water of a mutual company must include the right to decide where the water is received and how it is used, so long as a proposed change did not increase the company's costs or otherwise interfere with its ability to manage the water supply for the benefit of all shareholders. The state engineer's order did not interfere with East Jordan's ability to manage the company's water supply, but did provide that both East Jordan and the Utah Lake and Jordan River commissioners had the right to inspect Payson's meter to ensure that the city did not take more than its share of water. The order also provided that Payson's stockholders would remain liable for assessment to maintain East Jordan's canal and other company assets. If there were a water supply shortage, East Jordan could limit the amount of water Payson took through its well in the same proportion as applied to the other shareholders. The only difference was that Payson would take water from its own well rather than from the company canal. In Durham's view, the majority's approach increased the costs for everyone involved without providing any benefits.

In conclusion, preventing shareholders from changing the points of water diversion interferes with the ability of users to respond to new demands. In short, it prevents a market in water rights from allocating water to its highest and best use. Unhappily, the Utah Supreme Court decision prevented this salubrious result from occurring.

Despite the ruling, the matter of who owns the water rights is still alive in Utah. In the 2001 legislative session, a bill was introduced that would permit individual irrigators to transfer water rights without company approval. It should come as no surprise that the bill was opposed by the officials of many water companies, and even the state engineer expressed doubts about it (Spangler 2001). In the end, however, the bill was not brought up for a vote, and the matter was referred to a special task force on water rights. Appointed by the governor, this body will make recommendations to the legislature for future action.

CONCLUSIONS AND RECOMMENDATIONS

What conclusions can be drawn from the discussion presented here, and what institutional changes are required to effectuate desirable changes?

The office of the state engineer is not now equipped to implement a social welfare criterion for assessing applications to transfer water rights, nor can it be expected to do so regardless of how large its personnel and budget might be. The concept of social welfare is much too broad and too murky to be a workable standard for a regulatory agency evaluating thousands of change applications each year. Even though the pre-Bonham criterion of "impairment" of other water rights may neglect important factors in some instances, at least the impairment criterion is operational and is buttressed by hydrologic science that the state engineer is fully capable of applying.

Many of the challenges to the impairment rule come from interests that are concerned with potential harmful effects of water transfers on fish and wildlife habitat and recreation. However, if instream users were legally eligible to compete for water rights, then the market would properly account for these uses that now may be neglected in the market that permits only water diversions.

The argument that state administrative agencies, such as the state engineer, can utilize the impairment rule to protect existing water rights has been challenged by critics who believe that the impairment rule under prior-appropriation law needs to be modified by public trust criteria that give due regard to "public" values.

The modern-day erosion of the prior-appropriation doctrine's past virtues undermines the doctrine's prospective utility as the pre-eminent water allocation mechanism in the West into the 21st century, and thus increases the necessity for operating a more flexible version of the doctrine in conjunction with parallel allocation doctrines better equipped to distribute water to a number of meritorious competing public uses . . . (e.g., the public-trust doctrine and the emerging doctrine of federal regulatory rights). (Huffaker, Whittlesey, and Hamilton 2000, 271)

The primary basis for this conclusion is that "changes in on-farm irrigation technology have increased consumptive water use at the expense of other use-dependent rights, and have resulted in illegal water spreading with the blessing of state and federal water agencies. In short, the impairment rule has ceased to operate well, and consequently, should not be allowed to severely restrict water transfers."[8]

The scholars propounding the deficiencies in the impairment rule may be correct that prior-appropriation law (including impairment rules) have ceased to function well in some areas under specific circumstances, but more empirical evidence is needed from across the region before definitive conclusions can be drawn for the entire West. It is quite possible that regulatory agencies in some states perform impairment evaluations under tighter rules and with higher degrees of objectivity (less political influence) than they do in others. The prior-appropriation doctrine and the impairment rule seem to have worked rather well in Utah. These state differences in water institutions provide an important laboratory for research. A comparative study among states may turn up empirical evidence of what is working and what is not in terms of efficient water reallocations. States can learn from each other, and the promise for improving the efficiency of water allocation is much greater than would be true if water policy had been federalized and were identical everywhere in the country.

And what if the state engineer utilizing the "objective" impairment rule to evaluate change applications were replaced by an agency with public trust responsibilities? This would clearly lead to a higher degree of politicization of water allocation decisions. If public trust evaluations were to replace, or even complement, impairment rules, some political body would decide what is in the public interest, and what criteria would guide its decisions. Which body would do that and how would relative "values" of alternative allocations be determined? This is an enormously important issue. Economists have long argued that only buyers and sellers of commodities can possibly know the values of that which is traded. Cost and utility functions are intrinsically subjective, and no outsider can know what they are. In such an environment, opportunities for political rent seeking by interest groups and rent extraction by politicians would be rampant and very costly (McChesney 2002). In the end, it would probably come down to which political interests would trump other interests.

In a time when competition for water is growing rapidly, forfeiture laws serve no purpose and should be repealed. Incentives to transfer water rights prematurely and inefficiently would be thus largely removed. Especially conducive to economically efficient water allocations would be modification of beneficial-use rules to permit short-run transfers of water, such as annual rentals that would occur during times of drought and pressures on supply. This might be accomplished by allowing water use of the renter to be regarded as beneficial use under the current rules. But it is time to ask whether the beneficial-use requirement itself ought to be repealed. Given high water values and emerging water markets, it is difficult to see how any use that could successfully bid water away from other uses could not be considered as "beneficial."

As to who should hold the right to transfer water in the case of mutual water companies, it is evident that it is the individual shareholders who already have the legal responsibility (right) to determine the point of diversion, the season of use, and the type of use. These are significant rights, but the most important right is missing if water is to be efficiently allocated—the right to transfer water to a higher-valued user. It is unfortunate that the Utah Supreme Court chose to give this right to the irrigation company—an entity that cannot possibly know what water is worth to the water user, and therefore cannot make economically efficient market decisions. Only the irrigator shareholders bear the opportunity costs and capture the benefits of water use. Therefore, it is they, and not the officials of the company, who should determine whether they should keep or dispose of the water right. It must be granted, however, that water transfers may produce effects on third parties, due mainly to alterations in return flows. These third-party problems can be largely overcome, however, by limiting water transfers to historic consumptive use, a practice already implemented by the state engineer in Utah as the *East Jordan v. Morgan* case demonstrates. Furthermore, the impairment rule as employed in western states for over a century to evaluate both water appropriations and change applications is designed primarily to deal with these return-flow problems.

It appears that none of the existing problems associated with the legal impediments to water transfers discussed in this chapter requires more than minor changes in water law and administrative practice. State legislatures should move to fix these impediments to allow clear property rights in water. Only markets can produce the movement of water that is required to maximize economic growth and associated wealth creation.

NOTES

The author is indebted to Professor Ray G. Huffaker for comments on an early draft. The editors of this volume have also made useful suggestions that have contributed to relevance and clarity.

1. Utah Code 73-3-3.
2. Utah Code 73-3-2.
3. Utah Code 73-3-8.
4. Utah Code 73-1-10.
5. Utah Code. 73-3-3.
6. Utah Code 73-1-4.
7. Utah Code 73-1-4.
8. Ray Huffaker, e-mail correspondence with the author, November 2001.

REFERENCES

Anderson, Terry L. 1983. Introduction: The Water Crisis and the New Resource Economics. In *Water Rights: Scarce Resource Allocation, Bureaucracy, and the Environment,* ed. Terry L. Anderson. San Francisco: Pacific Institute for Public Policy Research, 1–9.

Davis, Ray Jay. 1989. Utah Water Rights Transfer Law. *Arizona Law Review* 31(4): 841–64.

Economist. 2001. You Say Potato, I Say Electricity. July 14–20, 28.

Gardner, B. Delworth. 2001. Water Rights and Efficient Transfers. Fellows address presented at the annual meeting of the Western Agricultural Economics Association, Utah State University, Logan, July 9.

Hamilton, J., N. Whittlesey, and P. Halverson. 1989. Interruptible Water Markets in the Pacific Northwest. *American Journal of Agricultural Economics* 71: 63–73.

Hosemann, John K. 2003. Agriculture and the Environment: A Thirty-Year Retrospective. This volume.

Huffaker, Ray, N. Whittlesey, and J. R. Hamilton. 2000. The Role of Prior Appropriation in Allocating Water Resources in the 21st Century. *Water Resources Development* 16(2): 265–73.

Jensen, Dallin W. 1999. The Evolving Nature of Water Law Practice Before the State Engineer and the Courts: The Impact of Recent Utah Supreme Court Decisions. In *CLE International Water Law Conference Handbook.*

McChesney, Fred S. 2002. "Pay to Play" Politics Examined, with Lessons for Campaign Finance Reform. *Independent Review* 5(3): 345–65.

Pipes, Richard. 1999. *Property and Freedom.* New York: Knopf.

Spangler, Donna Kemp. 2001. Flood of Worry on Water Rights. *Deseret News,* January 28, B1–B2.

CASES CITED

Baird v. Upper Canal Irrigation Co., 257 P. 1060 (Utah, 1927).

Bonham v. Morgan, 788 P.2d 497 (Utah, 1989).

East Jordan Irrigation Company v. Morgan and Payson City, 860 P.2d 310 (Utah, 1993).

Nephi City v. Hansen, 779 P.2d 673 (Utah, 1989).

St. George City v. Kirkland, 409 P.2d 970 (Utah, 1966).

Wadsworth Ditch Co. v. Brown, 88 P. 1060 (Colo., 1907).

5

Agricultural Programs with Dubious Environmental Benefits: The Political Economy of Ethanol

Gary D. Libecap

Consider the following statements about ethanol: According to Richard Gephardt, Democratic leader in the House of Representatives, "Ethanol is good for our environment, our nation's energy security, and for American farmers. By increasing demand for corn, the ethanol program boosts the annual income of a typical Midwest farm by about $15,000" (*Ethanol Report* 1998). According to David Pimentel, a Cornell University scientist, "Abusing our precious croplands to grow an energy-inefficient process that yields low-grade automobile fuel amounts to unsustainable, subsidized food burning" (EurekAlert! 2001b). A study by Department of Energy scientists "showed that the use of ethanol fuels leads to increased levels of toxins called aldehydes and peroxyacyl nitrates" (EurekAlert! 1997). The state of California contends that it can meet federal clean air standards without the use of ethanol, "but the state has run headlong into a powerful bloc of Midwest lobbyists and legislators representing corn farmers and ethanol producers, who has successfully stymied every California effort at changing the federal law" (Carlsen 2002, A15).

These reflect the controversial nature of the $10 billion, and counting, ethanol subsidy. Ethanol is an oxygenate gasoline additive, primarily made from corn, that is used to reduce certain kinds of air pollution and meet Clean Air Act requirements. It is an expensive additive, costing approximately $1.74 per gallon to produce (Zandonella 2001, 17). And, ironically, it may have no overall environmental benefits. Ethanol and other oxygenates, such as methyl tertiary-butyl ether (MTBE), made from natural gas, have been subsidized since 1978. The largest component of the subsidy is exemptions from federal excise taxes that have ranged from $.50 to $.60 per gallon of ethanol or $.05 to $.06 per gallon of gasoline blended

with 10 percent ethanol. Currently the tax exemption equals $.54 per gallon
of ethanol. In addition, at least twenty states provide exemptions to state motor fuel excise taxes for ethanol, providing an added subsidy of $.20 to $.30
per gallon of ethanol. There also have been grants for the construction of
ethanol plants. The federal ethanol subsidy, a loss in federal motor fuels excise taxes that are waived for ethanol and ethanol-based fuels, amounted to
more than $10 billion between 1979 and 2000, and total state and federal
support was approximately $1 billion annually (General Accounting Office
[GAO] 1997; EurekAlert! 2001b). If ethanol's use expands to replace MTBE,
as is possible, due to federal clean air mandates in California, New York,
Maine, and elsewhere, ethanol subsidies would rise even more. Existing production of ethanol of about 2.3 billion gallons per year requires approximately 7 percent of the U.S. corn crop. Were ethanol to completely replace
MTBE, its production would have to increase to 6.1 billion gallons per year
with a corresponding rise in corn demand by 15 percent or more.[1] Currently,
ethanol raises the price of corn by about $.30 per bushel, so that any expan-
sion in demand could further boost corn prices and products made from or
relying on corn.

In many ways ethanol is a politician's dream. It is advertised as having significant environmental benefits through reducing harmful automobile emissions of carbon monoxide and other gases; promoting energy independence by
substituting ethanol from locally grown, *renewable* biomass for petroleum imported from unreliable foreign sources; and assisting a well-established, concentrated political constituency—Midwestern corn farmers and large ethanol
producers such as Archer Daniels Midland and Cargill. Archer Daniels Midland
is the major producer of ethanol from corn, with about 50 percent of the
ethanol market (Forster 2001, 41). The lobby group is effectively organized as
the Renewable Fuels Association (*Ethanol Report* 1998). The benefits to agriculture are made more politically attractive because they are presented as aid-
ing depressed, deserving rural economies that have not shared in the economic
expansion of more urban sectors.

On the face of it, there is very little to fault. Ethanol seems to have it all.
Indeed, if ethanol performed as advertised, its economic and social costs
would be the alternative uses of the resources involved in production, primarily corn and the capital and labor costs associated with ethanol plants,
plus the opportunity cost of the subsidy itself—increased taxes and transfers
from beneficiaries, particularly the highway program. These costs could be
weighed against ethanol's apparent benefits, and such a cost-benefit analysis could indicate whether promoting ethanol is wise public policy.

Unfortunately, ethanol fails to perform on two of the three accounts—its
use appears to have no net positive air quality benefits; its production may
entail other environmental costs—soil and water degradation, which would
grow if its production were expanded; and it most likely does not contribute

to energy independence, using more energy in its production than it provides (Pimentel 2002, 159–71). Further, it is apt to have other negative collateral effects, reducing exports of corn if corn prices were to rise through ethanol use, thereby exacerbating balance of trade concerns, and reducing demand for soybeans and other livestock feeds because of the availability of feed stock by-products from subsidized ethanol production. Only in providing direct benefits to corn growers and ethanol producers does ethanol pull through as advertised. And this explains ethanol's popularity among politicians and the tenacity in which the additive is promoted. The alleged benefits of ethanol are asserted as fact, not only by midwestern politicians, but also by national politicians, like President George W. Bush and other regional legislators who seek the support of Midwest voters and their representatives in elections and in logrolling trades.

Because ethanol seems to result in at least some environmental harm and reduced energy supplies, despite representations to the contrary, its advocates constantly must challenge and discredit conflicting evidence. Further, because ethanol is such a valuable subsidy, particularly at a time of low commodity prices, its advocates are aggressive in expanding ethanol's uses, at the expense of alternatives, such as MTBE, and in thwarting efforts to drop oxygenates altogether. In both instances ethanol advocates have been extremely successful. As such, ethanol is a prime example of a narrow agricultural subsidy that is marketed based on its broad social benefits. It illustrates the workings of the political process when there is an entrenched, well-organized beneficiary, much more heterogeneous opponents with less at stake, and technical information that makes it difficult for general voters to assess the claims and counterclaims made by proponents and opponents about its effects. No constituency, other than those backing recently discredited MTBE, has had incentive to critically evaluate the claims made on ethanol's behalf, and there has been limited information for making such evaluations. These conditions have given ethanol a long and durable history, and likely, an even longer future, despite its possible overall negative impact on the environment and energy supplies.

THE LEGISLATIVE HISTORY OF THE
ETHANOL SUBSIDY: OPPORTUNISTIC PROMOTION

The origins of the ethanol subsidy began with the Arab oil embargo of 1973 and the related oil price shocks.[2] These events made America's growing dependence on foreign oil supplies a political issue, and politicians searched for ways to promote domestic, renewable energy sources. Ethanol, produced from renewable sources of biomass, could be used to supplement gasoline used in fuel, thereby reducing oil imports and extending the life of local sources of oil supply. Unfortunately, then, as today, ethanol was known to be a costly solution. In 1980, the cost of producing ethanol was nearly twice that of gasoline, but forecasts of high future gasoline prices (as high as $4 per gallon) by 1990–91, issued by the U.S. National Alcohol Fuels Commission, made ethanol seem like a reasonable alternative (GAO 1990; U.S. National Alcohol Fuels Commission 1980, iv). The nineteen congressional members of the fuels commission were predominantly from agricultural states, most likely to benefit from greater ethanol production from corn. Members included Senators Birch Bayh of Indiana, Henry Bellman of Oklahoma, Robert Dole of Kansas, and George McGovern of South Dakota; Representatives Bill Alexander of Arkansas, Dan Glickman and Keith Sebelius of Kansas, and Toby Roth of Wisconsin; as well as Phil French of the Indiana Farm Bureau and Sharon Peterson of Women Involved in Farm Economics from Montana. The committee began what was to become a familiar theme throughout ethanol's political history: that the additive not only could contribute to energy independence but also provide cleaner burning fuels and thereby help the United States meet the 1970 Clean Air Act's mandates for reduced air pollution. Further, ethanol could promote needed rural economic development and reduce the costs of the farm program. The latter would occur through lower domestic corn stocks and higher corn prices as corn was diverted to ethanol production. These claims were stressed as justification for the ethanol subsidy (U.S. National Alcohol Fuels Commission 1981, iii).

The ethanol subsidy began with the Energy Tax Act of 1978, which authorized federal highway excise tax exemptions for biomass-derived fuels, such as gasohol, which would be a mixture of 90 percent gasoline and 10 percent ethanol. The Crude Oil Windfall Profits Tax Act of 1980 extended the highway excise tax exemption through 1992 and added income tax credits for blenders of ethanol and gasoline. The Energy Security Act of 1980 also set a goal for alcohol fuel production equal to 10 percent of motor fuel consumption by 1990 and provided more than $1 billion in loan guarantees for ethanol plants (Kane and LeBlanc 1989). As noted, the federal excise tax exemptions ranged from $.50 to $.60 per gallon of ethanol or $.05 to $.06 per gallon of gasoline blended with 10 percent ethanol. And states provided an added subsidy of $.20 to $.30 per gallon of ethanol (GAO 1997). In 1998 Congress overwhelmingly agreed to extend the ethanol tax incentive through 2007 as part of the six-year federal highway reauthorization bill.[3]

Ethanol demand for corn has been critical, not only for raising corn prices, but also camouflaging the costs of federal feed grain subsidy programs and thereby protecting those programs from budget cuts. Through 1996, federal programs to maintain farm incomes included commodity target prices and income deficiency payments.[4] When market prices fell below the target or support price, farmers who met the eligibility criteria (usually participation in other supply control programs) received deficiency payments equal to the difference between the target price and the market price. The total income payment received by each farmer was a function of the difference in those prices, multiplied by the number of eligible acres times the normal yield for each participating farm. Most corn producers participated in this lucrative program (Kane, LeBlanc, and Reilly 1989; LeBlanc and Reilly 1989). By using excise tax exemptions to promote demand for corn in ethanol production, the ethanol subsidy raised corn prices above what they otherwise might have been and thereby reduced the differential between target and market prices. Hence, ethanol demand lowered the size of income deficiency payments that had to be made. This role was vital, especially at times when commodity prices were very low. Indeed, a 1984 GAO report suggested that the cost of ethanol subsidies might have been offset by the reduced costs of agricultural price support programs (GAO 1984). Of course, the cost to taxpayers remained the same in either case, and if ethanol demand distorted corn production plans and diverted capital, labor, and other inputs to ethanol factories, as was likely, the ethanol subsidy involved higher economic or resource costs than did the income transfers in the deficiency payments.

In fact, the average market price for corn generally has been below target prices, especially between 1985 and 1995 when the market price exceeded the target only once. As a result, income deficiency payments have had to make up the shortfall, ballooning from $88 million in 1978 to $25.8 billion in 1986 (Johnson and Libecap 2001). Deficiency payments became one of the largest and most visible components of agricultural commodity program costs. In 1985, the Congressional Budget Office (CBO) estimated that elimination of deficiency payments would save taxpayers $28,900 million over five years (CBO 1984, 1985). Reducing deficiency payments became an option in the mid-1980s for reducing the deficit, but political sponsors of the agricultural program mobilized to counter this action. As part of their efforts, they reemphasized their support for the ethanol subsidy.

In the early 1980s, protecting ethanol was not much of a problem. Proponents were enthusiastic about the potential contribution of alternative fuels, such as ethanol, to energy independence, cleaner air, and rural development (U.S. House 1984; U.S. Senate 1980). There was little counterinformation on ethanol's environmental or energy effects, and there was no cohesive constituency disadvantaged by the subsidy to organize to oppose it. Even so, given the size of the subsidy and the strong claims made on its behalf, a broad cost-benefit analysis of its effects on the environment, energy use, and competing livestock feed stocks such as soybean meal would have been useful in determining deficit reduction policy. A complete analysis would have required considerable new information and modeling, but there was no constituency that pushed for it. The limited studies that were conducted recognized that ethanol required substantial financial support because of its high costs (GAO 1997, 10; Meekhof, Tyner, and Holland 1980; Tyner and Bottum

1979). And despite the subsidy, ethanol managed to obtain only a small fraction of the alternative fuels market, and barely a third of the larger oxygenate market even as late as the early 1990s.

The closest study to a general cost-benefit analysis was released in 1986 by the U.S. Department of Agriculture (USDA) at the height of concerns about the size of agricultural deficiency payments, but it turned out to be very critical of ethanol. Not surprisingly, midwestern politicians scrambled to discredit the report and mitigate its political damage. No other studies of its kind followed.

The 1986 study subsidy concluded that ethanol production could not survive through 1995 without "massive Government subsidies, given the outlook for petroleum prices." Further it suggested that "[i]f the principal argument for subsidizing ethanol is to boost farm income, we conclude from this analysis that it would be more economical to burn straight gasoline in our automobiles and pay corn growers a direct subsidy equal to the amount they would receive as a result of ethanol production" (Gavett, Grinnell, and Smith 1986, iv, 45).

Ethanol advocates moved quickly to repudiate the report's findings.[5] Secretary of Agriculture Edmund Lyng agreed to have another study performed, and Senator Robert Dole of Kansas added an amendment to the Farm Disaster Assistance Act of 1987 to require that the secretary of agriculture establish a seven-member panel, made up largely of industry representatives, to conduct an analysis of the cost effectiveness of ethanol production, the likelihood of new cost-saving technology, and the impact of ethanol on agriculture and government farm programs.[6] A 1988 USDA study argued that with ethanol production reaching 2.7 billion gallons by 1995, corn prices would increase substantially, reducing deficiency payments to such an extent that there would be a *net savings* to the government (LeBlanc and Reilly 1989, 39).

No new threats to the ethanol subsidy emerged until political competition with MTBE developed in the early 1990s. Amendments to the Clean Air Act adopted in 1990 provided a new opportunity to expand ethanol demand. The legislation required the use of gasoline blended with oxygenates, reformulated gasoline (RFG), in order to reduce volatile organic compounds (VOCs) and carbon monoxide emissions in areas where air quality was low. Either ethanol or MTBE could be added to gasoline to reduce carbon monoxide emissions, but ethanol was not as effective in reducing VOC emissions as was MTBE. The concept of reformulated gasoline was originally promoted by ARCO Petroleum in the late 1980s for use in California, using MTBE (Environmental Protection Agency [EPA] 1995; GAO 1996). Ethanol proponents, however, used this legislation to open new markets for the fuel, but to do so they had to prevent less costly MTBE from being adopted and to raise permissible VOC emissions. They attempted to do so through legislative and administrative mandates for ethanol.

Under the Clean Air Act, beginning with the winter of 1992–93, all gasoline sold in thirty-nine carbon monoxide (CO) nonattainment areas was required to contain 2.7 percent oxygen. Additionally, only reformulated gasoline could be sold in the nine worst ozone nonattainment areas. Efforts to use the legislation to promote ethanol instead of MTBE led to renewed emphasis by farm-state politicians on ethanol's contributions to energy independence. Only in this area did ethanol, made from renewable sources such as corn, have potential advantages relative to MTBE. Accordingly, farm-state politicians attempted to mandate the use of only *renewable* oxygenates in reformulated gasoline (U.S. House 1987). In response to their lobbying, the EPA in 1994 issued an administrative rule (a renewable oxygenate rule, or ROR) that required at least 30 percent of the oxygenates used in RFG come from renewable sources (EPA 1994; National Research Council 1996, 4). Carol Browner, the EPA administrator, emphasized the gains to farmers from the ethanol program as well as its ability to reduce oil imports and to provide environmental benefits, particularly assistance in combating global warming (U.S. Senate 1994a, 8). The EPA noted in passing that ethanol would have to be specially blended in order to avoid increasing VOC emissions, which would defeat one of the objectives of the Clean Air Act.

The EPA's actions in issuing the ROR naturally were controversial, and they led to another round of congressional hearings on ethanol. The benefits to the farm program and the environment were always emphasized by leading advocate, Senator Daschle of South Dakota: "If successfully implemented, the RFG program has the potential to reduce air pollution, reduce our dependence on foreign imports and petroleum, and create domestic jobs" (U.S. Senate 1993, 2). Senator Kerrey of Nebraska added that "ethanol production currently raises the price of corn by about 15 cents a bushel, and is expected to raise the price even more by the year 2000. Not only . . . would this give vital financial help to our nation's farmers, but it will also help to reduce the Federal farm outlays. Each one cent increase in the price of corn saves the taxpayers $55 million in lower corn program costs. Thus, the current benefits of ethanol production save about $825 million in annual USDA expenditures" (U.S. Senate 1993, 11).

The EPA's 30 percent renewable oxygenate rule, however, was challenged in the U.S. Court of Appeals for the District of Columbia by the American Petroleum Institute and National Petroleum Refiners Association. The petitioners argued that the EPA lacked the statutory authority to impose a mandate to use renewable oxygenates in RFG and that the mandate undermined the VOC emission reductions unambiguously outlined in the Clean Air Act. The court agreed with the petitioners, reversed the EPA ruling, and scolded the agency for taking action that could *increase* air pollution: "The sole purpose of the RFG program is to reduce air pollution, which it does through specific performance standards for reducing

VOCs and toxic emissions. EPA admits that the ROR will not give additional emission reductions for VOCs or toxics . . . and has even conceded that use of ethanol might possibly make air quality worse" (*American Petroleum Institute v. EPA* 1995, 1118). Nevertheless, efforts by proponents to advance ethanol continued (U.S. Senate 1995, 1996). In hearings before the Senate Committee on Agriculture, Nutrition, and Forestry in September 1995, Senator Lugar of Indiana warned that any decline in ethanol production due to displacement by MTBE "would cause significant increases in farm program payments due to decreased demand for corn production" (U.S. Senate 1995, 2). He argued that these added farm costs exceeded the costs of the ethanol subsidy. During a 1998 congressional debate over extension of the ethanol subsidy, the National Corn Growers Association sent "Save Ethanol" messages to members of Congress to promote renewal of the excise tax exemptions. Senator Daschle repeated the familiar argument about ethanol's advantages as if they were facts: "The contribution of renewable fuels to national environment, energy and transportation policy is well documented and widely acknowledged. . . . Over a dozen new ethanol plants . . . will help diversify the industry and bring needed economic development to rural America . . ." (*Ethanol Report* 1998). The attractiveness of the argument remained compelling so that in May Congress extended the ethanol subsidy through 2007. Fortunately for ethanol, by that time problems with MTBE were creating new opportunities for ethanol's expansion.

To meet the standards outlined in the Clean Air Act amendments the California Air Resources Board required that by 1996 all gasoline sold in the state be oxygenated during the four or five winter months. MTBE was the preferred oxygenate because reformulated gasoline with ethanol could not meet California's VOC limits. Ethanol when mixed with gasoline does not reduce emissions of VOCs as much as does MTBE. But MTBE was water soluble, and leakage from storage tanks potentially could contaminate groundwater supplies. MTBE has an unpleasant smell and taste, and it may be a carcinogen. In December 1997, the EPA issued a drinking water advisory regarding MTBE (EPA 1997). In November 1998, the EPA announced creation of a blue-ribbon panel to review use of MTBE and other oxygenates. Taking advantage of these groundwater concerns, ethanol supporters, such as the Renewable Fuels Association, lobbied for legislation that would lift California's volatility limits and allow for ethanol's use in reformulated gasoline (Renewable Fuels Association 1999).

Concerns about MTBE, however, also raised questions about the need for *any* oxygenates to meet the requirements of the Clean Air Act. H.R. 630 was introduced in the 105th Congress in 1998 to allow for the implementation of RFG without the use of MTBE or other oxygenates (U.S. House 1998). In hearings on the bill, John Dunlap, chairman of the California Air Resources

Board, argued that no oxygenate was required to meet air quality standards in the state. His conclusions were opposed by Eric Vaughn of the Renewable Fuels Association, but were supported by some environmental groups (U.S. House 1998).

In the face of growing concerns about groundwater quality, in March of 1999 Governor Gray Davis ordered the phase-out of MTBE from California gasoline supplies by December 31, 2002 (California Energy Commission 1999). California RFG regulations allowed refiners to produce complying fuel without oxygenates, but these regulations were challenged by ethanol supporters. Mandated access to the California market was too important for ethanol to allow oxygenates to be bypassed in the production of reformulated gasoline. Further, if used in RFG in California, ethanol most likely would be adopted in other states, such as New York, to meet Clean Air Act objectives.

A shift to ethanol in California alone could add an additional demand for 950 million gallons of ethanol, raising overall ethanol production by 25 to 30 percent and creating a 2 billion bushel demand for corn to be used toward the production of ethanol (Alvarez 2001, A1; Carlsen 2002, A1; EurekAlert! 2001a). In anticipation, ethanol boosters began building twelve new plants and expanding several dozen more (Simon 2001, A1).

As testimony to the political strength of the ethanol lobby, the new Bush administration in June 2001 denied California's request for a waiver from federal oxygenate requirements and ordered the state to include ethanol as a fuel additive. California resisted, with Governor Davis filing suit to block EPA requirements for ethanol use in reformulated gasoline. Ethanol not only involves higher production costs, with feared gasoline price hikes of $.50 a gallon in California, costing motorists an additional $800 million a year, but also involves significant transportation problems, questions about whether there is sufficient capacity to meet California demand, and high costs for modifying refineries and other infrastructure. The last includes construction or modification of distribution terminals, railroad spurs, and blending facilities. Ethanol does not flow well through pipelines and hence requires bulk transport via rail, truck, and barge shipment through the Panama Canal. Although 40 percent of California ethanol might arrive by ship, the remaining 60 percent will require "ethanol express" trains of one hundred cars or more. Refinery and infrastructure adjustments are estimated to cost about $100 million and take two to three years to complete (Carlsen 2002, A1–A15). Davis has argued that these costs outweigh any benefits because RFG without any oxygenates burns as cleanly as gasoline with ethanol. A political compromise that would allow California and other states to waive the oxygenate requirement for RFG, but still require mandated increases in ethanol production and use elsewhere, is under consideration (Alvarez 2001, A1; Carlsen 2002, A15).

ETHANOL, THE ENVIRONMENT,
AND ENERGY INDEPENDENCE

If it were possible to accept as factual the claims made for ethanol by its political champions, there would be no issue as to its contribution to the environment. But in fact, the air quality benefits of ethanol are not conclusive, and
indeed, much of the research on the issue suggests that on net ethanol has
negative effects. As described, strong environmental assertions have been
made by ethanol advocates since the early 1980s, but these certainly have not
been warranted, nor do they withstand more careful scientific examination.

More conclusive scientific assessments of the environmental roles played
by ethanol and other oxygenates were not completed until the early 1990s.
There were scientific studies by the EPA, National Academy of Sciences, the
White House National Science and Technology Council, and the Committee
on the Environment and Natural Resources of the National Science and Technology Council. None of these or other studies found conclusive air quality
benefits from the use of any oxygenate additive.[7] The GAO reported in 1997
that removal of ethanol subsidies (and hence, the end of costly ethanol production) would have little environmental impact or little effect on petroleum
imports (GAO 1997). Hence, these and other studies, based on the best
available data, provided no basis for the unequivocal announcements and
fervent advocacy of ethanol's air quality benefits made by corn-state politicians and other regulatory officials, such as EPA commissioner Browner. In
fact, during the 1994 policy debates over EPA administrative rules favoring
ethanol, environmental groups became actively involved in the ethanol subsidy for the first time, and they opposed the oxygenate mandates. Representatives of the Sierra Club, Environmental Defense, and Resources for the Future argued that neither the alleged benefits nor the environmental and
health costs were sufficiently established to justify the EPA's action. A. Blake-
man Early, Washington director for Environmental Quality Programs of the
Sierra Club argued

> that this program will either create a program that is a global warming loser or
> the benefits are negligible at best. I just wanted to point out that there has not
> been a lot of analysis of the additional global warming burden that will be cre-
> ated through increased corn production, which uses fertilizer, which generates
> nitrous oxide, which is a five times more significant global warming gas, more
> damaging global warming gas than CO_2 is. (U.S. Senate 1994a, 70)

As negative research findings were released, ethanol advocates had either
to discredit the reports or divert attention to other alleged gains from
ethanol, notably energy independence and rural economic development.
The environmental claims were never dropped. For example, in the 1994

hearings before the Subcommittee on Nutrition and investigations of the Committee on Agriculture, Nutrition, and Forestry on the EPA's renewable oxygenate rule for RFG, Senator Harkin of Iowa repeated the statement that use of renewable fuels, "can help clean up the air, cut dependence on foreign oil, create investment and jobs in America, reduce primary energy use by 20 percent or more as compared to nonrenewable oxygenates, and lower emissions of harmful greenhouse gases." He dismissed questions about ethanol's environmental contributions as "misinformation and misrepresentations" (U.S. Senate 1994b, 1–2).

The most recent information suggests that ethanol, when mixed with gasoline, has higher emissions of VOCs than does gasoline blended with MTBE, and the use of ethanol could *increase* release of nitric oxide and other pollutants such as carcinogenic aldehydes into the atmosphere. Whereas ethanol as an automobile fuel additive could improve air quality by reducing hydrocarbon and carbon monoxide emissions, as it is burned, other chemical emissions result in the buildup of toxins of aldehydes and peroxyacyl nitrates (PAN). Research done by the Department of Energy Argonne National Laboratory at Albuquerque, New Mexico (a city under Clean Air Act mandates to use ethanol gasoline blends during the winter), and reported in 1997 indicates that PAN lasts longer in cold weather, is highly toxic to plants, is a powerful eye irritant as part of the winter "brown cloud," and can be carried in the atmosphere around the globe (EurekAlert! 1997; Gaffney et al. 1997). A 1999 National Academy of Sciences study corroborated these results by not finding significant pollution reduction from ethanol's use and instead possible increases in pollutants that cause smog (National Research Council 1999; Simon 2001, A1). The observed drop in pollution in many U.S. urban areas in recent years is more attributable to automobile fleet changes and the associated use of catalytic converters than to the use of oxygenate fuels. Additionally, ethanol and nitric oxide, a common air pollutant, are highly reactive with one another, making nitric oxide an even more caustic pollutant in the atmosphere as acid rain than had been believed previously (EurekAlert! 2000).

Besides negligible air quality benefits at best and overall harm at worst, ethanol most likely does not contribute to energy independence. A critical study of ethanol's energy and environmental effects was published in the *Encyclopedia of Physical Science and Technology* in 2002 by David Pimentel of Cornell University, who chaired a U.S. Department of Energy panel that investigated the energetics, economics, and environmental aspects of ethanol production (Pimentel 2002). The study concluded that conversion of corn and other food/feed crops into ethanol by fermentation is an expensive *net energy user*. Pimentel noted that since the ethanol subsidy began in 1978, new technology has been promised, but nothing has materialized to substantially lower costs. Ethanol remains dependent upon federal subsidies for its use.

The production of corn requires significant resources in the use of machinery, labor, gasoline, fertilizers, seeds, herbicides, insecticides, irrigation, electricity, and transportation. Pimentel estimated that an acre of land producing 7,110 pounds of corn would yield 328 gallons of ethanol. This corn production, however, would require 1,000 gallons of fossil fuel, costing $347 per acre or $1.05 per gallon of ethanol. Additionally, large amounts of fossil energy are required to crush and ferment the corn and to remove ethanol from it. Three distillations plus other treatments are necessary to produce ethanol suitable for blending with gasoline. The total estimated cost is $1.74 per gallon. Pimentel reported that it takes 131,000 BTUs to produce a gallon of ethanol. Ethanol, however, has an energy value of only 77,000 BTUs. Accordingly, about 70 percent more energy is required to produce 1,000 liters of ethanol than the energy that can be released from burning ethanol as a fuel.[8] Further, ethanol does not have the energy equivalence of gasoline. The energy produced from a liter of gasoline requires 1.5 liters of ethanol, so that more of the fuel must be used in automobiles. According to Pimentel, the annual incremental consumer costs of ethanol could be greater than the $1 billion federal subsidy because higher corn prices result in higher meat, milk, and egg prices; 70 percent of corn grain is fed to U.S. livestock and poultry. Increasing ethanol production, if its use were mandated in California and other states, can be expected to inflate corn prices by perhaps as much as 1 percent. Pimentel noted other environmental costs associated with a major expansion in corn production to support ethanol requirements: "Corn production in the U.S. erodes soil about 12 times faster than the soil can be reformed, and irrigating corn mines ground water 25 percent faster than the natural recharge rate of ground water" (EurekAlert! 2001b). If corn production were to be extended into marginal areas in the Great Plains, the costs of wind erosion and additional fertilizers would increase. Pimentel conjectured that the added environmental costs of corn would be $.23 per gallon of ethanol. As a result the production and environmental costs of ethanol could be $1.97 per gallon or more.

CONCLUSION

The ethanol subsidy for agriculture is an example of a program that has well-defined beneficiaries and dedicated political sponsors with few active opponents. Historically, program costs have been broadly spread, reducing incentives for organized opposition. Moreover, the broad claims of environmental quality improvements and energy independence through the use of ethanol require technical information and sophisticated analyses for corroboration. These have not been available to general voters, nor would general voters easily be able to sort through the arguments made on ethanol's behalf. Absent a counterconstituency to provide such information and analyses and to convey the results to voters, there has been little to block ethanol's advance—except its costs. Because of ethanol's high costs, even an annual subsidy in excess of $1 billion has not been sufficient to lead to a dramatic increase in its use as a fuel. Ethanol's opportunities in California, New York, and elsewhere with the demise of MTBE also will be constrained by its costs. As indicated, the high costs of conversion to ethanol in California are leading to political compromise. Even so, ethanol will most likely end up with greater use mandates. These are justified on the basis of environmental quality, energy independence, and rural economic development. The best available evidence indicates that there are dubious environmental quality effects and no net energy independence benefits from ethanol. Yet the subsidy persists with these claims. Unless a constituency emerges in whose interest it is to expose ethanol, and can do so effectively, or unless the costs of the subsidy rises substantially due to corn crop failure in the United States or elsewhere, dramatically raising corn prices, this agricultural support program will continue.

NOTES

1. Renewable Fuels Association production figures for 1995. Because each bushel of corn yields about 2.5 gallons of ethanol, ethanol production accounted for about 7 percent of U.S. corn production in 1995. The impact on ethanol production and corn demand from a complete MTBE phase-out is from Gold (2001, 33).

2. This part of the chapter on the legislative history of ethanol draws from two earlier studies by Johnson and Libecap (2001, 2002).

3. The vote was 297 to 86 in the House, 88 to 5 in the Senate (see www.cq.com).

4. Deficiency payments were dropped in the 1996 farm bill.

5. For a more detailed discussion of the event, see Johnson and Libecap (2001). Other potentially negative government studies also were sharply criticized. See Associated Press (1994, 1).

6. The panel would consist of four members representative of the ethanol industry, and then two members shall be employed by the federal government. See National Advisory Panel on Cost-Effectiveness of Fuel Ethanol Production (1987).

7. For study results see Anderson et al. (1995); Environmental Protection Agency (1993, 1996, vi, 4, 24, 32); Kirchstetter et al. (1996); Mannino and Etzel (1996); Mayotte et al. (1994); National Research Council (1991, 1, 4, 13); National Science and Technology Council (1997, iii); and Tennessee Valley Authority (1985, 1, 6, 55–56).

8. Perhaps reflective of the intense political pressure to justify the ethanol subsidy, the U.S. Department of Agriculture (2002) disputes this finding.

REFERENCES

Alvarez, Lizette. 2001. Support Grows for Corn-Based Fuel Despite Critics. *New York Times,* July 22.

Anderson, Larry G., et al. 1995. The Effects of Oxygenated Fuels on the Atmospheric Concentrations of Carbon Monoxide and Aldehydes in Colorado. In *Alternative Fuels and the Environment,* ed. Frances S. Sterrett. Boca Raton: Lewis Publishers, 75–101.

Associated Press. 1994. Energy Department May Bury Study Criticizing EPA Ethanol Mandate. *Clean Air Report,* March 10.

California Energy Commission. 1999. Fuel Resource Office. *Timetable for the Phase-out of MTBE from California's Gasoline Supply,* Docket No. 99-GEO-1. Sacramento. June.

Carlsen, William. 2002. MTBE Ban May Choke Gas Supply, Raise Prices. *San Francisco Chronicle,* January 20.

Congressional Budget Office. 1984. *Crop Price-Support Programs: Policy Options for Contemporary Agriculture.* Washington, DC: Government Printing Office.

———. 1985. *Reducing the Deficit: Spending and Revenue Options: A Report to the Senate and House Committees on the Budget. Part II.* Washington, DC: Government Printing Office.

Environmental Protection Agency. 1993. *Assessment of Potential Health Risks of Gasoline Oxygenated with Methyl Tertiary Butyl Ether (MTBE).* Office of Research and Development, EPA/600/R-93/206, Washington, DC: Government Printing Office.

———. 1994. *Regulation of Fuels and Fuel Additives: Renewable Oxygenate Requirement for Reformulated Gasoline.* 40 Code of Federal Regulations §80.

———. 1995. *Origin of the Reformulated Gasoline Program.* Office of Mobile Sources, EPA 420-F-95-001. Washington, DC: Government Printing Office.

———. 1996. *Toxicological and Performance Aspects of Oxygenated Motor Vehicle Fuels.* Washington, DC: Government Printing Office.

———. 1997. *Drinking Water Advisory: Consumer Acceptability Advice and Health Effects Analysis on Methyl Tertiary-Butyl Ether (MTBE),* EPA-822-F097-009. Washington, DC: Government Printing Office.

Ethanol Report. 1998. Issue 72, May 7. Online: www.ethanolRFA.org/EReports/er050798.html?NS-search-set=\3c8f9\s1p.8f9baa&NS-doc-offset=1& (cited: March 13, 2002).

EurekAlert! 1997. *Ethanol Causes Pollution, Too, Argonne Scientists Say.* November 3. Online: www.eurekalert.org/pub_releases/1997-11/ANL-ECPT-031197.php (cited: March 12, 2002).

———. 2000. *Acid-rain Component May Be More Potent Pollutant than Previously Thought, UB Chemists Discover.* December 5. Online: www.eurekalert.org/pub_releases/2000-12/UaB-Acmb-0512100.php (cited: March 13, 2002).

———. 2001a. *A Change of Fuel.* January 16. Online: www.eurekalert.org/pub_releases/2001-01/NS-Acof-1601101.php (cited: March 13, 2002).

———. 2001b. *Ethanol from Corn Faulted as Energy Waster.* August 7. Online: www.eurekalert.org/pub_releases/2001-08/cuns-efc080701.php (cited: March 13, 2002).

Forster, Julie. 2001. Betting the Farm on Ethanol. *Business Week,* June 18.

Gaffney, Jeffrey S., et al. 1997. Potential Air Quality Effects of Using Ethanol-Gasoline Fuel Blends: A Field Study in Albuquerque, New Mexico. *Environmental Science and Technology* 31: 3053–61.

Gavett, Earle E., Gerald E. Grinnell, and Nancy L. Smith. 1986. Fuel Ethanol and Agriculture: An Economic Assessment. *Agricultural Economic Report 562,* U.S. Department of Agriculture, Office of Energy. Washington, DC: Government Printing Office.

General Accounting Office. 1984. *Importance and Impact of Federal Alcohol Fuel Tax Incentives.* GAO/RCED-84-1. Washington, DC: Government Printing Office.

———. 1990. *Alcohol Fuels: Impacts from Increased Use of Ethanol Blended Fuels.* RCED-90-156. Washington, DC: Government Printing Office.

———. 1996. *Motor Fuels—Issues Related to Reformulated Gasoline, Oxygenated Fuels and Biofuels.* GAO/RCED-96-121. Washington, DC: Government Printing Office.

———. 1997. *Tax Policy: Effects of the Alcohol Fuels Tax Incentives.* GGD-97-41. Washington, DC: Government Printing Office.

Gold, Ronald B., John H. Lichtblau, and Larry Goldstein. 2001. Moving to Ethanol Use Instead of MTBE to Have Major Impacts. *Oil and Gas Journal* August 20: 33–35.

Johnson, Ronald N., and Gary D. Libecap. 2001. Information Distortion and Competitive Remedies in Government Transfer Programs: The Case of Ethanol. *Economics of Governance* 2: 101–34.

———. 2002. Information Distortion by Politicians and Constituent Groups in Promoting Regulatory Transfers: The Case of Ethanol. In *The State, Regulation and the Economy: An Historical Perspective,* ed. Lars Magnusson and Jan Ottosson. London: Edward Elgar Publishers, 13–43.

Kane, Sally M., and Michael LeBlanc. 1989. *Ethanol and U.S. Agriculture.* AIB-559, U.S. Department of Agriculture, Economic Research Service. Washington, DC: Government Printing Office.

Kane, Sally M., Michael LeBlanc, and John M. Reilly. 1989. Economics of Ethanol Production in the United States. *Agricultural Economic Report 607,* U.S. Department of Agriculture, Economic Research Service. Washington, DC: Government Printing Office.

Kirchstetter, Thomas W., et al. 1996. Impact of Oxygenated Gasoline Use on California Light-Duty Vehicle Emissions. *Environmental Science & Technology* 30(2): 661–70.

LeBlanc, Michael, and John Reilly. 1989. *Ethanol: Economic and Policy Tradeoffs.* AER-585, U.S. Department of Agriculture, Resources & Technology Division, Washington, DC: Government Printing Office.

Mannino, David M., and Ruth A. Etzel. 1996. Are Oxygenated Fuels Effective? An Evaluation of Ambient Carbon Monoxide Concentrations in 11 Western States, 1986 to 1992. *Journal of the Air and Waste Management Association* 46(January): 20–24.

Mayotte, Stephen C., et al. 1994. Reformulated Gasoline Effects on Exhaust Emissions: Phase I: Initial Investigation of Oxygenate, Volatility, Distillation and Sulfur Effects. *SAE Technical Paper Series,* 941973. Warrendale, PA: Society of Automotive Engineers.

———. 1994. Reformulated Gasoline Effects on Exhaust Emissions: Phase II: Continued Investigation of Oxygenate Type, Volatility, Sulfur, Olefins, and Distillation Parameters. *SAE Technical Paper Series,* 941974. Warrendale, PA: Society of Automotive Engineers.

Meekhof, Ronald L., Wallace E. Tyner, and Forrest D. Holland. 1980. U.S. Agricultural Policy and Gasohol: A Policy Simulation. *American Journal of Agricultural Economics* 62(3): 408–15.

National Advisory Panel on Cost-Effectiveness of Fuel Ethanol Production. 1987. *Fuel Ethanol Cost-Effectiveness Study.* Washington, DC: Government Printing Office.

National Research Council. 1991. *Rethinking the Ozone Problem in Urban and Regional Air Pollution.* Committee on Tropospheric Ozone Formation and Measurement, Washington, DC: National Academy Press.

———. 1996. *Toxicological and Performance Aspects of Oxygenated Motor Vehicle Fuels.* Committee on Toxicological and Performance Aspects of Oxygenated Motor Vehicle Fuels, Board on Environmental Studies and Toxicology, Commission on Life Sciences, Washington, DC: National Academy Press.

———. 1999. *Ozone Forming Potential of Reformulated Gasoline.* Washington, DC: National Academy Press.

National Science and Technology Council. 1997. *Interagency Assessment of Oxygenated Fuels.* Committee on Environment and Natural Resources, Executive Office of the President. Washington, DC: Government Printing Office.

Pimentel, David. 2002. Limits of Biomass Utilization. In *Encyclopedia of Physical Science and Technology,* 3rd ed., vol. 2. San Diego: Academic Press, 159–71.

Renewable Fuels Association. 1999. Ethanol Industry Vows to Continue Fight to Open California Gasoline Market to Ethanol. Press release dated September 29, Washington, DC.

Simon, Stephanie. 2001. Farmers Fume as State Goes against the Grain. *Milwaukee Journal Sentinel,* August 20.

Tennessee Valley Authority. 1985. *Effect of the Use of Gasohol on Ozone Formation for Cities in the Tennessee Valley Region.* Office of Natural Resources and Economic Development, Muscle Shoals, AL.

Tyner, Wallace E., and Carroll J. Bottum. 1979. Agricultural Energy Production: Economic and Policy Issues. Bulletin 240. Purdue University Agriculture Experiment Station, Lafayette, IN.

U.S. Department of Agriculture. 2002. USDA Report finds Ethanol is Energy Efficient. Release no. 0322. 02. Washington, DC.

U.S. House of Representatives. 1984. *Developments in the Production and Use of Ethanol Fuels.* Hearings before the Subcommittee on Investigations and Oversight of the Committee on Science, Space, and Technology, and the Subcommittee on Wheat, Soybeans, and Feed Grains of the Committee on Agriculture, 98th Congress, 2nd sess. Washington, DC: Government Printing Office.

———. 1987. *Alternative Automotive Fuels, Hearings on H.R. 168, H.R. 1595, H.R. 2031, and H.R. 2052, Bills to Encourage the Replacement of Gasoline with Alternative Fuels.* Hearings before the Subcommittee on Energy and Power of the Committee on Energy and Commerce, 100th Congress, 1st sess. Washington, DC: Government Printing Office.

———. 1998. *Implementation of the Reformulated Gasoline Program in California.* Hearings before the Committee on Commerce, 105th Congress, 2nd sess. Washington, DC: Government Printing Office.

U.S. National Alcohol Fuels Commission. 1980. *Ethanol: Farm and Fuel Issues.* Washington, DC: Government Printing Office.

———. 1981. *Fuel Alcohol: An Energy Alternative for the 1980s, Final Report.* Washington, DC: Government Printing Office.

U.S. Senate. 1980. *Effect of Alcohol Fuels Development on Agricultural Production, Price Support Programs and Commodity Reserves.* Hearings before the Subcommittee on Agricultural Production, Marketing, and Stabilization of Prices of the Committee on Agriculture, Nutrition, and Forestry, 96th Congress, 2nd sess. Washington, DC: Government Printing Office.

———. 1993. *Alternative Transportation Fuels.* Hearing before the Subcommittee on Energy and Agricultural Taxation of the Committee on Finance, 103rd Congress, 1st sess. Washington, DC: Government Printing Office.

———. 1994a. *Environmental Protection Agency's Proposed Renewable Oxygenate Standard.* Hearings before the Committee on Energy and Natural Resources, 103rd Congress, 2nd sess. Washington, DC: Government Printing Office.

———. 1994b. *Hearings on Renewable Oxygenate Rules in the Reformulated Gasoline Program.* Hearing before the Subcommittee on Nutrition and Investigations of the Committee on Agriculture, Nutrition, and Forestry, 103rd Congress, 2nd sess. Washington, DC: Government Printing Office.

———. 1995. *Ethanol, Clean Air, and Farm Economy.* Hearing before the Committee on Agriculture, Nutrition, and Forestry. 104th Congress, 1st sess. Washington, DC: Government Printing Office.

———. 1996. *Renewable Fuels and the Future Security of U.S. Energy Supplies.* Hearings before the Committee on Agriculture, Nutrition, and Forestry, 104th Congress, 2nd sess. Washington, DC: Government Printing Office.

Zandonella, Catherine. 2001. Going Up in Smoke. *New Scientist,* August 18.

CASE CITED

American Petroleum Institute v. Environmental Protection Agency, 52 F.3d 1113 (D.C. Ct. App., 1995).

6

Agricultural Technology and the Precautionary Principle

Indur M. Goklany

Perhaps no human activity is more critical to human well-being and environmental quality than agriculture. Having sufficient food and adequate nutrition is the first step to better health, lower mortality rates, and a longer, more productive and more fulfilling life (Goklany 1999a, 2001a). Accordingly, modern agricultural technology gets a good share of the credit for ensuring that today's global population of 6.2 billion is far better fed, healthier, and longer lived than ever.

Agriculture has literally shaped the world's landscape, rivers, and waterways. Worldwide, agriculture accounts for 38 percent of land use, 66 percent of freshwater withdrawals, and 85 percent of water consumption (Food and Agriculture Organization [FAO] 2001a; Shiklomanov 2000). It is responsible for most of the habitat conversion and fragmentation that threaten the world's forests, biodiversity, and terrestrial carbon stores and sinks. Current agricultural practices, including those associated with the green revolution, have reduced the quantity of water available to the rest of nature, and are among the prime contributors to environmental and water quality problems—oxygen depletion, pesticide and fertilizer runoff, and soil erosion—which are the major threats to aquatic and avian species. Their effects are evident not only inland but are often felt in estuaries, oceans, and even in the atmosphere far from where the actual agricultural activities might have been undertaken.

For all these reasons, modern agricultural technology is the environmentalists' *bête noire*. This technology, more than anything else, raises the dreaded specter of a silent spring. But modern agricultural technology has, by increasing yields, also forestalled massive conversion of habitat into agricultural uses that would have magnified the already considerable global pressures on ecosystems and biodiversity (Goklany 1998, 1999b). Given this, does it deserve all the opprobrium heaped on it by many environmentalists? Considering both the positive and negative environmental impacts associated with modern agricultural technology, would the precautionary principle sanction its use?

This chapter attempts to address this issue by applying the precautionary principle to (1) "conventional" agriculture as it existed at the end of the twentieth century, which includes the green revolution, and (2) future agricultural technology as it might evolve over the next half century with the aid of bioengineering.

THE PRECAUTIONARY PRINCIPLE

There is hardly a person who hasn't heard "better safe than sorry." In the 1980s, dressed up as the so-called precautionary principle—and with the support of nongovernmental organizations and European governments eager to appear greener-than-thou—this piece of commonsense wisdom began making its appearance in a variety of environmental declarations and agreements. By 1992, it was ubiquitous: It appeared in the Rio Declaration, the United Nations Framework Convention on Climate Change, and the Convention on Biological Diversity (CBD). These precedents ultimately spawned the CBD's January 2000 Cartagena Protocol on Biosafety, which uses the principle as a basis for assessing the risk of international transfer, handling, and use of genetically modified organisms (CBD 2000). This protocol is considered a major victory for the precautionary principle and its advocates (Smith 2000).

A popular—and, by now, commonly accepted—formulation of the precautionary principle is the Wingspread Declaration: "When an activity raises threats of harm to human health or the environment, precautionary measures should be taken even if some cause and effect relationships are not established scientifically" (Raffensperger and Tickner 1999, 8).

This principle has been interpreted by many to require—as precautionary measures—policies to curb technologies that science cannot prove to be absolutely safe. For example, it had been invoked to justify a global ban on DDT. It has also been used as a rationale for a global ban on research, development, and deployment of genetically modified (GM) crops, as well as policies such as the Kyoto Protocol to aggressively control greenhouse gases beyond "no regret" actions (Friends of the Earth [FOE] 1999; Goklany 2001b). But as shown in great detail elsewhere, these particular justifications are flawed because they take credit for the public health and environmental risks that the policies might reduce, but ignore other public health and environmental risks that might concurrently be generated or prolonged. Therefore, such policy cures could do more harm than the diseases they seek to cure. Part of the problem seems to be that the principle provides no guidance in situations in which a policy could simultaneously generate uncertain benefits and uncertain harms.

To avoid counterproductive "precautionary" policies, I have proposed elsewhere (Goklany 2000, 2001b), a framework for applying the precautionary principle to evaluate policies that might result in ambiguous outcomes because the harms might offset, in whole or in part, their benefits. This framework, sketched below, allows us to evaluate whether the precautionary principle would support the use of current and future agricultural technology.

A FRAMEWORK FOR APPLYING
THE PRECAUTIONARY PRINCIPLE

The framework to evaluate a policy (or action) consists of a set of hierarchical criteria to rank the various threats that are reduced, modified, or created by that policy (or action) based on their certainty, nature, magnitude, severity, and other characteristics.

First and foremost among these criteria is the *human mortality criterion:* The threat of death to any human—no matter how lowly—outweighs similar threats to members of another species—no matter how magnificent. Moreover, the other nonmortal threats related to human health—such as blindness, stunting, additional days of sickness, or lowered educational attainment— should take precedence over threats to the environment, although exceptions might be made based on the nature, severity, and extent of the threat. This is the *human morbidity criterion.* These two criteria can be combined into the *public health criterion.*

Additional criteria must be considered if an action under consideration results in both potential benefits and harms to public health or the environment. These other criteria include:

> *The immediacy criterion.* All else being equal, more-immediate threats should be given priority over threats that could occur later. This criterion is based on the fact that people tend to partially discount the value of lives that might be lost in the distant future (Cropper and Portney 1992). Such discounting can be justified ethically on the grounds that if death can be delayed, new technology might postpone it even longer. For instance, between 1995 and 1999 estimated U.S. deaths due to AIDS dropped by more than two-thirds (from 50,610 to 16,273) while estimated cases increased by almost half (from 216,796 to 320,282) (Centers for Disease Control and Prevention [CDC] 2000, tables 23 and 26). Thus,

if an HIV-positive American survived between 1995 and 1998, he had a better chance in 1999 to live out his "normal" life span (Goklany 2001b).

The uncertainty criterion. Threats of harm that are more certain should take precedence over those that are less certain if otherwise their consequences would be equivalent.

The expectation value criterion. Other things being equal, precedence should be given to threats with higher expectation values. For example, actions resulting in fewer expected deaths should be preferred over those resulting in more expected deaths.

The adaptation criterion. To the extent technologies are available to cope with, or adapt to, an impact, then that impact ought to be discounted.

The irreversibility criterion. Greater priority should be given to outcomes that are irreversible, or likely to be more persistent.

CONVENTIONAL MODERN
AGRICULTURAL TECHNOLOGY TO THE PRESENT

For the purposes of evaluating whether the precautionary principle would have supported the use of conventional (i.e., non-GM) modern agricultural technology—henceforth, "conventional agriculture"—I will examine the pros and cons of the changes in agricultural technology that occurred between 1961 and 1998. Included in these changes are deeper penetration of technologies that were available but not fully utilized in 1961, e.g., the use of fertilizers. The changes between 1961 and 1998 include the technologies and practices associated with the green revolution. Notably, in 1998 only 27.8 million hectares (Mha) of the 1,509 Mha of total global cropland were planted in GM crops (FAO 2001a; James 2000). Thus, for practical purposes, the agricultural technology in use in 1998 can be considered to be conventional agriculture.

The Environmental Consequences of Conventional Agriculture

Had technology, and therefore crop yields, been frozen at 1961 levels, then producing the same amount of crops as was actually produced in 1998 would have required a more than doubling of agricultural land area. Such land would have increased from 12.2 billion acres to at least 26.3 billion acres, that is, from 38 to 82 percent of global land area (FAO 2001a: Goklany 2001c). This estimate optimistically assumes that productivity of the added acreage would be the same as that of the original land. Cropland alone would have had to more than double, from 3.7 to 7.9 billion acres. In effect, an additional area the size of South America minus Chile would have to be plowed under.

Those figures assume that 7.9 billion acres of cropland would indeed be available. Potential cropland is estimated at about 8.5 billion acres world-wide (Alexandratos 1995; FAO 2001a). But because the best agricultural land is probably already being cultivated, new cropland is unlikely to be as pro-ductive. Moreover, at least 45 percent of this cultivable but uncultivated area is forested (about 2.1 billion acres), and 12 percent (or 0.56 billion acres) is protected (Alexandratos 1995; Goklany 1998). Therefore, the requirement for 7.9 billion acres of cropland could have been met in theory, though per-haps not in practice. Freezing technology at 1961 levels would have magni-fied the already substantial environmental cost of agriculture in terms of land conversion, soil erosion, and loss of forests and other habitat, which today constitute the major global threats to biological diversity.

To further place in context the magnitude of habitat saved from conver-sion, consider that worldwide in 1999 only 2.10 billion acres were reserved in fully and partially protected areas (World Resources Institute 2000). Thus, despite its environmental flaws, agricultural technology has been crucial in conserving habitat and biodiversity globally.

In sum, there simply isn't enough productive land worldwide to support today's world population using yesterday's technology.

Imagine the devastation that would have occurred had agricultural tech-nology been frozen at 1961 levels, while mortality rates continued to drop worldwide in response to advances in public health, hygiene, and medicine, pushing up population. Massive deforestation, soil erosion, greenhouse gas emissions, and losses of biodiversity would have occurred with the more than doubling of the amount of land diverted to agriculture. Not only would hunger and starvation not have declined (see below), the additional pressure on the land would have increased land prices, making it more difficult to re-serve land for conservation (except, possibly in the deserts, the frozen polar regions, and the peaks of mountain ranges).

This almost certainly would have reaped a silent spring, but thanks to im-provements in productivity at each step of the food and agricultural system, that was avoided. To begin with, science-based varieties of seeds helped in-crease global yields for all cereals, the grains that are currently grown on 45 percent of the world's cropland. Cereal yields went up by 126 percent be-tween 1961 and 1998 (FAO 2001a). To more fully exploit these high-yielding crop varieties, farmers implemented a set of complementary technologies. Although these technologies caused numerous environmental problems, they also increased productivity, reducing the amount of land devoted to agriculture.

Irrigation. In the United States, 16 percent of harvested cropland is irrigated; it contributes nearly half the value of all crops sold (U.S. Department of Agriculture [USDA] 2001, 76). Irrigated acreage increased worldwide from

343 million acres in 1961 to 670 million acres in 1998, an increase of 95 percent (FAO 2001a). Although water diversions for agriculture are a major problem for many aquatic species, irrigating the land, on average, triples its productivity (Goklany 1998). In other words, one acre of irrigated land saves two more from being plowed under. Currently, 18 percent of global cropland is irrigated (FAO 2001a). Hence, if the amount of irrigated land were fixed at the 1961 level, then at least an extra 650 million acres would have been needed to compensate for the lost production (Goklany 2001c).

Fertilizers. Total global fertilizer use jumped 4.4-fold between 1961 and 1998 (FAO 2001a). This increased yields substantially—doubling them in some instances—but the use and abuse of fertilizers is the major source of nutrient loading in the world's waters. In Europe and the United States, only 18 percent of the nitrogen and 30 percent of the phosphorus in fertilizers are incorporated into crops, between 10 percent and 80 percent of the nitrogen and 15 percent of the phosphorus end up in aquatic ecosystems, and much of the remainder accumulates in the soil, to be later eroded into aquatic systems (Carpenter et al. 1998).

Mechanization. Tractor usage increased 2.3-fold between 1961 and 1998 (FAO 2001a). While increasing society's dependence on fossil fuels, it reduced the need for human and animal labor on the farm. This helped reduce food costs and lessened the need to cultivate additional land to feed work animals. In 1910, for example, about one-third of all U.S. cropland was used to feed working horses and mules (Goklany and Sprague 1991). Mechanization also reduced an incentive for a higher birth rate, and the use of child labor on the farm.

Pest control systems. In the absence of pesticides and other pest controls, an estimated 70 percent of the world's crop might be lost, instead of the current 42 percent (Oerke et al. 1994, 750). Thus, without them, at least 90 percent more cropland would be required to offset the loss in production. But as much as 99 (+) percent of pesticides are wasted and end up in the environment (Goklany 1998). Even so, a number of cost-benefit analyses indicate that aggregate economic, public health, and environmental benefits of pesticide use may outweigh the aggregate costs (Pimentel 1997; Pimentel and Greiner 1997). These studies do not take into account the environmental benefits that come from reduced habitat conversion, a major conceptual error in their analyses.

Other factors that also contributed to farm productivity include innovations in animal husbandry, technologies for storage, handling and processing (e.g., plastic bags, refrigeration, canning, and preservation), and a wider—largely fossil fuel driven—global infrastructure for the efficient transportation, storage, distribution, and trade of agricultural inputs and outputs (which also helped reduce waste and spoilage) (Goklany and Sprague 1991).

Whereas the extent of cropland is probably the single most important indicator of agriculture's impact on the environment, as mentioned, it does not capture the full range of those impacts, such as pesticide residues in tissues of human beings and avian and aquatic species; excess nitrates and phosphorus; and reductions in dissolved oxygen levels in water.

Nevertheless, the experience of developed countries indicates that with technology and wealth, these problems might be surmountable if a long-term effort is undertaken to reverse them. Trends for various pollution indicators related to agricultural sources in the United States and Europe show recent reductions in their rates of growth, if not outright improvements (Council on Environmental Quality [CEQ] 1992, 1993, 2001; Goklany 1994, 1996, 1998).

Since the early 1970s, due to pressure from environmental laws, concentrations of many pesticides such as DDT, toxaphene, dieldrin, and chlordane have declined in human adipose tissue, freshwater fish, and some avian species. For example, between 1974 and 1996, levels of various pesticide metabolites and residues (DDE, dieldrin, mirex, and HCB) in herring gull eggs from each of the five Great Lakes of North America declined by more than 80 percent (CEQ 1999). In the United States, DDT and related compounds declined 65 percent between 1971 and 1984 in national samples of freshwater fish (Schmitt, Zajicek, and Peterman 1990). Between 1980 and 1988, DDT in fall run coho salmon declined 40 and 60 percent in Lakes Erie and Michigan, respectively (CEQ 1992). Between 1966 and 1985, levels of DDE, a derivative of DDT, in waterfowl dropped from 0.70 to 0.09 ppm in the Atlantic flyway, from 0.65 to 0.05 ppm in the Pacific flyway, and from 0.15 and 0.25 ppm to below detection levels in the Mississippi and Central flyways (CEQ 1993). Partly as a result of such reductions, some species, such as bald eagles and peregrine falcons, that were once endangered in the United States by these chemicals have now rebounded and are no longer on the endangered species list (Goklany 1998).

Such improvements are not limited to the United States. They also extend to the other richer nations. For example, from the 1960s to the 1990s, studies on various aquatic and avian species in the Baltic show that total DDT (including its metabolites) declined 8 to 12 percent per year for herring and cod, and 11 percent per year in guillemot eggs (Olsson et al. 2000; Skei et al. 2000).

All these improvements have also reduced pesticide residues entering the human food chain. Monitoring of pesticide residues on various food commodities in the United States indicates that between 1973 and 1986, 3 percent of the samples tested violated pesticide residue standards, whereas between 1997 and 1998 that level had dropped to 1 percent (CEQ 2001).

Significantly, DDT and related compounds have declined in human adipose tissue and breast milk. DDT in human adipose tissue dropped by 80 percent between 1970 and 1983 (U.S. Bureau of Commerce [USBOC] 1987). Similarly, DDT concentrations declined from 1.066 mg/kg of human adipose tissue to 0.066 mg/kg in Canadian citizens (United Nations Environment Programme/Global Environment Monitoring System [UNEP/GEMS] 1991). DDT concentrations in such tissue also dropped by an order of magnitude in the Netherlands. Also, based on a review of about a hundred studies, Smith (1999) concludes that DDT levels in human breast milk declined 11 to 21 percent per year in the United States and Canada since 1975, and between 9 and 13 percent per year in Western Europe. Notably, Smith's analysis suggests that DDT levels in human breast milk have also declined substantially since the early to mid-1970s in parts of Asia, the Middle East, Latin America, and Eastern Europe, although data for these regions are sparser.

Water quality in developed countries has also improved for other agriculture-related pollutants. From 1975–77 to 1995–97, violation rates in the United States for water quality standards declined from 7 to 1 percent for dissolved oxygen (CEQ 2001), but for fecal coliform they rebounded to 31 percent in 1993–95 after having declined from 34 percent in 1975–77 to 23 percent in 1986–88 (CEQ 2001). But since water-borne disease rates have dropped over the long term and are at relatively low levels, the significance of this trend (or lack of it) for public health is unclear (Goklany 1996).

There has been a general improvement in other water quality indicators that are potentially sensitive to agricultural inputs and practices. Nitrogen fertilizer usage in the United States in 1996–98 was 8 percent above the 1978–80 level, which is a marked improvement over the previous eighteen-year period, during which it increased 195 percent (FAO 2000). That, coupled with a decline in air pollution emissions of nitrogen oxides, contributed in the 1980s to a 25 percent reduction in the number of water monitoring stations with "extreme" concentrations of nitrates (in excess of 3 mg/L) (Smith, Alexander, and Lanfear 1993). Moreover, large investments in sewage treatment plants and limitations on phosphate content of detergents in the 1960s and 1970s supplemented by point-source controls and an 18 percent drop in phosphorus fertilizer usage since 1978–80 have led to widespread reductions in phosphorus loading of water bodies (CEQ 2000; Goklany 1994). As a result, between 1975–77 and 1995–97, violation rates for water quality standards for total phosphorus declined from 5 to 2 percent (CEQ 2001). Finally, soil erosion from agricultural practices has dropped by 40 percent in the United States between 1982 and 1997 (USDA 2001, 75).

As a result of similar efforts and large investments in point sources over the past few decades, there has, by and large, been substantial improvement in the condition of rivers in the rest of the developed world. Dissolved oxygen levels have slowly but steadily improved (Goklany 1994, 1996). For example, the number of species in the sediment of the Rhine, one of Western Europe's major rivers, increased from 27 in 1971 to 97 in 1997.

Comparing the Environmental Consequences

The "precautionary" framework outlined previously can be used to compare the above environmental benefits and costs of conventional agricultural technologies in order to evaluate whether—with the benefit of hindsight—the precautionary principle would support their use today.

Some might argue, based on experience with DDT and other relatively long-lived organic pollutants, that under the irreversibility criterion of the framework the impacts of persistent pesticide pollution, in particular, ought to take precedence. But we have seen that the worst of these impacts, namely the declines in populations of various bird species, and levels in fish and mammalian tissues, are, in the long term, reversible, albeit at some cost.

Moreover, the impacts of land conversion do not seem any less irreversible, particularly if such conversion threatens or endangers species. More important, because of the magnitude and the certainty of the environmental problems resulting from massive land conversion as compared with the problems created by agricultural inputs, it seems that the former outweigh the latter. Accordingly, if one is concerned only with environmental impacts, the expectation value criterion, coupled with the adaptation criterion, indicates that the precautionary principle would support the use of conventional agricultural technology. As we shall see, consideration of the range, magnitudes, and certainties associated with its public health consequences only reinforces this conclusion.

Recognizing the benefits of conventional agricultural technology does not mean that we should excuse the tendency to overuse inputs such as water, fertilizers, pesticides, and energy, in part because of subsidies compounded, in the case of water, by the lack of clear property rights. So although total environmental benefits of conventional agricultural technology probably exceed total environmental costs, the marginal benefits may not always be exceeded by the marginal costs.

Public Health Consequences of Conventional Agriculture

As shown in table 6.1, between 1961 and 1998, global population increased by 92 percent, while global cropland only increased by 12 percent. Accordingly, had agricultural technology (and its extent) been frozen at its 1961 level, then in 1998, per capita global food supplies would have dropped from 2,257 kilocalories (kcal)/day to 1,321 kcal/day, that is, by 41 percent. According to the FAO (1996a), this only barely meets the minimum energy requirement of 1,300 to 1,700 kcal/day an adult needs to keep basic metabolic activities functioning at rest in a supine position! In the absence of modern agricultural technology, mass starvation and death would have been inevitable. But, in fact, global daily food supplies per capita increased by 24 percent to 2,798 kcal/day (FAO 2001a).

As indicated by table 6.1, similar calculations for developing countries as well as India and China individually indicate that in 1998 their food supplies per capita would have been between 1,006 and 1,121 kcal/day in the absence of post-1961 improvements in agricultural technology. These calculations assume that food supplies would increase in proportion to cropland, and that net imports would also change in proportion to domestic production.

Because of modern agricultural technology, despite a 76 percent increase in developing countries' populations between 1969–71 and 1997–99, the number of people suffering from chronic undernourishment in developing countries shrank from 917 million to 790 million during that period (FAO 1996b, 2001b). As a result, in this period the portion of their population suffering from chronic undernourishment actually declined from 35 percent to 17 percent instead of escalating, as would inevitably have been the case had conventional technology, including the green revolution, not come to the rescue (FAO 1996b, 2001b; Goklany 1998). Merely freezing the proportion of the chronically undernourished at 35 percent would have meant their numbers would have more than doubled to 1.6 billion people.

Arrayed against these public health benefits are the health problems associated with conventional agricultural practices. The FAO estimates that exposure to pesticides causes at least 3 million cases of acute poisoning and 20,000 deaths each year (UNEP/World Health Organization [WHO]/FAO 1999). Irrigation and dams can lead to increases in a number of water-borne or water-related diseases, e.g., malaria, bilharziasis (schistosomiasis), and river blindness (onchocerciasis), whose vectors proliferate in irrigation waters (FAO 1997). They can be contained by improving soil drainage, proper construction of drainage canals, and a variety of public health measures. But comparing the relative magnitudes of risks reduced against those created by agricultural water projects and pesticide and fertilizer use, one must conclude that the public health criterion specified in the precautionary framework (coupled with the adaptation criterion) strongly supports the notion that conventional agricultural technology has been more of a boon than a bane to mankind.

The Precautionary Principle and Conventional Agriculture

Thus, with respect to either the environment or public health, the comparison of net consequences suggests that the precautionary principle favors the use of post-1961 agricultural technology, including the suite of technologies associated with the green revolution.

Table 6.1. Changes in Population, Cropland Area, and Food Supplies Per Capita, 1961–1998

| Area | 1961 to 1998 Changes (% increase) | | | 1998 Food Supplies (kcal per capita, per day) | |
	Population	Cropland	Food Supplies Per Capita	Actual (with technology)	Estimated (without technology)
World	92	12	24	2,798	1,321
Developing countries	119	26	39	2,676	1,112
China	87	29	87	3,052	1,121
India	117	5	16	2,399	1,006

Source: Based on data from FAO (2001a).

Some have argued that conventional agricultural technology, by making more food available, merely postponed the Malthusian day of reckoning, leading to a larger population, which in turn increased net conversion of wildlife habitat. In response to this claim, I would first argue that agricultural technology, by reducing starvation and hunger, helped reduce maternal and infant mortality rates. Not only has this reduced misery worldwide, but it has also directly improved human well-being.

Second, population growth can, at least for a time, be fueled by reductions in mortality rates due to nonagricultural technologies (e.g., control of infectious and parasitic diseases, better food distribution) that precede declines in birth rates, without improvements in agricultural technology. For example, between 1918 and 1945, India's population increased 25 percent and food supplies per capita declined by a like amount (Cipolla 1978), and by 1950–51, its food supplies per capita stood at 1,635 kcal/day. Thus, population can increase without a substantial improvement in agricultural technology per se.

Third, failure to produce enough food would not necessarily have led to protection of habitat for the rest of nature. Consider the statistics about India. In 1961, daily food supplies per capita in India were 2,073 kcal. At that time, 398 million acres of India's total land area of 734 million acres (or 54 percent) was devoted to crop production (FAO 2001a).

Between 1961 and 1998, as shown in table 6.1, India's population increased by 117 percent, food supplies per capita grew 16 percent, and India became, at least temporarily, a net grain exporter. Yet cropland increased by only 5 percent (to 420 million acres). Forest and woodland area expanded 21 percent between 1961 and 1994 (from 141 to 170 million acres) (FAO 2001a).

Assuming no improvement in agricultural production since 1961 or any change in the 1998 population level, available daily food supplies per capita would have slid to an unacceptably low 1,006 kcal.

Would that have translated into more wildlife habitat? Faced with such hunger, it seems unlikely that India's population and—because it's a democracy—its policy makers would have been more willing to set land aside for conservation. India would have been fortunate not to have lost much of its remaining forests, let alone "reserve" as much as the 35 million acres that are currently in partially or fully protected areas (World Resources Institute 2000).

By reducing hunger, agricultural technology has not only improved human welfare and reduced habitat loss but also has made it easier to view the rest of nature as a source of wonder and not merely as one's next meal or the fire to cook it with. It also decreased the socioeconomic cost of conservation.

These factors helped create the conditions necessary for support of conservation within the body politic. In the absence of technological progress, would the World Conservation Union's (IUCN) Red List, which classifies about a quarter of all mammalian species as threatened (IUCN 2000), been larger because more species would be threatened, or smaller because more species were extinct?

FUTURE AGRICULTURAL
TECHNOLOGY: GM CROPS

In the future, perhaps the world's biggest environmental challenge will be to meet the growing demand of a larger and wealthier population for food, nutrition, fiber, timber, and other natural resource products while conserving habitat and biodiversity. Biotechnology could be key to reconciling these opposing goals (Goklany 2001b).

Environmental Consequences of GM Crops

Benefits

As we have already seen, there is always a tradeoff between increased agricultural productivity and increased land conversion (Goklany 1999b). Assuming that population will be 8.9 billion in 2050 and that crop production per capita will grow at the same rate between 1997 and 2050 as it did between the early 1960s and late 1990s, and if conventional agricultural productivity increases 1 percent per year between 1997 and 2050, then 325 million hectares (about 800 million acres) of forests or other habitat will have to be converted to new cropland. That's a 21.5 percent increase over the 1.5 billion hectares of existing cropland (FAO 2000). This would inevitably increase pressure on terrestrial biodiversity. Given existing, but unused, opportunities to increase productivity, such increases are plausible with conventional agriculture (Goklany 1998, 2001b). First, the historic rate of productivity growth between 1961–63 and 1996–98 was approximately 2 percent per year (FAO 2001a). Second, if the average global cereal yield was raised to the same level as that of Belgium-Luxembourg's in 1996–98, then cereal production would increase by 163 percent. This substantially exceeds the cumulative 76 percent increase that is equivalent to the 1 percent increase per year from 1997 to 2050 assumed in the previous calculation. But such increases might also mean greater use of the inputs employed in conventional agriculture, namely, fertilizers and pesticides, particularly in areas where the human and capital resources needed for precision agriculture are, for whatever reason, unavailable.

What is possible with conventional agriculture is more probable with GM crops. Numerous GM crops, in various stages between research and commercialization, could make such gains more likely. For example, GM crops could be bioengineered to tolerate poor climatic and soil conditions, including acidic soils, drought, and high salinity levels, conditions that prevail in many developing countries. For instance, 43 percent of tropical soils are acidic, and one-third of the world's irrigated land has been lost to salinity (Frommer, Ludewig, and Rentsch 1999). Moreover, if biotechnology increases productivity by 1.5 percent per year—corresponding to a cumulative 30 percent increase in productivity by 2050 due to biotechnology alone—then agriculture could return 98 million hectares of current cropland to nature. An increase to 2 percent per year would return 422 million hectares (Goklany 2001b).

GM crops can also make agriculture more environmentally sustainable. Higher productivity leads to less cropland, less soil erosion, less silt, and less carbon in the water and the atmosphere. GM crops could also be bioengineered to fix their own nitrogen, increase nitrogen and phosphorus uptake from the soil, and resist pests (Goklany 2001b, and references therein). Such crops would lower environmental loading of nutrients, pesticides, and nitrous oxide. In the United States, for example, in 1999, cultivation of corn genetically modified to express the *Bacillus thuringiensis* (*Bt*) gene—which repels pests without the need for chemical pesticides—reduced pesticide usage by 1 million acre-treatments. Production also increased by 66 million bushels, equivalent to the output of half a million acres (Carpenter and Gianessi 2001).

A four-year study done by the USDA Agricultural Research Service in a 7,000-square-mile watershed in the Mississippi Delta comparing insecticide runoff from *Bt* cotton and conventional cotton sites found that the former had lower levels of pyrethroid insecticides (Environmental Protection Agency [EPA] 2001, IIE42).

Since the introduction of *Bt* cotton, the use of conventional insecticide on cotton has declined substantially. Comparing the period prior to the introduction of *Bt* cotton (1993 to 1995) to the latest year available (2000) shows a two-thirds decrease for the pesticides that are most toxic to birds and fish, and a one-third decrease for those most toxic to humans (EPA 2001, IIE36). Perhaps more important, this dramatic reduction in the toxicity of pesticides coincides with substantial increases in average bird counts in cotton growing areas in the South. The USGS's North American Breeding Bird Survey shows that bird counts have increased from the five years prior to the introduction of *Bt* cotton (1991 to 1995) to the five years after (1996 to 2000), and are positively correlated with the *Bt* adoption rates, the reduction in insecticide use, and the relative presence of the species in cotton fields (EPA 2001, IIE38-40). These increases, on average, range from 10 percent for Texas to 37 percent for Mississippi.

Bioengineering could also enhance feed to reduce phosphorus in animal waste, lowering its runoff into streams, lakes, and other waters. Similarly, in

1999 the use of the herbicide-resistant 'Roundup Ready' soybean, reportedly lowered pesticide usage by 19 million acre-treatments while simultaneously increasing yields and facilitating no-till cultivation, a very effective method of containing erosion (Carpenter and Gianessi 2001).

Risks

In spite of the potential environmental benefits of deploying bioengineered crops, there has been much hue and cry about the risks inherent in this new agricultural technology. Some fear that GM crops may lead to pesticide-resistant insects and superweeds, harm beneficial insects, and have adverse effects on human health.

Perhaps the most familiar environmental concerns about GM crops center on pest-resistant and herbicide-tolerant crops. One risk is that target pests will become resistant to toxins produced by pest-resistant GM crops, such as *Bt* corn or *Bt* cotton. Recent studies from Arizona, Mississippi, and Australia, however, indicate that the bollworm, for instance, did not increase its resistance to *Bt* toxin produced by a GM *Bt* cotton (Kershen 2000; Tabashnik et al. 2000).

Conventional strategies to deter pest resistance to conventional pesticide, such as maintaining refuges of non-*Bt* crops, crop rotation, and expanded monitoring, can be adapted for GM crops (EPA 2000a). Other strategies include developing crops with more than one toxin gene acting on separate molecular targets and inserting the bioengineered gene into the chloroplast—a type of cell in the green part of plants that is critical to the process of photosynthesis. These alterations allow more *Bt* toxin to be expressed, so that more of the pest insects die and fewer live to develop resistance (Conway 2000; Daniell 1999).

Another source of risk is that *Bt* plants could harm nontarget species. Earlier studies in non-field conditions had shown higher mortality in monarch butterflies fed with leaves dusted with pollen from *Bt* corn or from areas adjacent to *Bt* cornfields (Jesse and Obrycki 2000; Losey, Rayor, and Carter 1999). But a set of papers recently published in the *Proceedings of the National Academy of Sciences* suggests that the risk to monarchs is negligible under field conditions (Hellmich et al. 2001; Sears et al. 2001; Zangerl et al. 2001). Studies have also shown that green lacewing larvae, a beneficial insect, that ate corn borers fed with *Bt* corn were more likely to die (Hilbeck et al. 1998). Whether—and the extent to which—these studies represent real-world conditions is also debatable (EPA 2001, IIC39–IIC40; Ferber 1999; Richard 2000).

Earlier, the EPA (2000b, 17) had concluded that "the weight of evidence" indicates "no hazard to wildlife from the continued registration of *Bt* crops," and *Bt* corn is unlikely to cause widespread harm to monarchs. This basic conclusion was reaffirmed in the EPA's decision to reregister various *Bt* corns and cottons until 2008 and 2006, respectively (EPA 2001, I1–I2, I18–I19).

Another concern is that bioengineered herbicide- or pest-tolerant crops might escape into wild relatives leading to "genetic pollution" and creating "superweeds." Because that would defeat the very justification for such GM crops, farmers and GM seed vendors have substantial economic incentives for preventing the creation of herbicide-tolerant superweeds and, failing that, keeping such weeds in check.

Gene escape is possible if GM crops are planted near wild relatives; however, the most common GM crops—soybeans and corn—have no wild relatives in the United States. Also, conventional breeding has rendered many crops—corn and wheat, for example—"ecologically incompetent," that is, the hybrid forms in common use can't easily reproduce in natural conditions and are unlikely to cross-pollinate with other species. A ten-year British study of four different herbicide-tolerant or pest-resistant GM crops—oilseed rape, corn, sugar beet, and potato— shows that they are no more invasive or persistent in the wild than their conventional counterparts (Crawley et al. 2001). This study also provides reassurance that superweeds perhaps can't invade natural ecosystems, and confirms that such GM plants have no competitive advantage in natural systems.

Moreover, had any herbicide-tolerant or pest-resistant weeds begun to spread, available crop management techniques—such as applying an herbicide to which the GM plant had not been engineered to be resistant— could have been used to control them. Finally, the chances of gene escape from GM to non-GM crops can be further reduced by maintaining a buffer between the two crops. Gene escape could also be limited with greater certainty if the GM plants were engineered to be sterile or prevented from germinating using, for instance, "terminator technology." An alternative approach would be to insert the gene into the chloroplast, which would preclude spread through pollen or fruit, as well as prevent root leakage (Chamberlain and Stewart 1999; Daniell 1999; Royal Society 1998).

Notably, based on its examination of the risks to the environment, the EPA recently concluded that *Bt* crops "will not significantly increase the risk of unreasonable adverse effects to the environment." Accordingly, it has allowed these crops to be reregistered for continued use for the next five years for *Bt* cotton and seven years for *Bt* corn (EPA 2001, I1–I2, I18–I19).

Finally, there is a concern that in the quest to expand yields, herbicide-tolerant and pest-resistant GM plants would work too well and further simplify agricultural ecosystems, decreasing biodiversity.

Public Health

Benefits

Sufficient food is the first step to a healthy society (Goklany 1999a, 2001a; WHO 1999). Despite unprecedented progress in the past half century, as indicated in table 6.2, 815 million people still suffer from hunger and malnourishment (FAO 2001b), and as many as 4 to 5 billion people might suffer from some form of micronutrient deficiencies (WHO 2001c). GM crops could reduce public health problems worldwide arising partly or wholly from deficiencies in the quantity or nutritional quality of food, from malnutrition to heart disease. Cumulatively, hunger and malnutrition are estimated to contribute to at least 5.4 million deaths worldwide in children younger than five years (WHO 2001a) and stunting in 182 million children (de Onis, Frongillo, and Blossner 2000). According to the WHO (2001b), about 2 billion suffer from anemia mainly due to iron deficiency. Between 100 and 140 million children suffer from vitamin A deficiency, which can cause clinical xerophthalmia—a condition of the eye, caused primarily by a lack of vitamin A, that causes thickening and drying of the conjunctiva and cornea and could lead to blindness. As a result, between 250,000 and 500,000 children become blind from vitamin A deficiency, of whom half die within a year (WHO 2001c).

Bioengineering can increase the quantity as well as the nutritional quality of food, as exemplified by "golden rice," which is rich in beta-carotene, a precursor to vitamin A. Crossed with another bioengineered strain, such rice could help reduce deaths and diseases globally that occur from vitamin A and iron deficiencies.

Bioengineered crops can also help battle the so-called diseases of affluence. In 1998, these diseases—heart disease, hypertension, and cancer—accounted for 4.8 million deaths in high-income countries, and 14.9 million deaths in low- and middle-income countries. GM crops that could reduce this toll include low-fat soybeans; higher protein rice; tomatoes with increased antioxidant content; higher-starch potatoes; and vitamin-fortified fruits and vegetables.

Finally, pest resistant GM plants can—by reducing the amount, toxicity, or persistence of pesticides—reduce accidental poisonings and other health effects on farmworkers.

Risks

Some fear that the new genes inserted into GM plants could be incorporated into a consumer's genetic makeup. But plant and animal DNA has always been a part of the daily human diet. In fact, an estimated 4 percent of human diet is composed of DNA, which is naturally present in meats and plants (Chassy and Sheppard 1999).

Table 6.2. Current Public Health Problems That Could Be Alleviated Using GM Crops

Health Problem	Current Extent (Year)	Likelihood That GM Crops Would Reduce the Problem
Undernourishment	815 million people (1997–99)	Very high
Malnutrition	5.4 million deaths per year in children <5 years	Very high
Stunting	182 million people (2000)	High
Iron-deficiency anemia	~2,000 million people	High
Vitamin A deficiency	100–140 million children; 0.25–0.5 million children blinded per year, of whom half die	High
Ischemic & cerebrovascular diseases	2.8 million deaths per year in moderate HIC (1998) 9.7 million deaths per year in LIC/MIC (1998)	Moderate
Cancers	2.0 million deaths per year in HIC (1998) 5.2 million deaths per year in LIC/MIC (1998)	Moderate

Notes: HIC = high-income countries; LIC = low-income countries; MIC = middle-income countries. Data for cancers and ischemic and cerebrovascular diseases include deaths due to smoking. Data are for the years noted in parentheses.
Sources: de Onis, Frongillo, and Blossner (2000); FAO (2001b); WHO (1999, 2001a, 2001b, 2001c).

Another concern is that GM crops could trigger allergies in unsuspecting consumers. One to 3 percent of adults and 5 to 8 percent of children in the United States suffer from food allergies, and each year food allergies cause 135 fatalities and 2,500 emergency room visits. But GM foods can and have been tested and, most important, rejected, prior to commercialization for their allergic potential. In fact, the precision of bioengineering could be used to render allergenic crops nonallergenic (Buchanan 1999).

Antibiotic-resistant markers used to identify whether a gene has been successfully incorporated into plants could accelerate the trend toward antibiotic-resistant diseases. But this threat is slight compared with that due to overuse of antibiotics in livestock feed and by humans (Royal Society 1998). Moreover, alternative markers have been devised for many crops, with more in the offing.

Applying the Precautionary Principle to GM Crops

Clearly, there are risks associated with using or not using GM crops. The precautionary framework presented earlier offers a way to evaluate actions that could result in uncertain costs and uncertain benefits. Ideally, each criterion should be applied separately to the public health and to the environmental consequences of using or not using GM crops. But because there are variations in the severity, certainty, and magnitude associated with the various competing costs and benefits regarding each of these sets of consequences, I will apply several criteria simultaneously.

Public Health

Population could increase 50 percent between 1998 and 2050, and with it undernourishment, malnutrition, and their consequences, assuming global food supply increases by a like amount and all else remains equal. Thus, unless food production outstrips population growth significantly over the next half century, billions in the developing world may suffer from undernourishment, hundreds of millions may be stunted, and millions may die from malnutrition. Based on the sheer magnitude of people at risk of hunger and malnutrition and the degree of certainty attached to their public health consequences, limiting GM crops will, by limiting the rate at which food production can expand, almost certainly increase death and disease, particularly among the world's poor.

By contrast, the negative health consequences of ingesting GM foods—for example, the effects due to ingesting transgenes—are speculative. Other risks are relatively minor in magnitude, such as a potential increase in antibiotic resistance, or both speculative and relatively minor, such as a potential increase in the incidence of allergic reactions. Moreover, as noted, many of these impacts can be contained, if not eliminated.

Thus, based on the uncertainty, expectation value, and adaptation criteria applied either singly or in conjunction, GM crops must be favored over conventional or alternative agricultural production systems. Hence, the precautionary principle requires that we continue to research, develop, and commercialize—with appropriate safeguards, of course—those GM crops that would increase food production and generally improve nutrition and health, especially in the developing world.

Some have argued that many developed countries are "awash in surplus grain," and they do not need larger harvests (Christison 1999). But reducing those surpluses would harm public health in developing countries, which currently import about 10 percent of their cereals. Without these surpluses, food supplies would be lower and food prices would be higher, as would undernourishment, malnutrition, and associated health problems. Developing countries' deficits are expected to rise because of future population and economic growth and, possibly, global warming. Therefore, developed countries' surpluses will continue to be critical for future food security in developing countries, just as it is today.

The above argument against GM crops also assumes that they will provide little or no public health benefits to developed countries. But GM crops are also being engineered to combat diseases of affluence, which claim 4.8 million annually in the developed countries. Even a small reduction in these numbers due to GM crops would translate into relatively large declines in the death toll. Moreover, the health benefits of golden rice, for instance, do not have to be confined to developing countries. Thus, even in developed countries the potential public health benefits of GM crops ought to outweigh in magnitude and certainty the speculative health consequences of ingesting GM foods.

Another argument against developing GM foods is that hunger and malnutrition are rooted in maldistribution and unequal access to food and not in food shortages; therefore, there is no compelling need for biotechnology (MacIlwaine 1999). This argument tacitly acknowledges that GM crops would boost quantities more rapidly than would conventional agriculture. More important, GM crops do not decrease access. In fact, by increasing production, they would lower prices, which would increase access, particularly for the lower rungs of society. In addition, a factor contributing to poor food distribution is crop spoilage. But various GM crops could increase shelf life, reducing spoilage and wastage (Goklany 2001b). In addition, nutritional quality is just as important as food quantity, and GM foods can enhance the former far easier than conventional agriculture.

Bioengineered crops do not have to be the sole solution for hunger and malnutrition. It is sufficient that they contribute to—and are among the most efficient—solutions. If the argument that there is sufficient food is truly compelling, then it should be equally valid for arguing against increases in production using conventional technologies. Perhaps, then, developing countries like India and Bangladesh should forgo increasing agricultural productivity altogether, and focus only on improving access and distribution. For obvious reasons, no one makes this argument.

Environment

Regardless of the level of demand, GM crops would increase yields per unit of land used. And higher yields mean less land for mankind, and more for the rest of nature. Moreover, reduced land demand for mankind means lower land prices and socioeconomic opportunity costs for sequestering land for conservation and preservation, which would facilitate conservation of species and biodiversity in the wild—a major goal of the Convention on Biological Diversity (Glowka, Burhenne-Guilmin, and Synge 1994).

Also, by reducing amounts of cropland, fertilizers, and pesticides, GM crops would reduce soil erosion and releases of nutrients, pesticides, carbon, and nitrous oxide emissions into the environment.

Compare these tangible ecological benefits of GM crops to the more speculative environmental benefits of limiting pest-resistant and herbicide-tolerant GM crops even without factoring in the environmental costs of conventional farming. Assuming GM crops actually do harm nontarget pests and weeds more than conventional farming practices, banning GM crops may increase the diversity of the flora and fauna, but this is an uncertain benefit. In addition, the possibility of gene escape to weeds and non-GM crops is also uncertain.

Hence, with respect to the environmental consequences of the use or nonuse of GM crops, one must conclude, based on the uncertainty and expectation value criteria, that the precautionary principle requires cultivation of GM crops. This would conserve the planet's habitat, biodiversity, and carbon stores and sinks, provided due caution is exercised, particularly with respect to herbicide-tolerant and pest-resistant GM crops.

It may be argued that although gene escape to "natural" ecosystems might be a low-probability event, under the irreversibility criterion, GM crops ought to be banned. But increased habitat clearance and land conversion resulting from such a ban may be at least as irreversible, particularly if it leads to species extinctions.

The precautionary principle supports using terminator-type technology because it would minimize the possibility of gene transfer without diminishing any of the public health or environmental benefits of GM crops.

The Precautionary Principle and GM Crops

The precautionary principle has often been invoked to justify a prohibition on GM crops (FOE 1999). But whereas this justification touts the potential public health and environmental benefits of a ban on GM crops, it ignores any harm caused by delaying or forgoing benefits that GM crops would bring.

Worldwide, more than 800 million people suffer from hunger and undernourishment, and more than 2 billion suffer from malnutrition; as a result, millions suffer death and disease annually. But in comparison with conventional crops, GM crops would, in fact, increase the quantity and nutritional quality of food supplies. This should reduce mortality and morbidity rates worldwide. And by increasing productivity and reducing chemical inputs, GM crops would increase land available for the rest of nature and reduce global pollution by fertilizers, pesticides, and carbon. Thus, GM crops would also better protect habitat, biological diversity, water quality, and the current climate than would conventional agriculture.

Hence, contrary to conventional environmental wisdom, the precautionary principle—properly applied, with a more comprehensive consideration of the public health and environmental consequences of a ban—argues for a sustained effort to research, develop, and commercialize GM crops, provided reasonable caution is exercised during testing and commercialization of the crops.

In this context, a "reasonable" precaution is one whose public health and environmental benefits are not negated by the harm incurred due to reductions or delays in enhancing the quantity or quality of food or of the environment. Any such harm to public health would be disproportionately borne by the poorest and most vulnerable segments of society.

The Convention on Biological Diversity is dedicated to conserving biodiversity, preferably through conservation in the wild (Glowka, Burhenne-Guilmin, and Synge 1994). But a GM crop ban is more likely to magnify threats to biodiversity and reduce land and water available for such conservation. Such a ban, therefore, would be directly counter to the CBD's very reason for existence, and that of any subsidiary agreements such as the Biosafety Protocol.

Finally, slowing down commercialization of GM crops would, by reducing the future quantity and quality of food available, arguably abridge the "right to a standard of living adequate for the health and well-being . . . including food, clothing" and the "inalienable right to be free from hunger and malnutrition" as specified in the Universal Declaration of Human Rights (United Nations [UN] 1998) and the Universal Declaration on the Eradication of Hunger and Malnutrition (UN 1974), respectively, thereby violating Article 10 of the Declaration on Human Rights Defenders, which states that "no one shall participate, by act or failure to act where required, in violating human rights and fundamental freedoms . . ." (UN 1999).

In summary, although it might be a mistake to go full steam ahead on GM crops, it might be an even larger mistake to stop them in their tracks. The wisest policy on GM crops, therefore, would be to move forward with all deliberate speed.

CONCLUSION

Some fear that conventional modern agricultural technology, which includes practices associated with the green revolution, presages a silent spring. Indeed it has brought several problems in its wake, but despite that, it has been instrumental in ensuring that silent spring does not become reality. Had technology—and therefore yields—been frozen at 1961 levels, then producing as much food as was actually produced in 1998 would have been virtually impossible given the amount of global land suitable for cultivation. At the very minimum, that would have required at least a doubling of cropland and conversion of over four-fifths of the world's area to agricultural pursuits. This would have devastated the rest of nature. Alternatively, if yields had stalled at 1961 levels, and the amount of cropland was allowed to grow to the 1998 level, then the average daily food supply per capita in the developing world would have been significantly below the minimum needed for survival, and only barely above that worldwide. And that would have been devastating to mankind. Thus, conventional agricultural technology has so far been a net benefit to both humanity and the rest of nature.

Just as yesterday's technology would have been unable to support today's population without further harming the environment, today's technology cannot sustain tomorrow's population while also maintaining, if not improving, environmental quality. And that is what agricultural biotechnology promises in the foreseeable future.

REFERENCES

Alexandratos, N. ed. 1995. *World Agriculture: Towards 2010.* Chichester, UK: FAO and John Wiley.

Buchanan, Robert. 1999. *Statement to the Senate Committee on Agriculture, Nutrition, and Forestry.* October 6, 1999. Online: www.senate.gov/~agriculture/buc99106. htm (cited: January 11, 2000).

Carpenter, Janet E., and Leonard P. Gianessi. 2001. *Agricultural Biotechnology: Updated Benefit Estimates.* Washington, DC: National Center for Food and Agricultural Policy.

Carpenter, S., et al. 1998. Nonpoint Pollution of Surface Waters with Phosphorus and Nitrogen. *Issues in Ecology* 3 (Summer). Online: esa.sdsc.edu/carpenter.htm (cited: February 10, 2000).

Centers for Disease Control and Prevention. 2000. U.S. HIV and AIDS Cases Reported through June 2000. *HIV/AIDS Surveillance Report* 12 (1). Online: www.cdc.gov/ hiv/stats/hasr1201.htm (cited: February 21, 2001).

Chamberlain, D., and C. N. Stewart. 1999. Transgene Escape and Transplastomics. *Nature Biotechnology* 17: 330–31.

Chassy, Bruce, and Lisa Sheppard. 1999. GMO Food Safety Risk Is Negligible. *ACES News,* November 23. Online: www.ag.uiuc.edu/news/articles/943382465.html (cited: December 10, 1999).

Christison, Bill. 1999. *Statement of Bill Christison, President—National Farm Family Coalition.* December 14. Online: www.psrast.org/usfarmlawst.htm (cited: March 29, 2002).

Cipolla, C. 1978. *The Economic History of World Population.* Brighton, UK: Harvester.

Convention on Biological Diversity (CBD). 2000. *Cartagena Protocol on Biosafety to the Convention on Biological Diversity.* Online: http://www.biodiv.org/biosafety/ (cited: March 13, 2002).

Conway, Gordon. 2000. Food for All in the Twenty First Century. *Environment* 42: 9–18.

Council on Environmental Quality. 1992. *Environmental Quality.* Washington, DC.

———. 1993. *Environmental Quality.* Washington, DC.

———. 1999. *Environmental Quality Statistics.* Washington, DC. Online: ceq.eh.doe. gov/nepa/reports/statistics/aquatic.html (cited: March 12, 2002).

———. 2000. *Environmental Quality Statistics.* November 29. Online: ceq.eh.doe. gov/nepa/reports/statistics/ (cited: March 29, 2002).

———. 2001. *Environmental Quality Statistics.* October 17. Online: ceq.eh.doe.gov/ nepa/reports/statistics/ (cited: April 2, 2002).

Crawley, M. J., et al. 2001. Biotechnology: Transgenic Crops in Natural Habitats. *Nature* 409: 682–83.

Cropper, Maureen L., and Paul R. Portney. 1992. Discounting Human Lives. *Resources* 108: 1–4.

Daniell, Henry. 1999. The Next Generation of Genetically Engineered Crops for Herbicide and Insect Resistance: Containment of Gene Pollution and Resistant Insects. *AgBiotechNet,* vol. 1, August, ABN 024. Online: www.agbiotechnet.com/ reviews/aug99/html/Daniell.htm (cited: February 12, 2000).

de Onis, Mercedes, Edward A. Frongillo, and Monika Blossner. 2000. Is Malnutrition Declining? An Analysis of Changes in Levels of Child Malnutrition Since 1980. *Bulletin of the World Health Organization* 78(10): 1222–33.

Environmental Protection Agency. 2000a. *Bt Corn Insect Resistance Management Announced for 2000 Growing Season.* EPA Headquarters Press Release. January 14, 2000.

———. 2000b. *October 18–20, 2000 FIFRA SAP Meeting: Bt Plant Pesticides Risk and Benefits Assessment.* Online: www.epa.gov/scipoly/sap/2000/october/questions. pdf (cited: April 2, 2002).

———. 2001. *Biopesticides Registration Action Document:* Bacillus thuringiensis *Plant-Incorporated Protectants, 10/16/2001.* October 23. Online: www.epa. gov/pesticides/biopesticides/reds/brad_bt_pip2.htm (cited: April 2, 2002).

Ferber, Dan. 1999. Risks and Benefits: GM Crops in the Cross Hairs. *Science* 286: 1662–66.

Food and Agriculture Organization. 1996a. *Assessment of Feasible Progress in Food Security.* Technical Background Documents 12–15, vol. 3. Rome, Italy.

———. 1996b. *The State of Agriculture.* Rome, Italy.

———. 1997. *Irrigation Potential in Africa: A Basin Approach.* FAO Land and Water Bulletin 4. Rome, Italy.

———. 2000. FAOSTAT Database. apps.fao.org. December12, 2000.

———. 2001a. FAOSTAT Database. apps.fao.org. October 12, 2001.

———. 2001b. *The State of Food Insecurity in the World 2001.* Online: www.fao.org/docrep/003/y1500e/y1500e00.htm (cited: April 2, 2002).

Friends of the Earth. 1999. *FoE Supports Tory GM Moratorium Call. What about the Precautionary Principle Mr Blair.* February 3. Online: www.foe.co.uk/pubsinfo/infoteam/pressrel/1999/19990203170456.html (cited: May 15, 2000).

Frommer, Wolf B., Uwe Ludewig, and Doris Rentsch. 1999. Taking Transgenic Plants with a Pinch of Salt. *Science* 285: 1222–23.

Glowka, L., F. Burhenne-Guilmin, and H. Synge. 1994. *A Guide to the Convention on Biological Diversity.* Gland, Switzerland: World Conservation Union (IUCN).

Goklany, Indur M. 1994. *Air and Inland Surface Waters: Long Term Trends and Relationship to Affluence.* Washington, DC: Office of Policy Analysis, U.S. Department of the Interior.

———. 1996. Factors Affecting Environmental Impacts: The Effects of Technology on Long Term Trends in Cropland, Air Pollution and Water-related Diseases. *Ambio* 25: 497–503.

———. 1998. Saving Habitat and Conserving Biodiversity on a Crowded Planet. *BioScience* 48: 941–53.

———. 1999a. *The Future of the Industrial System.* International Conference on Industrial Ecology and Sustainability, University of Technology of Troyes, Troyes, France, September 22–25, 1999.

———. 1999b. Meeting Global Food Needs: The Environmental Trade-offs between Increasing Land Conversion and Land Productivity. *Technology* 6: 107–30.

———. 2000. Applying the Precautionary Principle in a Broader Context. In *Rethinking Risk and the Precautionary Principle,* ed. Julian Morris. Oxford, UK: Butterworth-Heinemann, 189–228.

———. 2001a. Economic Growth and the State of Humanity. *PERC Policy Series,* PS-21. Bozeman, MT: PERC, April.

———. 2001b. *The Precautionary Principle: A Critical Appraisal of Environmental Risk Assessment.* Washington, DC: Cato Institute.

———. 2001c. Agriculture and the Environment: The Pros and Cons of Modern Farming. *PERC Reports* 19(March): 12–14.

Goklany, Indur M., and Merritt W. Sprague. 1991. *An Alternative Approach to Sustainable Development: Conserving Forests, Habitat and Biological Diversity by Increasing the Efficiency and Productivity of Land Utilization.* Washington, DC: Office of Program Analysis, Department of the Interior.

Hellmich, R. L., et al. 2001. Monarch Larvae Sensitivity to *Bacillus thuringiensis*—Purified Proteins and Pollen. *Proceedings of the National Academy of Sciences* 98: 11925–30.

Hilbeck, A., et al. 1998. Effects of Transgenic *Bacillus thuringiensis* Corn-fed Prey on Mortality and Development Time of Immature *Chysoperla carnea* (Neuroptera: Chrysopidae). *Environmental Entomology* 27(2): 480–87.

James, Clive. 2000. *Global Status of Commercialized Transgenic Crops: 1999.* ISAAA Brief No. 17, 2000. Online: www.isaa.org/publications/briefs/Brief-17.htm (cited: October 15, 2001).

Jesse, L. C. H., and J. J. Obrycki. 2000. Field Deposition of *Bt* Transgenic Corn Pollen: Lethal Effects on the Monarch Butterfly. *Oecologia* 125: 241–48.

Kershen, Drew L. 2000. The Risks of Going Non-GMO. *Oklahoma Law Review* 53(4): 631–52.

Losey, John E., Linda S. Rayor, and Maureen E. Carter. 1999. Transgenic Pollen Harms Monarch Larvae. *Nature* 399: 214.

MacIlwaine, Colin. 1999. Access Issues May Determine Whether Agri-Biotech Will Help the World's Poor. *Nature* 402: 341–45.

Oerke, E. C., et al. 1994. Conclusion and Perspectives. In *Crop Production and Crop Protection: Estimated Losses in Food and Cash Crops,* ed. E. C. Oerke et al. Amsterdam: Elsevier, 742–70.

Olsson, Mats, et al. 2000. Comparison of Temporal Trends (1940s–1990s) of DDT and PCB in Baltic Sediment and Biota in Relation to Sediment. *Ambio* 29: 195–201.

Pimentel, D. 1997. Pest Management in Agriculture. In *Techniques for Reducing Pesticide Use: Economic and Environmental Benefits,* ed. D. Pimentel. Chichester, UK: John Wiley, 1–11.

Pimentel, D., and A. Greiner. 1997. Economic and Socio-Economic Costs of Pesticide Use. In *Techniques for Reducing Pesticide Use: Economic and Environmental Benefits,* ed. D. Pimentel. Chichester, UK: John Wiley, 51–78.

Raffensperger, Carolyn, and Joel Tickner, eds. 1999. *Protecting Public Health & the Environment.* Washington, DC: Island Press.

Richard, Cindy Lynn. 2000. *CBS News Covers Iowa Researcher's Study on Bt Corn Pollen and Monarch Butterfly Larvae.* Council for Agricultural Science and Technology. Online: www.cast-science.org/biotechnology/20000821.htm (cited: February 13, 2001).

Royal Society. 1998. *Genetically Modified Plants for Food Use.* Online: www.royalsoc.ac. ukfiles/statfiles/document-56.pdf (cited: April 2, 2002).

Schmitt, C. J., J. L. Zajicek, and P. H. Peterman. 1990. National Pesticide Monitoring Program. *Archives of Environmental Contamination and Toxicology* 19: 748–81.

Sears, Mark K., et al. 2001. Impact of *Bt* Corn Pollen on Monarch Butterfly Populations: A Risk Assessment. *Proceedings of the National Academy of Sciences* 98: 11937–42.

Shiklomanov, Igor A. 2000. Appraisal and Assessment of World Water Resources. *Water International* 25(1): 11–32.

Skei, Jens, et al. 2000. Eutrophication and Contaminants in Aquatic Ecosystems. *Ambio* 29: 184–94.

Smith, Daniel. 1999. Worldwide Trends in DDT Levels in Human Breast Milk. *International Journal of Epidemiology* 28(2): 179–88.

Smith, Frances B. 2000. The Biosafety Protocol: The Real Losers Are Developing Countries. *BRIEFLY: Perspectives on Legislation, Regulation, and Litigation* 4(3). National Legal Center for the Public Interest, Washington, DC.

Smith, R. A., R. B. Alexander, and K. J. Lanfear. 1993. Stream Water Quality in the Conterminous United States—Status and Trends of Selected Indicators During the 1980's. In *National Water Summary 1990–91, Stream Water Quality,* Water Supply Paper No. 2400. Reston, VA: U.S. Geological Survey.

Tabashnik, Bruce E., et al. 2000. Frequency of Resistance to *Bacillus thuringiensis* in Field Populations of Pink Bollworm. *Proceedings of the National Academy of Sciences* 97: 12980–84.

United Nations. 1974. Universal Declaration on the Eradication of Hunger and Malnutrition. Adopted on 16 November 1974 by the World Food Conference convened under General Assembly resolution 3180 (XXVIII) of December 1973, and endorsed by General Assembly resolution 3348 (XXIX) of 17 December 1974. Online: www.unhchr.ch/html/menu3/b/69.htm (cited: June 29, 2002).

———. 1998. Fiftieth Anniversary of the Universal Declaration of Human Rights. Online: www.un.org/rights/50/decla.htm (cited: June 29, 2002).

———. 1999. *Declaration on the Right and Responsibility of Individuals, Groups and Organs of Society to Promote and Protect Universally Recognized Human Rights and Fundamental Freedoms.* General Assembly resolution 53/144. Online: www.unhchr.ch/huridocda.huridoca.nsf/(Symbol)/A.RES.53.144.En?OpenDocument (cited: June 29, 2002).

United Nations Environment Programme/Global Environment Monitoring System. 1991. *Environmental Data Report 1991–92.* Cambridge, UK: Blackwell.

United Nations Environment Programme/World Health Organization/Food and Agriculture Organization. 1999. *Guidelines for the Management of Small Quantities of Unwanted and Obsolete Pesticides.* FAO Pesticide Disposal Series 7. Rome, Italy: FAO.

U.S. Bureau of Commerce. 1987. *Statistical Abstract of the United States, 1987.* Washington, DC.

U.S. Department of Agriculture. 2001. *Food and Agricultural Policy: Taking Stock for the New Century.* Washington, DC.

World Conservation Union (IUCN). 2000. *Confirming the Global Extinction Crisis.* IUCN Press Release, September 28, 2000. Online: www.iucn.org/redlist/2000/news.html (cited: November 7, 2001).

World Health Organization. 1999. *The World Health Report 1999.* Geneva, Switzerland.

———. 2001a. *WHO Nutrition.* Updated October 24, 2001. Online: www.who.int/nut/index.htm (cited: November 16, 2001).

———. 2001b. *Iron Deficiency Anemia.* Updated July 23, 2001. Online: www.who.int/nut/ida.htm (cited: November 16, 2001).

———. 2001c. *Vitamin A Deficiency.* Updated July 23, 2001. Online: www.who.int/nut/vad.htm (cited: November 16, 2001).

World Resources Institute. 2000. *World Resources 2000–01.* Washington, DC.

Zangerl, A. R., et al. 2001. Effects of Exposure to Event 176 *Bacillus thuringiensis* Corn Pollen on Monarch and Black Swallowtail Caterpillars under Field Conditions. *Proceedings of the National Academy of Sciences* 98: 11908–12.

7

High-Yield Conservation: More Food and Environmental Quality through Intensive Agriculture

Alex Avery and Dennis Avery

The world faces a significant challenge to conserving environmental assets over the next fifty years. Public sentiment supports greater protection of wildlife habitats and undeveloped areas. Farm and forestry product demands of the growing, more affluent global population are adding pressure to increase the area that is intensively managed at the expense of less developed areas. Simultaneously achieving the goals of (1) increased food, fiber, and resource availability for the growing global human population and (2) conservation of natural landscapes and wildlife habitats requires that people use existing farmlands and managed forest areas more intensively and efficiently.

More food for more people and greater protection of environmental assets require that we evaluate our farming regulations to ensure that they do not needlessly limit productivity or innovation. One way to increase land use efficiency is to liberalize trade of agricultural and forestry products under the World Trade Organization. That would allow greater resource use efficiencies. Further increases in productivity also require biotechnology to play a key role. Therefore, international food and trade regulations on agricultural biotechnology products need to be liberalized to ease the development and adoption of this technology by farmers.

As discussed in greater detail by Goklany (2003) in the previous chapter, agriculture has been the human activity that has affected the natural landscape to the greatest extent. As Goklany notes, agriculture accounts for 38 percent of the land use and the majority of water consumption. Agriculture is also related to most of the habitat conversion issues and the fragmentation that threaten the world's forests. The most significant environmental impacts of agriculture have often come from its most basic aspects. For example, because farming replaces natural biodiversity with a heavily managed human landscape of just a few species (this is true even for mixed agro-forestry systems, often billed as more environmentally benign, that use three or four different crop and tree species in combined plots), loss of natural biodiversity and so-called ecosystem complexity occurs when land is converted to farming regardless of the type of farming system adopted. Simple plowing, as another example, causes much of the soil erosion and instream sedimentation that arises from agriculture. Thus, the most important feature of a given agricultural system—in terms of its total environmental impact—is its productivity per acre, or land use efficiency.

In a recent report, *Common Ground, Common Future,* the World Conservation Union (IUCN) and Future Harvest state, "The challenge is to protect wild species and conserve habitat while increasing agricultural production" (McNeely and Scherr 2001, 3).[1] The report succinctly covers the conservation challenge of meeting the needs of the still-growing human population without converting additional land from forests and other habitat to farmland, and, at the same time, making agriculture even more sensitive to its off-farm impacts. The report notes that in tropical wilderness areas, the population is still growing at more than twice the world average and that more than 20 percent of the population lives within the twenty-five "most-threatened biodiversity hotspots." Many of these populations are poor, which creates special concerns. Population increases do not necessarily mean reductions in natural biodiversity. But when such increases occur in poverty-stricken areas, which usually means a lack of secure property rights and other factors, such as political instability, destruction of natural resources are more likely to occur (Norton 2002). For example, more than 750,000 Rwandan refugees fleeing tribal genocide used Virunga National Park in Zaire for food and firewood in the early 1990s, destroying more than 20,000 acres of forest and killing protected wildlife (most silver-backed mountain gorillas were killed). Although these unfortunate, destitute people had no other choice, most observers would agree that it would be better if such areas could be protected against such destruction.

The IUCN and Future Harvest sensibly conclude in their report that designating areas as game parks and wildlife reserves will not adequately conserve natural areas and biodiversity, especially when local farmers are poor and inefficient. The groups recommend higher crop yields and livestock productivity to decrease encroachment pressures on unmanaged areas. The strategy to protect biodiversity is to "reduce habitat destruction by increasing agricultural productivity and sustainability on lands already being farmed" (McNeely and Scherr 2001, 4). This "high-yield conservation" strategy—producing more per acre to leave more for nature—has been a hard concept for many conservation groups to accept.

Agriculture and environmental groups have largely been antagonistic toward each other, with environmentalists seeing farmers as part of the problem, and farmers wanting to be left alone to run their farms. The evolving partnership between Future Harvest (farmers) and the IUCN (environmentalists) is significant because it demonstrates recognition that high-yield farming is part of the solution to balancing the food needs of humanity with biodiversity. There is no practical alternative, given the projected increases in demand resulting from the world's growing, more affluent population. The demographic and economic trends outlined below indicate that if we are to meet food needs and protect wildlife habitat, then significant increases in agricultural efficiency and productivity are critical.

POPULATION GROWTH: MYTH VERSUS REALITY

Biologist and biodiversity advocate E. O. Wilson claims that species extinctions are inevitable until the world's population stops growing. "I call that the bottleneck, because we have to pass through that scramble for remaining resources in order to get to an era, perhaps sometime in the 22nd century, of declining population" (Gibbs 2001, 49). The "bottleneck" is much shorter than Wilson appreciates: The world's population will likely peak before the middle of this century. Humanity passed a significant milestone in the late 1990s, when the population growth rate shifted into decline. The peak growth year was 1997, when world population grew by 90 million. The next year, 85 million were added, and fewer have been added in each year since (World Bank 2000, 41, fig. 2.1). This is the first time in modern history that the population growth rate has declined. The peak population is projected to reach 9 billion people, roughly 50 percent higher than the year 2000 population. And because nearly every developed nation has settled into a below-replacement level fertility rate, world population will begin to fall after the peak, likely around 2050. That's the bottleneck: 50 percent increase in population in 50 years.

Earlier predictions of a peak population of 15 billion people (and more extreme scenarios offered by Ehrlich and others of 20 billion or more) failed to account for the widespread and rapid decline in fertility rates across the globe over the past thirty years—especially in developing countries (Seckler and Cox 1994). Moreover, few predicted that fertility rates would settle at levels below replacement. (Replacement level is the fertility rate needed to maintain a population at a steady level, which is about 2.1 children per couple.) Several factors have contributed to the rapid fertility rate declines: lower infant and child mortality rates, increased education and workforce participation by women, access to reproductive health information and contraceptives, and an economic shift in many countries from subsistence agriculture to more urban manufacturing. The single biggest factor in the fertility rate decline has been higher and rising living standards, especially in Asia.

Although increases in living standards are helping to lower population growth rates, higher incomes also mean increased consumption of resource-costly foods and therefore higher resource demand. As a result, the actual food and fiber demand increases of the next fifty years will be significantly greater than just the 50 percent rise in population (fig. 7.1). High-income urbanites eat higher-quality foods: better cereals, more meat and dairy products, and more fresh fruits and vegetables. Consider one example of the significant impact affluence can have on consumption patterns: China more than doubled its total meat consumption (and personal incomes) during the 1990s (U.S. Department of Agriculture [USDA] 2001b).

Animal protein calories take between two and five times more resources (feed, land, water, nutrients, etc.) per calorie to produce than cereal or plant-based calories. But significant portions of animal diets are often composed of human inedible resources such as grass, forage, crop residues, or food processing by-products, and so some resource costs are mitigated. For example, some high-yielding forage crops when fed to animals can provide more human-edible food product per acre than many grain or vegetable crops. After factoring in all feed inputs, animals use about 1.4 kilograms of human edible protein to produce 1 kilogram of human food protein. But this protein has about 1.4 times higher biological value (protein) than plant proteins, so the tradeoff is worthy in terms of dietary quality and diversity—especially for children (Council on Agricultural Science and Technology 1999).

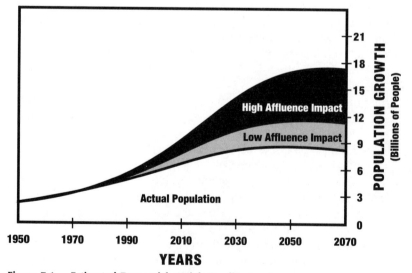

Figure 7.1.   Estimated Demand for High-Quality Foods.

Similarly, demand for fiber products increases with living standards. Global cotton consumption has increased by 40 percent above 1970 levels as increased incomes translate into larger wardrobes (USDA 2001a). Whereas once two outfits were all many people could afford, more affluent developing world consumers own six or ten outfits. As family size decreases, house pets become more popular. If China were to reach the same dog and cat ownership rates as in the U.S. population, China would be feeding an extra half-billion animals. When all such factors are combined, it's easy to see why the debate in development circles is whether the world will have to double or even triple farm output over the next half century to keep up with demand. Either way, a significant increase in the efficiency and productivity of our farms must occur if we are to avoid converting massive amounts of uncultivated land to agriculture.

LAND USE: BATTLEFRONT OF THE BIODIVERSITY CONSERVATION WAR

Habitat preservation is a key factor for conservation. Overhunting caused several extinctions and near extinctions—such as the passenger pigeon, great auk, and bison. Even though hunting remains a threat to some species (i.e., tigers and gorillas), land use competition is the primary threat for many species, especially in densely populated areas throughout Asia and increasingly in Africa. According to the Food and Agriculture Organization of the United Nations (1999), farms occupy 38 percent of the earth's land area—11 percent in crops and 27 percent in pasture/rangeland. If the ice-covered land area is removed from this equation, farming takes nearly half of the land area of the globe. In contrast, cities, highways, and industrial complexes combined take up less than 2 percent of global land area (Richards 1990). Assuming a 50 percent increase in population, it seems unlikely that urban land uses would take more than 5 percent of the global land area. Farms, not urban areas, are where humanity competes with nature for real estate.

How might there be a balance between man and nature as we confront the burgeoning demands for food? Should there be areas we farm differently in deference to nature? Since 1981, the Netherlands has subsidized so-called eco-fields in which farmers are paid either to delay farming activities on specific fields until after wild nesting birds have hatched their chicks or to limit mowing and fertilizer use on pastures to promote grassland biodiversity. Such agri-environmental schemes currently cover about 20 percent of Europe's farmland and account for 4 percent of European Union (EU) farm expenditures. Plans are in place to increase agri-environmental funding to 10 percent of EU farm expenditures in the near future.

Eco-fields are touted as the middle way toward a more "balanced" landscape that is friendlier to Mother Nature. In practice, they can lead to the wasting of prime farmland productivity, and thereby, expansion into land not now farmed. Furthermore, Dutch eco-fields were found to have less plant diversity and fewer birds than comparable intensively farmed fields, according to a team of researchers from the Nature Conservation and Plant Ecology group at Wageningen University. The Dutch team reports that a survey of 78 paired fields found fewer birds and wild plants, and only modestly higher numbers of fly species, in the eco-fields (Kleijn et al. 2001). The decreased nesting of wading birds was particularly unwelcome because the Netherlands is the nesting site for nearly half the European populations of wading birds such as the black-tailed godwit and oystercatcher.

The wading birds preferred to nest in the more intensive fields, apparently because of the greater food abundance as a result of more intensive fertilizer use. "Birds avoided the eco-fields because the soils contained fewer earthworms. They feared going hungry," notes David Kleijn, the lead researcher (Pearce 2001). This means that the eco-fields were a waste of taxpayer dollars and are perhaps a net negative to Europe's wildlife as well. It wasn't supposed to work that way. It was always assumed that these eco-schemes would pay noticeable dividends in increased bird numbers and plant diversity.

Defenders of the eco-field policies have suggested that this research merely indicates the need to closely monitor such schemes to make sure they are working as planned and adapt them as needed. It seems more likely that the eco-fields concept should be limited to special situations in which desired or endangered wildlife has a particular dependence upon farmed areas for habitat.

The belief that we can tweak our farms into harboring significant populations of wildlife now permeates government agricultural policy throughout the developed world. The EU is not alone in such subsidy schemes. The United States has the Conservation Reserve Program (comprising more than 30 million acres) and there are plans to tie government farm payments to eco-services and environmental stewardship programs.

The fundamental flaw is the belief that farmland is critical wildlife habitat that is best utilized in an eco-friendly manner. But farmland is poor wildlife habitat at best. As the Dutch researchers noted in their report, "The primary concern of farmers is necessarily to secure an income. As a result, nature conservation will be of secondary importance to them, and will be fitted into a farming system that, owing to economic pressure, is still increasing in intensity" (Kleijn et al. 2001, 724). Further, for those who want "natural" biodiversity, the more land area we can leave unfarmed, the better. Otherwise, the biodiversity that is fostered will be that favored under the specific management practices of farmers—an artificial biodiversity at best.

Organic Isn't Necessarily Eco-Friendly

Some environmental groups advocate a return to low-input organic farming out of concern over the off-farm impacts of inputs such as herbicides and insecticides. This leads to the mistaken belief that low input will mean low impact. On a global scale, this is clearly not the case.

Organic farming is often cited as a low-input farm system that is more environmentally friendly than conventional farm practices. Some consumers choose to pay higher prices for organic foods and products because of perceived health and environmental benefits. But mandating organic farming globally would be an unprecedented disaster for biodiversity. The restriction on synthetic nitrogen fertilizers is sufficient to eliminate organic farming as a strategy for biodiversity conservation. According to Vaclav Smil, author of *Enriching the Earth: Fritz Haber, Carl Bosch and the Transformation of World Food Production,* it would take the manure from about 8 billion additional cattle to replace the world's current annual use of synthetic nitrogen fertilizer.[2] Considering that the world's population of 1.3 billion cattle is already consuming much of existing grasslands, where would humanity find the forage for that many extra cattle? The United States alone would need the manure from an additional 1 billion cattle to replace current synthetic nitrogen fertilizer use. Simply growing the feed for that many extra cattle would require all of the farmland of the conterminous forty-eight states. This is not to say that organic farming is necessarily wasteful of resources. Organic nitrogen sources enhance soil quality and can produce high yields; however, there simply is not enough organic nitrogen available to supply the needs now, let alone for the year 2050. And to the extent that organic farmers fall short in productivity—whether due to lower nutrient availability, the "green manure" requirements for additional land, excessive weed pressures, or excessive pest damage—then organic farming adds to pressures to convert more land to agriculture and away from current use, such as wildlife habitat.

GULF OF MEXICO HYPOXIA AND THE PRECAUTIONARY PRINCIPLE

Synthetic nitrogen fertilizer is in this sense a powerful wildlands conservation tool. Yet regulatory agencies around the world are considering various levels of fertilizer use restrictions on the basis of water quality. Taken too far, this could throw the biodiversity baby out with the conservation bathwater. Regulations that significantly curtail fertilizer use at the expense of farm productivity add pressure to convert natural lands to farmlands. The U.S. government's Mississippi River/Gulf of Mexico Watershed Nutrient Task Force, for example, has stated that a 20 to 30 percent reduction in total nutrient fluxes to the Gulf of Mexico is needed to address the seasonal low oxygen content of some Louisiana coastal waters (Mississippi River/Gulf of Mexico Watershed Nutrient Task Force 2001). But the ecological benefits of improved water quality must be weighed against the costs of reduced farm productivity. In the case of Gulf of Mexico hypoxia, the task force failed to document a serious environmental problem, let alone justify potentially onerous fertilizer and land use regulations. Nor did the task force consider possible benefits of nutrient fluxes to the Gulf of Mexico.

Hypoxia in the Gulf of Mexico is a transient, seasonal zone of low oxygen that occurs in summer along the coast of Louisiana. As the sediment and nutrient-laden waters of the Mississippi flow into the Gulf of Mexico, the less-dense fresh water from the Mississippi floats atop the denser salt water of the Gulf and is carried west along the continental shelf by Gulf currents. The nutrients within the river water (primarily nitrogen and especially during high spring river flows) fuel the growth of algae and phytoplankton in the water. Algae blooms and wastes from phytoplankton then sink to the bottom where bacteria degrade the organic matter, thereby consuming dissolved oxygen. In the summer months, when the weather is calm, the still upper layer prevents the bottom waters from being reoxygenated. The bottom waters become hypoxic, or low in dissolved oxygen. When this occurs, mobile organisms swim away or to upper, more oxygenated water layers. Bottom-dwelling organisms that cannot swim or crawl, such as mudworms, are believed to weaken or die depending on the length and severity of hypoxia. The hypoxia ends when storms and waves disrupt the stratified water column.

The Gulf hypoxic zone, or "dead zone" as environmental groups have dubbed it, has been surveyed and its size estimated only since 1985. The annual hypoxia survey is conducted on a single cruise. Dissolved oxygen levels are measured in a grid across the Gulf shelf along the Louisiana and Texas coasts. The hypoxic zone is extrapolated from the grid measurements and is defined by the area of bottom water oxygen levels below 2 mg/liter (fig. 7.2). At its largest, in 2001, the area measured 20,000 square kilometers or about 1 percent of the Gulf area. Many factors affect the size, duration, and intensity of hypoxia, especially Mississippi River flows and weather conditions—which raises the question of how hypoxia researchers know which week in the year to time the research cruise. Moreover, only estimated maps of the hypoxic area, not the data used to extrapolate the area, have ever been published. The five-year running average size of the measured hypoxic zone for 1996–2000 is about 14,000 kilometers, although in drought years, such as 1988, there was essentially no hypoxic zone, and in flood years it has been larger.

The questions left unresolved include the ecological impacts of the hypoxia, its causes, and what, if anything, should be done about it. We have no

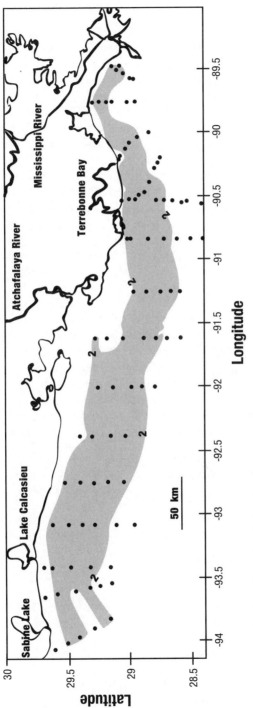

Figure 7.2. **Gulf of Mexico Hypoxic Zone.** Source: Rabalais (1998).

measurements of the hypoxic zone previous to 1985, although sediment analysis indicates an increase in nutrient fluxes out of the Mississippi beginning about the time the prairies were first plowed and increasing through the past century of farming, human settlement, and river management. It is likely that there has been a hypoxic zone of some size along the northern Gulf Coast for at least a century. Several factors likely exacerbate hypoxia, including increased nutrient loadings into the basin—via human wastes, industrial sources, and of course farming and livestock production—and changes to the river system. Levees for flood control and channeling of the river for shipping have altered Mississippi River dynamics. Much more of the river's sediment and nutrients now make it into the Gulf, rather than being deposited in the coastal wetlands of the Mississippi Delta. The effect of this can be seen in the new "bird's-foot" delta, located at the river outlet (see fig. 7.2). Eighty percent of U.S. annual wetlands loss is Louisiana coastal wetlands sinking into the Gulf because they are no longer replenished by additions of sediment each year (U.S. Geological Survey 1995).

The Gulf of Mexico Hypoxia Work Group, created by the Clinton administration and assigned in the mid-1990s to assess the situation and recommend government policy, failed to find any "detrimental ecological and economic effects" of hypoxia to the Gulf environment or its fisheries. Moreover, the work group did not consider possible ecological and economic benefits of hypoxia. The area contains a fishery that generates more than a half-billion dollars annually. In 1994, when the hypoxic zone was near peak size, fisheries landings off the Louisiana coast surpassed 1.7 trillion pounds, the most valuable catch in nearly a decade. Louisiana fisheries officials reported at an Environmental Protection Agency (EPA) hypoxia conference in 1995:

> Louisiana's fisheries, and to a large extent those of the northern Gulf of Mexico, depend on the Mississippi River for their existence. The sediments and nutrients carried by the river built the Louisiana coastal marshes. Today, as a result of leveeing [*sic*] the river, nutrients and sediments that once built and maintained Louisiana's coastal marshes are being deposited off the Continental Shelf in the abyssal depths of the Gulf of Mexico. Decreasing the nutrient levels in the Mississippi River may serve to lessen the severity of hypoxia in coastal waters, but also may impact the food web of the northern Gulf and decrease fisheries production. (Hanifen et al. 1997, 92)

Indeed, a pod of roughly 500 endangered sperm whales has now taken up permanent residence at the mouth of the Mississippi River, presumably due to the abundant food supply.

Despite the failure to document any significant negative ecological or economic impacts of hypoxia, the work group concluded that nutrient fluxes should be cut by 20 to 30 percent, apparently based on the precautionary principle that harm to fisheries or the Gulf may eventually occur.

The work group concluded, "Currently, there are no hypoxia effects on fisheries," but warned that conditions could worsen, adding that "in the face of worsening hypoxic conditions, at some point fisheries and other species will decline, perhaps precipitously." The group knows, however, that there is no clear trend toward worsening conditions. It is also clear that too few measurements have been taken for too short a time to predict ecological catastrophe from hypoxia, especially considering the apparent resiliency of Gulf fisheries.

The group's plan contains no specific regulations for controlling nonpoint sources of pollution. Instead it envisions expanded funding for existing incentive-based programs under the Clean Water Act, the Farm Bill, and other programs. Given the uncertain science of the matter, it is questionable whether such concerted nitrogen-reduction efforts could produce conservation benefits. If fertilizer reduction causes output reduction, then the environmental side effect could be the conversion of more lands into croplands.

THINKING GLOBALLY, ACTING LOCALLY MEANS FREE TRADE

Conservation of nonagricultural lands means using trade as a tool to more efficiently allocate and utilize existing farming resources. A number of so-called environmental groups advocate regional food self-sufficiency. Consider the following excerpt of a policy paper from the Sierra Club of Canada:

> The overall policy goal of sustainable farm production must be food security and not more trade. If we are to reverse present trends we must, as environmentalists, confront the onslaught of global corporations with grand ambitions. We can begin by identifying those policies that will begin to restore agricultural production and trade to a sustainable footing by reducing the distance between farm and consumer (between garden and table) which would in turn reduce the need for food processing and packaging and transportation . . . in other words by making the transition from global dependence to self reliance. (Shrybman 1997)

They claim that trade in farm products wastes resources, especially fuel for transportation. They also see this as a community sustainability issue: For a community to be "sustainable" it must also be food/fiber self-sufficient. This ignores the resource costs of regional self-sufficiency, especially the tropical forests that will be destroyed to make densely populated regions such as Asia food self-sufficient. They also radically overestimate the amount of energy used to transport food long distances by today's fuel-efficient trains and ships. The agricultural sector of the United States uses only 2 percent of the nation's total energy consumption (direct energy use and energy used to manufacture and transport agrochemicals and fertilizers), and transportation comprises a small fraction of that 2 percent (USDA 1994).

Agricultural trade also is a stabilizing force in global food security. Droughts and crop and livestock disease outbreaks tend to be localized; global food production is quite stable. Even regional self-sufficiency is a bad food security policy: Any one region can suffer crop failures and other catastrophes that limit food availability. In such times, it is the world market that offers real food security.

Sustainability itself is a term with only limited application and may not be environmentally "friendly." For example, low-yield slash-and-burn farming systems are perfectly sustainable when population levels are low and land is abundant. Land rotations can be kept quite long under such circumstances, and forests have time to regenerate and restore nutrients to the soil. Also, enough land is kept in a seminatural state to satisfy biodiversity needs. But when population pressures rise and land becomes scarcer, rotation cycles must be shortened and the system eventually becomes unsustainable.

The best rationale for free trade in agricultural products, however, is land use efficiency or productivity per acre. Wheat yields in Brazil are about half as high as wheat yields in Argentina, almost entirely due to climatic differences. Environmentally and economically it makes sense for Argentina to concentrate on wheat and for Brazil to focus on citrus and other warm-climate crops. Instead of India attempting to supply itself entirely with dairy products (as currently with high import tariffs), India's farmland would be more efficiently utilized growing cotton, legumes, and tropical crops better suited to its climate. Conversely, it is a waste of prime cropland resources and consumer dollars for the U.S. government to limit sugar imports, artificially inflate sugar prices, and attempt to supply itself with sugar by growing sugar beets in northern states. Cane sugar production in tropical climates is significantly more efficient in land and water resources than sugar beet production in northern climates. For example, Hawaii in the early 1990s produced 20 percent of U.S. raw sugar from only 7 percent of total U.S. sugar acreage. Tropical cane production results in almost ten tons of raw sugar per acre, compared with only two to three tons per acre from beet sugar production in northern U.S. states (Nakamoto 1996). The United States could significantly reduce the amount of land needed to meet its sugar needs—and reduce consumer sugar prices—if it simply allowed more tropical cane sugar imports from land-efficient producers such as Cuba and Mexico.

There are ongoing efforts to liberalize trade through the World Trade Organization. The aim is to end all farm export subsidies and lower tariff and nontariff barriers. Liberalizing agricultural trade is politically unpopular and will not be easy to achieve. The sooner farm trade is liberalized, the sooner the land pressures can be relieved in such areas as Asia, where trade barriers and self-sufficiency goals are pushing agricultural encroachment upon uncountable numbers of species.

BIOTECHNOLOGY: A KEY TO
HIGH YIELDS AND SUSTAINABILITY

Biotechnology will play an enormous role in agriculture and the conservation challenge of the next half century. An estimated 125 million acres of genetically modified crops were planted by the end of 2001. In the year 2000, 34 percent of the soybeans, 16 percent of the cotton, 11 percent of the rapeseed, and 7 percent of the maize crops worldwide were genetically modified. In western Canada, 61 percent of the 2001 canola crop was genetically modified (Auxenfans 2001). Thirteen countries are producing or importing biotech crops and twenty-nine are conducting biotech field trials. Biotech crops have already decreased production costs and pesticide use significantly. More important, they are helping to conserve water and topsoil through herbicide-tolerant no-tillage crops. No-till and reduced-tillage practices have helped cut soil erosion drastically, to the point that in some areas we are building, rather than losing topsoil.

But this is just the tip of the biotech iceberg. Biotechnology has isolated genes from wild crop relatives that significantly increase crop yields in modern crop varieties. For example, researchers found two wild rice genes that each increased yields by nearly 20 percent in the highest-yielding Chinese rice hybrids. Rice is a crop in which yield gains had leveled off in recent years, yet these two natural genes offer the prospect of a 35 percent increase in yields. A wild tomato gene was found that increases tomato solids yield by nearly 50 percent (Tanksley and McCouch 1997).

Biotechnology has also found solutions to other critical productivity problems. Aluminum toxicity, for example, severely limits yields on 40 percent of the arable land in the tropics. After decades of failed traditional breeding efforts for aluminum tolerance, biotechnology may solve the problem with a single gene for citric acid excretion from the plant roots (de la Fuente et al. 1997). This is a biotech copy of a natural plant aluminum tolerance strategy—the citric acid excreted by the roots into the soil binds to the aluminum and prevents its absorption by the crop. Yields from aluminum-tolerant crops should be significantly higher, perhaps as much as twice as high, alleviating pressure to cultivate additional land area, especially in tropical regions where aluminum toxicity is a major yield constraint. To date, this transformation has been successfully conducted in papaya, rice, and wheat but it is a strategy that might be employed on nearly any crop.

Even salt tolerance, the goal of plant breeders for decades because of salinization in irrigated soils, is being addressed through biotechnology. This strategy not only provides the ability to grow crops in saline conditions but also allows the remediation of salt-contaminated fields. Researchers at the University of California–Davis were able to create tomato and canola plants that grow in 40 percent seawater (Zhang and Blumwald 2001). This was achieved not by adding any "foreign" genes to these crops, but by getting the plants to produce more of a plant protein they already had. This strategy, like aluminum tolerance, is also applicable to nearly every crop species.

Of course, salt-tolerant crops could be used to justify the destruction of salt marshes and other wild habitats. But the costs of transforming such environments are usually high, and the incentive to do so will be undercut by the significant productivity gains of salt-tolerant crops and from reducing salt contamination in existing irrigated lands. Overall, the benefits of biotechnology will weigh in on the side of conservation, not increased destruction.

CONCLUSION

The scope of the humanitarian/biodiversity conservation challenge ahead is huge. It will require a concerted global effort on the part of governments, private institutions, and the agricultural sector to foster increased agricultural productivity at a time when many are calling for decreased intensity and productivity from existing farmland. To make the most efficient use of farmland, international farm trade laws must be liberalized. Food safety standards, labeling laws, and such will have to be harmonized for genetically modified crops and foods, a process that is occurring but faces strong opposition from various special interests. Finally, it would benefit greatly from a shift in thinking among both agriculturists and conservationists. The IUCN and Future Harvest have taken a bold step toward abandoning the traditional antagonism and are coming together toward the goal of a healthy humanity and environment.

NOTES

1. The World Conservation Union, or IUCN, is a nature organization consisting of 112 government agencies, 10,000 scientists, and 735 non-governmental organizations. Future Harvest is the nonprofit outreach arm of the Consultative Group on International Agricultural Research.

2. Vaclav Smil, telephone conversation with author, October 16, 2001.

REFERENCES

Auxenfans, Bernard. 2001. *Protracted Introduction of New Technologies in European Agriculture: Plant Biotechnology*. Presentation at Rabobank UK Food & Agribusiness Advisory Board meeting, September 22, Foxhills, UK.

Council on Agricultural Science and Technology. 1999. *Animal Agriculture and Global Food Supply*. Task Force report 135. Ames, Iowa.

de la Fuente, Juan Manuel, et al. 1997. Aluminum Tolerance in Transgenic Plants by Alteration of Citrate Synthesis. *Science* 276(5318): 1566–68.

Food and Agriculture Organization. 1999. FAOSTAT Database. Online: apps.fao.org (cited: March 25, 2002).

Gibbs, W. Wayt. 2001. On the Termination of Species. *Scientific American* 285(5): 40–49.

Goklany, Indur M. 2003. Agricultural Technology and the Precautionary Principle. This volume.

Hanifen, James G., et al. 1997. *Potential Impacts of Hypoxia on Fisheries: Louisiana's Fishery-Independent Data.* Proceedings of the First Gulf of Mexico Hypoxia Management Conference. EPA-55-R-97-001. Washington, DC. Online: web.archive.org/web/20010818114254/pelican.gmpo.gov/nutrient/front.html (cited: October 10, 2001).

Kleijn, David, et al. 2001. Agri-environment Schemes Do Not Effectively Protect Biodiversity in Dutch Agricultural Landscapes. *Nature* 413: 723–25.

McNeely, Jeffrey A., and Sara J. Scherr. 2001. *Common Ground Common Future: How Ecoagriculture Can Help Feed the World and Save Wild Biodiversity.* IUCN and Future Harvest. May. Online: www.futureharvest.org/pdf/biodiversity_report.pdf (cited: March 29, 2002).

Mississippi River/Gulf of Mexico Watershed Nutrient Task Force. 2001. *Action Plan for Reducing, Mitigating, and Controlling Hypoxia in the Northern Gulf of Mexico.* Washington, DC.

Nakamoto, Stuart. 1996. *Trade Liberalization and the U.S. Sugar Industry.* Revised February 1996. Online: ag.arizona.edu/AREC/WEMC/papers/TradeLibSugarInd.html (cited: March 25, 2002).

Norton, Seth. 2002. Population Growth, Economic Freedom, and the Rule of Law. *PERC Policy Series,* PS-24. Bozeman, MT: PERC, February.

Pearce, Fred. 2001. Green Farming Can Be an Expensive Failure. October 15. Online: www.newscientist.com/news/news.jsp?id=ns99991433 (cited: March 25, 2002).

Rabalais, Nancy N. 1998. Oxygen Depletion in Coastal Waters. National Oceanic and Atmospheric Administration's State of the Coast Report. Online: state-of-coast.noaa.gov/bulletins/html/hyp_09/hyp.html (cited: March 29, 2002).

Richards, John F. 1990. Land Transformation. In *The Earth as Transformed by Human Action,* ed. B. L. Turner and William C. Clark. Cambridge, UK: Cambridge University Press, 163–78.

Seckler, David, and Gerald Cox. 1994. *Population Projections by the United Nations and the World Bank: Zero Growth in 40 Years.* Discussion paper 21. Winrock International Institute for Agricultural Development, Center for Economic Policy Studies, Arlington, VA.

Shrybman, Steven. 1997. An Environment Guide to the World Trade Organization. May. Online: www.sierraclub.ca/national/trade-env/env-guide-wto.html (cited: March 25, 2002).

Tanksley, Steven D., and Susan R. McCouch. 1997. Seed Banks and Molecular Maps: Unlocking Genetic Potential from the Wild. *Science* 277(5329): 1063–66.

U.S. Department of Agriculture. 1994. *Agricultural Resources and Environmental Indicators.* Economic Research Service, AH-705. Washington, DC.

———. 2001a. Cotton: World Markets and Trade. Foreign Agricultural Service, Circular Series FC-05-01, May. Online: www.fas.usda.gov/cotton/circular/2001/05/circular.pdf (cited: March 29, 2002).

———. 2001b. Livestock and Poultry: World Markets and Trade. Foreign Agricultural Service, Circular Series DL&P 2-01, October. Online: www.fas.usda.gov/dlp/circular/2001/01-10LP/dlp2_01.pdf (cited: March 29, 2002).

U.S. Geological Survey. 1995. *Fact Sheet on Louisiana Wetlands*. November. Marine and Coastal Geology Program. Online: marine.usgs.gov/fact-sheets/LAwetlands/lawetlands.html (cited: March 29, 2002).

World Bank. 2000. *2000 World Development Indicators*. Washington, DC.

Zhang, Hong-Xia, and Eduardo Blumwald. 2001. Transgenic Salt-Tolerant Tomato Plants Accumulate Salt in Foliage But Not in Fruit. *Nature Biotechnology* 19(8): 765–68.

8

Carbon Emissions, Carbon Sinks, and Global Warming

*Joshua A. Utt, W. Walker Hunter,
and Robert E. McCormick*

This chapter is a report on a long-term project to assay the relation between the terrestrial-atmospheric carbon stock and per capita income over time within the United States. Carbon, in various forms, flows naturally between the aquatic, atmospheric, and terrestrial spheres. We pursue this research agenda for two reasons. First, there is concern in the environmental movement about the relation between economic activity and something called global warming. In this world, human economic activity leads to the burning of fossil fuels and plant matter, releasing carbon dioxide. Other human activities release other gases, such as methane and chlorofluorocarbon compounds. In turn, increases in CO_2, CH_4, and other carbon compounds in the atmosphere are argued to cause the earth to retain additional heat from the sun and thus warm the earth in what is said to be an unnatural way. Why warming is a concern is sometimes, but rarely, carefully discussed.[1] We do not join that debate here, but we do believe that the question of how human, read economic, activity relates to the environment is a very important and interesting one. Therefore, we want to know what the relation is between economic activity and the net emissions of certain gaseous carbon compounds.

This version of our research agenda is focused on several agricultural issues. Specifically we ask what role has agricultural enterprise played in affecting global warming either through carbon emissions or sequestrations? We address this question in several formats: examining forest product changes over time and linking animal stocks over time and cross-sectionally within the United States. Together these paint a picture of the relation between human agricultural activity and airborne carbon stocks.

The terrestrial stock of carbon is increased by the growth of carbon sinks such as forests or other biomass. A sink is an object or group of objects, such

151

as a tree or a forest, in the terrestrial sphere that stores more carbon in a given year than it emits. The terrestrial stock of carbon is decreased by the burning of sources of carbon, such as fossil fuels, for energy. A source is an object, or activity, in the terrestrial sphere that emits more carbon into the atmosphere than it stores. So a growing forest is a sink, and a forest fire is a source, but the exact delineation requires measurement to determine whether growing trees add to the stock of solid carbon or increase the stock of gaseous carbon. Intuition suggests the former.

Carbon sequestration is the process whereby gaseous carbon is removed from the atmosphere and stored in the terrestrial sphere. Sequestrations can take place either as deliberate human practices, such as removing CO_2 from the air and cooling it to liquid for transport to some place for some other purpose, such as for use as a coolant, or as the result of natural processes or human-induced activities with unintended consequences.

We speculate that carbon emissions grow with income, but that carbon storage in the terrestrial sphere does as well. The question becomes, which grows faster? Do the causes and effects of the income growth when the economy is relatively poor—dirty energy consumption, growth in agriculture, and deforestation—spur a net surplus of sources over sinks? Does growth when the country is relatively richer—the shift to service industries, afforestation, and less dirty energy use—lead to a decrease in the disparity or perhaps a net surplus of sinks over sources? We will estimate these relations in a two-part process. First we analyze the relation between emissions and income by itself. Then we estimate the sequestration-income connection, also by itself. We view these as two blades of a pair of scissors by first estimating the size and shape of each blade, then determining how the pair cut together. This includes analyzing the correlation between net emissions, the amount of carbon emitted in a year less the amount of carbon sequestered, and per capita income.

By analyzing the link between emissions and per capita income we look for the presence of an environmental Kuznets curve or at least a modified version of one (Yandle, Vijayaraghavan, and Bhattarai 2002). According to the literature, pollution increases with industrial and income growth until some turning point. After this inflection, additional income growth leads to enhanced environmental quality. There are two possible reasons for this parabolic relation between income and the environment. First, environmental consumption is almost surely a normal or superior good. As incomes rise, individuals become more willing to trade consumption of basic food and shelter for an enhanced quality of life and environmental quality. This argument is augmented by the distinct possibility that there is simply less pollution emitted to create the products demanded of a rich economy. Pollution is heavy when countries are poor as most consumption creates, coincidentally, unpleasant by-products. Agriculture produces less unpleasant side products than does industrial production. Pollution falls farther as a nation shifts from industry to a service-based economy (Moomaw and Unruh 1998).

International treaties such as the Kyoto Protocol propose to set caps on carbon emissions in order to limit the growth of atmospheric carbon. Because this will almost surely reduce energy production in the short term, it is quite possible this will cause a contraction in national income. If it is true that net carbon emissions rise and then fall with income, this policy might have the perverse effect of keeping a country at an income level at which there is a wide disparity between source and sink. In the end, a cap on emissions might actually increase the amount of airborne carbon. And to those worried about global warming, this might conceivably make the world warmer.

Several statistics point to the possibility that economic growth in the United States may lead to a decrease in net carbon emissions. First, carbon emissions from energy production by Annex 1 (developed plus transition economies) nations fell from 1980–89 to 1990–99.[2] During the same period emissions increased by more than 50 percent for other, low-income nations in the world. Second, emissions from the second largest source, land-use change, such as conversion of forests to cropland, diminished from 1980–89 to 1990–99 (Intergovernmental Panel on Climate Change [IPCC] 2000). As agriculture has become more productive, the amount of cropland in temperate regions has fallen. Although these statistics are global in nature, they may be similar to those of the United States.

GREENHOUSE ISSUES

In the mid-1980s, the world was introduced to the concept of human-induced climate change said to be caused by the greenhouse effect.[3] About half of the sun's incoming energy reaches the earth while the other half is reflected back into space or absorbed by the atmosphere. Of the energy that reaches the surface, most is absorbed and re-emitted as heat. Gases in the atmosphere trap some of this rising heat and return it to the earth's surface. Human activities may intensify this effect when growing amounts of heat-trapping gases are released into the atmosphere. For purposes of our project, whether this is true or not is irrelevant.

In 1988, two United Nations organizations, the U.N. Environment Programme and the World Meteorological Organization, set up the IPCC, which was assigned the responsibility to make comprehensive assessments of the science and impacts of climate change induced by a warming of the earth's atmosphere. The IPCC's first report in 1990 concluded that emissions resulting from human activities were substantially increasing the atmospheric concentrations of the greenhouse gases: carbon dioxide, methane, chlorofluorocarbons, and nitrous oxide. The IPCC also concluded that the global mean surface air temperature increased by 0.3 to 0.6 degree centigrade over the past 100 years, perhaps caused by the built-up concentrations of greenhouse gases (IPCC 1990).

The IPCC report and subsequent meetings of United Nations members produced the United Nations Framework Convention on Climate Change (UNFCCC), a treaty signed in 1992 by forty-one nations including the United States. This treaty was a formal agreement under which member nations would aim to curb their 2000 carbon emissions levels to those of 1990. The word *aim* was a specifically weak term used so that the United States would sign the treaty despite questions regarding the scientific evidence for global warming put forth by the IPCC.

When it became apparent by 1997 that very few countries would meet the goals set forth in the UNFCCC, the member nations sought to amend the treaty. At the third Conference of Parties to the UNFCCC held in Kyoto, Japan, in December 1997, member nations signed an amended treaty containing legally binding agreements as to future levels of carbon emissions. This treaty, known as the Kyoto Protocol, further increased the commitment of nations such that by 2008, emissions would be reduced to at least 5 percent less than levels in 1990. The protocol included many improved features, including emissions permits, trading between nations, and the Clean Development Mechanism (CDM). The CDM allows nations to substitute carbon sequestration for emissions reduction.

Allowing a firm or nation to choose between reducing emissions or increasing sequestration stands to save resources. Nations face very different costs of reducing emissions. Therefore, trading can take place when, for example, a high-cost nation pays a low-cost nation to plant trees to act as a sink. One concept that seems to have been overlooked is whether growth in income leads naturally to growth in carbon sinks. A keen understanding of the relation between income and changes in the atmospheric carbon stock might be valuable as the United States considers implementing new legislation that caps emissions.

OCEANIC CARBON SINK

The ocean holds fifty times as much carbon as the atmosphere in the form of dissolved inorganic and organic carbon (IPCC 2000, 31). In the ocean, carbon is sequestered by plantlike phytoplankton, which in turn is consumed by sea animals. Some of this carbon rains down toward the ocean floor as waste and dead organisms. Bacteria feed on this particulate organic carbon and produce CO_2, which dissolves, while the rest of the detritus ends up on the sea floor (Preuss 2001). Scientific evidence shows that although the ocean removes three times more carbon, and holds nineteen times more in storage from the atmosphere per year than the terrestrial system, it is the transfer between the atmosphere and land that primarily explains variability between annual measurements of change in atmospheric carbon (IPCC 2000). This results from the fact that ocean carbon sequestration is a far slower process. The rate of carbon uptake is limited by the solubility of CO_2 in seawater and by the slow transfer between the surface and deep waters (IPCC 2000, 32). The limited solubility of CO_2 can be pictured by considering how quickly a carbonated beverage goes flat after being exposed to air. Carbon is stored more effectively at greater depths; however, carbon cycles very slowly within the ocean. Waters circulate between surface and deep layers on varying time scales from 250 years in the Atlantic Ocean to 1,000 years for parts of the Pacific Ocean (U.S. Department of Energy [DOE] 1999).

There are also transfers between land and ocean. The ocean gains carbon in the form of runoff from the terrestrial system and carbon is removed from the oceanic reservoir through the process of sedimentation of organic remains and inorganic carbonate shell material. Although the store of carbon and the annual flux of carbon are both greater for the ocean than the terrestrial system, studies have found that year-to-year variations in the rate of CO_2 accumulation in the atmosphere are influenced primarily by the carbon flux from land.

Because our focus is on the United States, it is difficult to analyze any carbon storage transfers involving the ocean aquatic system. Oceanic carbon fluxes are general rather than local, preventing an accurate measurement of the flux occurring within U.S. controlled territory. There are several proposed ways of actually harnessing the ocean's sequestration power. Liquid CO_2 can be poured directly into the ocean or iron can be added to ocean waters to spur a very large growth in phytoplankton to sequester more carbon. Until these technologies are fully realized, we make no assumption about the relation between income in the United States and changes in ocean carbon storage.

TERRESTRIAL CARBON SOURCES AND SINKS

Another transfer between land and the aquatic system occurs within terrestrial waterways such as reservoirs and rivers. Studies have shown that a growing amount of carbon sediment is accumulating at the bottom of U.S. reservoirs. As well, carbon accumulates in alluvium, the detrital material deposited by running water. Although the total carbon storage in the terrestrial aquatic system, lakes, rivers, reservoirs, and so forth is small relative to that of forests and soil, its growth rate in carbon storage is significant enough that it may account for more than 5 percent of the carbon sequestered within the United States between 1980 and 1990 (Pacala et al. 2001). Rivers also export a small but important quantity of sequestered carbon to the sea. The total export of dissolved inorganic carbon and particulate organic carbon to the sea may account for another 5 percent of U.S. carbon sequestration.

The primary relation to be analyzed here is the one between carbon in the atmosphere and carbon on land in the United States. In order to estimate changes in the U.S. carbon budget, we will estimate the total amount of carbon transferred from the terrestrial sphere to the atmosphere in a given year and vice versa. Carbon cycles from the terrestrial sphere to the atmosphere primarily when fossil fuels storing carbon are used in energy production. Some of the fossil fuels used for energy include petroleum, motor gasoline, coal, and natural gas. The U.S. Department of Energy provides detailed statistics on all greenhouse gases emitted by type, sector, state, and year. Between 1950 and 1970 energy consumption per person rose from 229 (million BTU) to 334. Between 1970 and 2000, the change was much less drastic, with a final consumption level of 350 million BTU per person. Between 1949 and 2000, energy consumption per dollar of gross domestic product (GDP), fell by half from 20.63 to 10.57 thousand BTU per (1996) dollar of GDP (DOE 2001). Energy production itself has also become more efficient. Over the century, natural gas has replaced coal in industrial, commercial, and residential energy use to become the second biggest energy source behind petroleum. In 1999, natural gas use produced 1.32 pounds of CO_2 per kilowatt-hour, whereas coal produced 2.09 (DOE and EPA 2000).

There are also many sources that naturally emit methane (and therefore carbon) including livestock, rice paddies, and natural wetlands. During animal digestion, methane is produced through the process of enteric fermentation, in which microbes residing in animal digestive systems break down the feed consumed. Although livestock include cattle, swine, poultry, and others, cattle are responsible for more than 90 percent of methane produced by enteric fermentation. Enteric fermentation accounts for 19 percent of all methane produced by the United States in 1998, following only that produced by landfills (Environmental Protection Agency [EPA] 2000). Between 1927 and 2000, the number of milk-producing cattle dropped from 21.4 to 9.2 million. The amount of enteric fermentation is based on the number of animals, as well as emission factors that are based on the animals' diet. During that same time, milk production doubled from 89 to 167 billion pounds due to the four-fold increase in cattle productivity (U.S. Department of Agriculture [USDA] 2001). To correctly understand how enteric fermentation has changed due to increased production technology, further research must be done to determine how larger quantities of feed, necessary to provide higher milk production, have increased emissions per animal.

Livestock agriculture plays another role in methane emissions. The decomposition of organic animal waste in an anaerobic environment produces methane. The amount of methane produced depends on how the manure is managed, because certain types of storage and treatment systems promote an oxygen-free environment. Liquid systems tend to encourage anaerobic conditions and produce significant quantities of methane, whereas solid waste management produces little or no methane. Between 1990 and 1998 emissions from this source increased by 53 percent due to a shift in the composition of the swine and dairy industries toward larger facilities that tend to use liquid management systems.

Wetlands are most likely the largest natural, not human-induced, source of methane to the atmosphere. Methanogenic bacteria, found in wetlands, produce methane by anaerobic decomposition of organic materials. Between 1986 and 1997, a net of 644,000 acres of wetlands were drained. The U.S. Fish and Wildlife Service reported to Congress that the estimated wetland loss rate in 1997 was 58,500 acres (U.S. Fish and Wildlife Service 2001). Although the benefit of preserving wetlands is debatable, draining them reduces the annual amount of methane produced. Highly local controls such as temperature, topography, water table, and organic content as well as episodic events such as hydrostatic pressure changes and wind also have a large effect on methane fluxes (Augenbran, Matthews, and Sarma 2001). Further research needs to be done to understand how income or technology has affected these variables.

The level of atmospheric carbon can increase when terrestrial sinks are altered or destroyed. This occurs when biomass is burned or cleared and replaced by some inferior sink (or not at all), such as happens when trees are replaced with cropland. Terrestrial carbon stocks include rocks and sediments, swamps, wetlands and forests, forest soils, grasslands, and agricultural biomass. During the latter part of the century, forests were replaced primarily by developed land such as roads, and residential and commercial areas. Between 1982 and 1997, more than 10 million acres of forestland were converted to developed land, greater than the sum of all other newly converted types of land use (USDA 2000). Nevertheless, this deforestation was more than replaced by afforestation, as other types of land were converted to forest during the same period.

The level of atmospheric carbon is decreased when terrestrial stocks of carbon grow over time. The primary terrestrial sinks are forest and soil. The forest ecosystem stores carbon in four major forms: forest trees, forest soils, understory, and the forest floor. The tree portion includes all above- and below-ground portions of all live and dead trees: the merchantable stem; limbs; tops and cull sections; stump; foliage; bark and root bark; and coarse tree roots (greater than 2 mm). The soil component includes all organic carbon in mineral horizons to a depth of one meter, excluding coarse tree roots. The forest floor includes all dead organic matter above the mineral soil horizons except standing dead trees: litter, humus, and other woody debris. Understory vegetation encompasses all live vegetation besides live trees (Birdsey and Heath 1995).

There are many variables that affect the forest carbon stock. Forest tree volume is added to by new plantings or growth in old trees. Forest tree volume is reduced by the harvesting of trees for products or fuel. Several variables affect the growth of old trees including stand age, weather conditions, fire suppression, and prevalence of understory biomass. When forests are being harvested regularly, stand age is less of an issue. However, when old-growth forests are allowed to grow indefinitely, they reach a point where carbon flux is essentially zero. Fire suppression beginning after the 1930s had a large impact on carbon sequestration. Between 1919 and 1929, more than 26 million acres of wildland burned each year; during the next decade, the number increased to almost 40 million acres. As a result of enormous expenditures on fire suppression, the average annual burn area between 1990 and 1999 was 3,647,597 acres, a reduction of more than 90 percent (National Interagency Fire Center 2001). Between 1994 and 2000, federal agencies spent more than $4 billion on fire suppression, which along with carbon sequestration, is obviously affected positively by growth in U.S. income.

Another factor affecting the growth of forest volume is technology in the field of silviculture involving variables such as shade, seeding requirements, elevation, location, and spacing to maximize growth and return. The increasing understanding of silviculture may have promoted further carbon sequestration over time. Because the technology and science of silviculture are positively affected by economic growth, it is reasonable to assume income growth may have an additional relation to carbon sequestration.

The planting of trees is also affected by changes in income and stages of economic growth. During the earlier part of the twentieth century, the number of U.S. farms was increasing. Between 1910 and 1935, the number of farms grew 6 percent, before the beginning of a steady decline that persisted into the 1990s (USDA 2001). The USDA has statistics on total farm acreage as far back as 1950, when 1.20 billion acres of the United States were used as farmland. The area used for farming would increase to a high of 1.21 billion acres in 1955, and then decrease steadily until today. In 1999, only 947.44 million acres of land were used for farming. Many farms were built on previously forested lands, and many of the farms that have been abandoned reverted back to forest. Between 1982 and 1997, 1,108,400 net acres of prime farmland were converted to forest. During the same period, land areas with biomass containing the lowest carbon content, pastureland, and rangeland were reduced (USDA 2000).

Another factor affecting carbon sequestration is the rate of harvest of existing forests. The rate of harvest is influenced by the demand for wood used for fuel or wood products. Harvested wood no longer accumulates carbon; however, it can act as storage for differing periods. Wood harvested for fuel acts as carbon storage until the wood is burned and the carbon is released.

Wood harvested for wood or paper products may exist as carbon storage indefinitely because treated or sealed wood may decay at a very slow rate.

Wood harvest and clearcutting for agriculture grew as the United States was settled in the eighteenth century. As wood fuel was replaced with fossil fuels midway through the nineteenth century, harvest rates slowed in many regions. Fuel-wood consumption nearly disappeared only to reemerge during the Depression and the oil shocks of the 1970s. By the 1950s and 1960s, many forest regions began to accumulate carbon faster than it was harvested, resulting in overall carbon sequestration. Between 1976 and 1996, harvest rates remained constant in the northeastern states and fell dramatically in the Pacific Northwest and Rocky Mountains. In the South, a resurgence in fuel-wood use and increasingly intensive use of forests for wood products caused harvest rates (already the highest in 1976) to increase by more than 50 percent.[4] The net effect was a 12 percent national increase in removal between 1976 and 1996. This is independent of the flux in the forest carbon stock attributable to tree growth.

Technology in wood harvesting also affects carbon sequestration. The efficiency of industrial wood harvesting improved over time, so that more wood was removed per hectare and less left as slash (dead vegetation). Whether this affects carbon sequestration positively or negatively depends on the use of the harvested wood. If it is used to produce wood products, the slash will decay at a relatively faster rate. If the harvested wood is to be burned for energy, the slash will store carbon for a longer period than the harvested wood. Because the majority of wood is used for products rather than fuel, the conclusion can be drawn that the reduction in slash over time has had a positive impact on carbon sequestration.

Another very important sink that has been growing over time is woody biomass outside of forests. Savanna ecosystems are composed of two major competing types of biomass: grasslands and woody plants (woody plants include shrub-steppe, desert scrub, woodland, or forest). Over the past century, woody plants have occupied an increasing percentage of the land. This woody encroachment stores most of the carbon contained in nonforest, noncropland biomass. Many theories have been proposed as to the growing encroachment including fire suppression, overgrazing, and nitrogen deposition. The area of the United States that burns on an annual basis has been reduced by 95 percent since 1850 (Pacala et al. 2001). As a result, woody plants that historically have been burned are covering a much larger area. Changes in soils and microclimate accompanying long-term heavy grazing may have shifted the balance in favor of woody plants better adapted to nutrient-poor soils. This growth would be further exacerbated by grazing-induced reductions in herbaceous competition (Archer, Boutton, and Hibbard 2000). This increase in woody plants previously was unaccounted for in studies of the U.S. carbon budget.

There is more carbon stored nationally in soil than in vegetation. Soil organic carbon (SOC) makes up about two-thirds of the carbon pool in the terrestrial biosphere (Allmaras et al. 2000). This carbon is in the form of plant, animal, and microbial residues in all stages of decomposition. The only significant vegetation that stores carbon is located in forest biomass and woody plants. Soils, however, store carbon regardless of local vegetation (IPCC 2000). Temperate and tropical forests (not located in the United States) store more carbon in the local vegetation than the local soil, but biomass in most other areas contains less carbon than the corresponding soil. It is therefore important that a study of carbon sequestration account for soil organic carbon in addition to carbon stored in biomass.

Agricultural practices are the most important variable affecting the accumulation of soil organic carbon. In 1997, 25 percent of the 1.5 billion acres of U.S. nonfederal land were considered cropland. The conversion of natural vegetation to cultivated use inevitably leads to an immediate loss of SOC. Some estimates suggest that cultivated croplands in the United States lose about 2.7 terragrams of carbon (of C) per year (Gebhart et al. 1994). This loss in carbon can be attributed to reduced inputs of organic matter, increased decomposability of crop residues, and tillage effects that decrease the amount of physical protection to decomposition (Post and Kwon 2000). Tillage-induced changes of perennial grasses to annual crop species reduce root biomass and inputs of carbon from roots to soils. Fluxes in carbon are therefore tied to the area of land that is taken in and out of agriculture each year as well as the technology of agriculture used on existing croplands.

As mentioned earlier, the square acreage of total U.S. farmland has declined over most of the past century. Because cropland is for the most part a net source, abandoning this land may reduce net emissions regardless of whether the land reverts to forest or other significant biomass. In fact, conversion to grassland may lead to significant gains in carbon due to large increases in soil organic carbon. The Conservation Reserve Program (CRP) was established to reduce water and wind erosion through the establishment of perennial grass cover on as much as 45 million acres of highly erodible and environmentally sensitive cropland. Studies have shown that, averaged across locations, soil organic carbon levels for the CRP plantings were significantly greater than those of croplands, indicating that only five years after restoration, 21 percent of soil organic carbon lost during tillage was restored. The authors of this study estimate that cropland enrolled in CRP may have the potential to sequester 45 percent of the 38.1 terragrams of carbon (of C) per year emitted into the atmosphere by U.S. agriculture (Gebhart et al. 1994).

Soil organic carbon in existing cropland depends partly on tillage intensity. Tillage, in addition to mixing and stirring of soil, exposes deeper organo-mineral surfaces otherwise inaccessible to decomposers, further reducing soil organic carbon. Therefore, the shift toward lower tillage intensity over the past few decades has deceased net carbon emissions from agriculture. Agriculture has made a shift from heavy to minimum tillage in which the soil is lightly tilled only a few times a year. The final shift is to zero tillage, in which crops are seeded directly into stubble without tilling the soil first. This system conserves moisture, controls soil erosion, uses less fuel, and reduces labor costs. The decision to zero-till depends on the availability and cost of new seeding equipment and herbicides. As incomes rise and technology develops, agriculture has naturally moved toward a system that favors fewer net carbon emissions from soil use.

The level of atmospheric carbon also decreases when the carbon stock in anthropogenic (man-made) sinks grows. Such sinks include landfills, buildings, manufactured agricultural products, automobiles, manufactured wood products, and living bodies. Wood and agricultural products store a significant amount of carbon for varying amounts of time, depending on end use. By tracking both wood and agricultural products through their production, end use, and then disposal, it is possible to estimate changes in terrestrial carbon storage attributed to these products over time.

Approximately 16 percent of all discarded municipal sold waste is incinerated. The remainder is disposed of in landfills. It is estimated that 41 percent of U.S. landfill volume is taken up by paper and paperboard, 7.9 percent is food waste, and 17.9 percent is yard waste. Therefore, the majority of cellulose and hemicellulose in landfills originates from forest and agricultural products. This represents a large amount of carbon being sequestered each year. The USDA Forest Service has estimated that only up to 3 percent of the carbon from wood and an average of 26 percent of the carbon from paper is potentially released into the atmosphere as carbon dioxide and methane once the material has been put into landfills (Micales and Skog 1998).

The percent that is susceptible to release has fallen over time as waste disposal areas have changed in nature. Originally waste was disposed of in dumps where, prior to 1972, a portion of wood and paper products was burned without energy, and the remaining material was exposed to oxygen and released carbon through decay. Legislation required a phase-out of dumps by 1986 and waste was disposed of in landfills instead. Landfills seal the waste periodically, limiting the amount of decay from oxygen. Although this slows the decay rate of wood products and increases the life span of stored carbon, there is a higher proportion of methane emissions relative to carbon dioxide due to the lower level of oxygen. Because methane has a greater impact on global warming potential, the flux in net carbon emissions must be weighted by this effect. Global warming potential is outlined in more detail later in this paper.

The amount of carbon stored in buildings, automobiles, animals, and people is a function mainly of the growth in the total number of those goods and organisms over time. Because the flux is positive for many or all of these categories, the reasonable assumption to be made is that carbon storage has risen accordingly. In order to correctly monitor this flux over time, it is necessary to have not only the total numbers in each year but also an average carbon content with which to create a total carbon content. Finding and applying these numbers is left for future research.

The United States exports more in the form of wood and food than it imports. Agricultural products—especially grains, oil seeds, and oil seed cakes—are exported in large numbers, creating this imbalance (Pacala et al. 2001). This net export surplus is additional carbon storage by the United States. (We derive this relation mathematically in the following section on methodology.) Essentially, without accounting for exports, a count of stock on hand at the beginning and end of each year would not include the quantity of wood or agricultural products that were put into storage and then moved to a foreign nation. It is left to future studies to determine whether the fate of this exported storage belongs with the nation that stored the carbon or the nation that emits it later. It seems appropriate at this point to credit the storage as sequestration by the nation that was responsible for removing it from the atmosphere.

METHODOLOGY

The IPCC reports that for technical reasons only emissions and sequestrations of CO_2 can be determined directly as changes in carbon stocks. The emissions and sequestrations of other greenhouse gases, such as methane and nitrous oxide, cannot be estimated as part of an overall carbon budget without accounting for their magnified effect on heat trapping within the atmosphere. We are unable at this point to verify the validity of this statement. As such, we estimate methane changes within the carbon budget using two separate methods. First we estimate the contribution to carbon flux of methane and other greenhouse gases by using the pure carbon weight of each gas, similar to how the carbon weight of CO_2 is measured.

Second, we engage the normative issue of global warming, weighting each carbon molecule by some factor, called the global warming potential. The relation between the chemical carbon and the question of global warming is held by many to differ depending on its exact compound. Thus, the global warming impact of carbon as carbon dioxide is said to be different from the global warming impact of carbon as methane. Moreover, carbon gases in the atmosphere are said to contribute to the greenhouse effect both directly and indirectly. Direct effects occur when the gas itself leads to warming; indirect radiative forcing occurs when chemical transformations of the original gas produce a gas or gases that are said to be greenhouse gases, or when a gas influences the atmospheric lifetimes of other gases. The concept of global warming potential has been developed to compare the ability of each greenhouse gas to trap heat in the atmosphere relative to another gas.[5] Carbon dioxide was chosen as the reference gas to be consistent with IPCC guidelines. Global warming potentials have not yet been developed for certain compounds (CO, NO, and SO_2) because there is no agreed upon method to estimate the contribution of gases that have only indirect effects on radiative forcing (EPA 2000; IPCC 1996).

In the second method, all gases are converted to units of million metric tons of carbon equivalents (MMTCE). Carbon comprises 12/44 of carbon dioxide by weight. The relation between gigagrams (Gg) of a gas and MMTCE is:

$$\text{MMTCE} = (\text{Gg of gas}) \times (\text{MMT}/1{,}000 \text{ Gg}) \times$$
$$(\text{global warming potential}) \times (12/44).$$

Table 8.1 lists global warming potential values for various greenhouse gases.

Without accounting for global warming potential, the sum of the carbon weight of all other greenhouse gases besides CO_2, including CH_4, N_2O, HFCs, PFCs, and SF_6, comprises less than 1 percent of the total carbon emitted to the atmosphere by the United States. When accounting for the magnified impact of greenhouse gases besides carbon dioxide, their relative weight in terms of the total MMTCE transferred to the atmosphere each year is 18 percent.

Table 8.1. Global Warming Potentials (100-Year Time Horizon)

Gas	Global Warming Potential
Carbon dioxide (CO_2)	1
Methane (CH_4)	21
Nitrous oxide (N_2O)	310
HFC-23	11,700
HFC-125	2,800
HFC-134a	1,300
HFC-143a	3,800
HFC-152a	140
HFC-227ea	2,900
HFC-236fa	6,300
HFC-4310mee	1,300
CF_4	6,500
C_2F_6	9,200
C_4F_{10}	7,000
C_6F_{14}	7,400
SF_6	23,900

Source: IPCC (1996).

SOME FINDINGS

In environmental Kuznets analysis, some measure of ambient environmental quality is measured over time or cross-sectionally against income. Typically, income growth is linked with environmental decay at low levels of income, and this decay rises as income increases, to a point, after which environmental quality improves with income. Our analysis is focused on carbon emissions and sinks, which is about changes, not levels of environmental quality. Hence, we depart slightly from the classical analysis.

If there were some agreed upon standard for atmospheric carbon, we would gladly adopt it. But there is absence of consensus on, first, the amount of carbon in the air on a regular or daily basis and, more important, no general agreement about the quality of life as the amount of carbon varies in the atmosphere. Put simply, there is no standard of agreement about whether carbon emissions cause global warming, and there is no standard of opinion about whether a warmer climate is good or bad.

Emissions

Total emissions of CO_2 in the United States from all sources for 1929 to 1996 in carbon equivalents reveal that these emissions grow over time and income, but not on a per capita basis except a long time ago and at low levels of income. As income has risen, total emissions per capita are essentially stable over the past twenty-five years or so. A carbon equivalent measures the amount of carbon in a compound. For instance, the atomic weight of CO_2 is 44 of which carbon is 12. Therefore, a ton of carbon equivalent CO_2 actually weighs 3.6667 tons. Put differently, 3.667 tons of CO_2 contain 1 ton of carbon (see our earlier discussion of MMTCE). Carbon emissions have been on the increase, basically without interruption for the entire past century. There are two exceptions: the early 1930s and the early 1980s. The first can be traced to the Depression and the second to some other force, perhaps, to the decade of greed. To explore this straightforward question we estimated the relation between emissions per capita and GDP per capita using the 1929–96 sample period. To wit,

$$CO_2 \text{ per capita} = f(\text{GDP per capita}).$$

Figure 8.1 plots the emissions per capita in the United States versus income for 1929–1996.[6] Emissions rise with real income, up to about $5,000 per per-

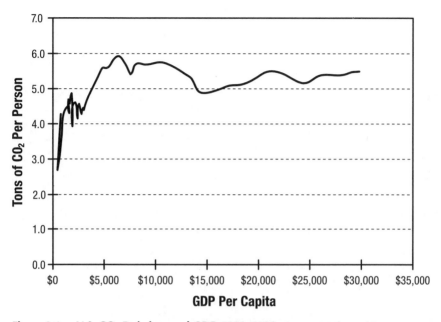

Figure 8.1.   U.S. CO_2 Emissions and GDP, 1929–1996. Source: U.S. Dept. of Energy (2000).

son per year (in year 1999 dollar terms). After that they are relatively flat. We estimated the precise relation by ordinary least squares regression, correcting for autocorrelation in the residuals and by including polynomial terms until the $(n+1)$th order was insignificant. In our sample, $n = 4$. The fifth order term was not significant. The results of this estimation reveal that emissions per capita grow with income but in a complex way and not over all ranges of income, mostly at low levels. At higher levels of income the relation is cyclical but essentially flat.

There are three inflection points in this fourth order polynomial. There are two peaks at about $8,000 and $28,000 and a trough at about $20,000. Figure 8.2 plots the estimated function. Insofar as these estimates are appropriate, they suggest that gross emissions decline at income levels above the $30,000 (1999 dollars) range.

To test for structural stability, we divided the sample at the median of the income data, $3,462, and estimated the emissions-income relation separately over the two samples. The fourth order polynomial structure remains and although the coefficients are different, the differences are not fundamental.

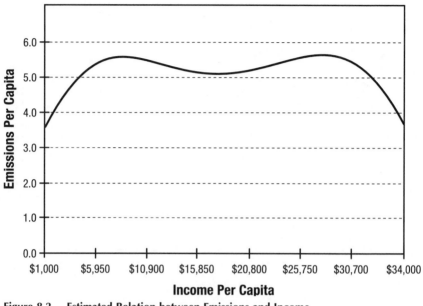

Figure 8.2.   Estimated Relation between Emissions and Income.

Sequestrations

Of course, the real impact of income on atmospheric carbon depends upon the net emissions, that is the gross emissions minus the sinks or sequestrations. Here we report initial data to determine the basic underlying relations.

To give some bare insights into our inquiry to date, consider the forest as a potential sink. We have forest carbon content for the United States, in usable form, from 1950 through 2000. We plot in these in figure 8.3. This graph reveals that forests in the United States, while relatively constant in acreage, are sequestering less and less carbon, most likely due to the age of the trees.

We are in the process of acquiring data on other agricultural carbon sinks and can report now some distinctly preliminary results on cattle and hog populations as they relate to income. These data come from a pooled time-series and cross section of states in the United States from 1900 through 2000.

We regressed the stock of hogs and cattle on real income per capita. This is far from a perfect methodology because these markets are clearly *not* state markets. Hence production in one state does not imply consumption there. Moreover, there are international imports and exports. Nevertheless, the technique has probative value, at least in our minds. The results using a fixed-effects model and not withstanding these shortcomings reveal that carbon sequestration as captured in the fat, bones, meat, and skin of hogs and cattle, rises with income (fig. 8.4).

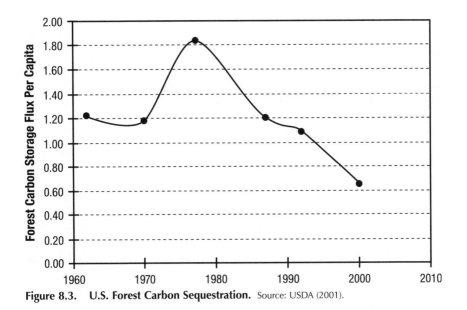

Figure 8.3. U.S. Forest Carbon Sequestration. Source: USDA (2001).

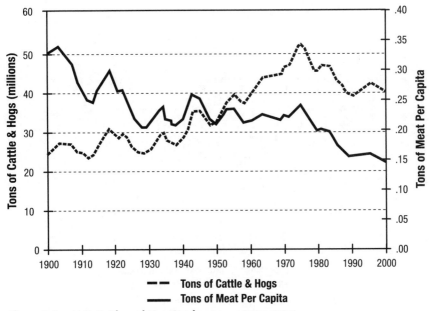

– – – Tons of Cattle & Hogs
—— Tons of Meat Per Capita

Figure 8.4. U.S. Cattle and Hog Stocks. Source: USDA (2001).

To explore the extent of carbon sequestration in animal stocks, we added the weights of hogs and cattle and then plotted the totals per year in the United States. We assume that cattle weigh 700 pounds each and hogs weigh 125 pounds each. We also plot the per capita amounts of these sequestration stocks. As the chart clearly reveals, we have been adding to our stocks of carbon sequestered in these types of animals, but not on a per person basis.

We then repeated this estimation for hogs. These results also reveal that hog production and carbon sequestration are associated with higher income. These animal results together lead us to believe that carbon sequestration, in the loins and hams of cattle and hogs, is rising with income.

Figure 8.5 plots annual wheat production in thousands of bushels and also the per capita amount of wheat produced in the United States each year from 1900. Wheat production is temporary carbon sequestration. Once eaten, the wheat produces heat and waste; therefore, only a portion of the total wheat produced leads to sequestration. The point here is that the amount is on the rise. This chart reveals a story similar to the others, and work on other crops and animals is proceeding. The United States is sequestering carbon in many forms.

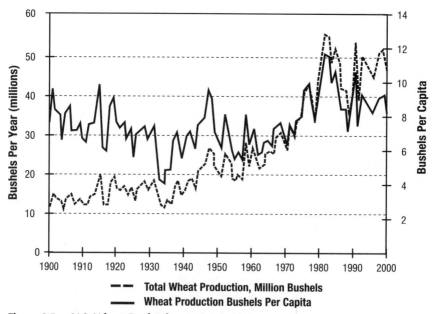

Figure 8.5.   U.S. Wheat Production. Source: USDA (2001).

INTERIM CONCLUSIONS

We started this inquiry with one simple objective. Do increases in economic activity lead an economy to take carbon out of the air? Our investigation is not finished; there is ample evidence to continue the inquiry. It does appear that richer economies take more carbon out of the air than poorer ones. Hence a unidimensional focus on carbon emissions stands to make severely grave errors in analysis and policy by only looking at what comes out of the tailpipe of automobiles. Preliminary results lead to speculation that richer people do suck carbon out of the air into animals, trees, landfills, buildings, and other material possessions. We do not yet know, and may never find out, but there is enough evidence here to ask the question, "Does the United States economy actually take carbon out of the air?" If yes, and it is certainly not unreasonable to wonder, then the Kyoto Protocol and other regulations on economic activity may do more harm than good (assuming they intend what they say).

There is a widely held view that the United States is primarily responsible for carbon emissions and global warming. We have no quarrel with that view insofar as it goes. We do now, however, given the state of our research, have a relatively strong opinion about the proper way to analyze regulation of carbon emissions. That view is actually quite simple and obvious. Regulation of carbon emissions should take great care not to kill the goose that lays the golden egg.

The remainder of this project is dedicated to converting all forms of carbon sequestration into the same annual units of emissions so that we can see whether the United States is a net emitter. There is ample evidence that the U.S. economy sinks a lot of carbon, but until we make the conversions and compare, we simply do not know the answer.

NOTES

1. For a more detailed discussion of this and related topics, see Simon (1995, 1999).

2. The list of Annex 1 countries is available at www.ictp.trieste.it/~moltenif/UN_climate/annex1.htm.

3. Webster's dictionary offers the following definition of greenhouse effect—"warming of the surface and lower atmosphere of a planet that is caused by the conversion of solar radiation into heat in a process involving selective transmission of short wave solar radiation by the atmosphere, its absorption by the planet's surface, and reradiation as infrared which is absorbed and partly reradiated back to the surface by atmospheric gases."

4. Brad Smith, forest inventory and analysis, USDA Forest Service, Washington, DC, telephone interview, July 2001.

5. We are *not* addressing the normative issue of global warming. We only address the question of net emissions and their relation to income. Others, concerned about warmer temperatures, have made the judgment that cool is better. We are neither accepting nor rejecting this idea. But to the extent that others desire to engage that debate using our data, methods, and conclusions, we have, for their uses, incorporated the global warming potential analysis.

6. This period was chosen because of data limitation on GDP for the United States. We have not found any reliable measure of income per capita for the earlier period.

REFERENCES

Allmaras, Raymond R., et al. 2000. Soil Organic Carbon Sequestration Potential of Adopting Conservation Tillage in U.S. Croplands. *Journal of Soil and Water Conservation* 55(3): 365–73.

Archer, Steven R., Thoms W. Boutton, and Kathy A. Hibbard. 2000. Trees in Grasslands: Biogeochemical Consequences of Woody Plant Expansion. In *Global Biogeochemical Cycles in the Climate System,* ed. E. D. Schulze et al. San Diego, CA: Academic Press, 115–37.

Augenbran, Harvey, Elaine Matthews, and David Sarma. 2001. The Global Methane Cycle. *Global Methane Inventory Website.* Institute on Climate and Planets, National Aeronautics and Space Administration. Online: icp.giss.nasa.gov/research/methane/index.html (cited: March 25, 2002).

Birdsey, Richard A., and Linda S. Heath. 1995. Carbon Changes in U.S. Forests. In *Productivity of America's Forests and Climate Change,* ed. Linda A. Joyce. Fort Collins, CO: USDA Forest Service, 56–70.

Environmental Protection Agency. 2000. *Inventory of U.S. Greenhouse Gas Emissions and Sinks: 1990–1998.* Office of Atmospheric Programs. EPA 236-R-00-001, April. Online: www.epa.gov/globalwarming/publications/emissions/us2000/index.html (cited: March 18, 2002).

Gebhart, Dick L., et al. 1994. The CRP Increases Soil Organic Carbon. *Journal of Soil and Water Conservation* 49(5): 488–92.

Intergovernmental Panel on Climate Change (IPCC). 1990. *Climate Change—The IPCC Scientific Assessment,* ed. John T. Houghton, G. J. Jenkins, and J. J. Ephraums. Cambridge, MA: Cambridge University Press.

———. 1996 *Revised 1996 IPCC Guidelines for National Greenhouse Gas Inventories,* ed. John T. Houghton et al. Bracknell: UK Meteorological Office.

———. 2000. *Special Report on Land Use, Land-Use Change, and Forestry,* ed. Robert T. Watson et al. Cambridge, MA: Cambridge University Press.

Micales, Jessie A., and Kenneth E. Skog. 1998. The Decomposition of Forest Products in Landfills. *International Biodeterioration & Biodegradation* 39(July/August): 145–58.

Moomaw, William R., and Gregory C. Unruh. 1998. Are Environmental Kuznets Curves Misleading Us? *Environment and Development Economics,* special issue, 2(4): 451–63.

National Interagency Fire Center. 2001. Wildland Fire Statistics. Online: www.nifc. gov/stats/wildlandfirestats.html (cited: March 18, 2002).

Pacala, Stephen W., et al. 2001. Consistent Land- and Atmosphere-Based U.S. Carbon Sink Estimates. *Science Magazine* 292(June 22): 2316–20.

Post, Wilfred M., and Kyung C. Kwon. 2000. Soil Carbon Sequestration and Land-Use Change: Processes and Potential. *Global Change Biology* 6(3): 317–27.

Preuss, Paul. 2001. Climate Change Scenarios Compel Studies of Ocean Carbon Storage. *Science Beat*, February 1. Ernest Orlando Lawrence Berkeley National Laboratory, Berkeley, CA. Online: www.lbl.gov/Science-Articles/Archive/sea-carb-bish.html (cited: March 18, 2002).

Simon, Julian L. 1995. *The State of Humanity*. Malden, MA: Blackwell Publishers.

———. 1999. *Hoodwinking the Nation*. New Brunswick, NJ: Transaction Press.

U.S. Department of Agriculture. 2000. *1997 National Resources Inventory*. U.S. Department of Agriculture and Iowa State University Statistical Laboratory. Online: www.nhq.nrcs.usda.gov/NRI/1997/summary_report/report.pdf (cited: April 2, 2002).

———. 2001. *Published Estimates Database*. National Agriculture Statistics Service (NAAS). Online: www.nass.usda.gov:81/ipedb/ (cited: March 18, 2002).

U.S. Department of Energy. 1999. *Carbon Sequestration: Research and Development*. December. Online: www.fe.doe.gov/coal_power/sequestration/reports/rd/index.shtml (cited: March 18, 2002).

———. 2001. *Annual Energy Review 2000*. Online: www.eia.doe.gov/aer/ (cited: March 18, 2002).

U.S. Department of Energy and Environmental Protection Agency. 2000. *Carbon Dioxide Emissions from the Generation of Electric Power in the United States* (July). Online: www.eia.doe.gov/cneaf/electricity/page/co2_report/co2emiss.pdf (cited: April 2, 2002).

U.S. Fish and Wildlife Service. 2001. *Report to Congress on the Status and Trends of Wetlands in the Conterminous United States 1986 to 1997*. January. Online: wetlands.fws.gov/bha/SandT/SandTReport.html (cited: April 2, 2002).

Yandle, Bruce, Maya Vijayaraghavan, and Madhusudan Bhattarai. 2002. The Environmental Kuznets Curve: A Primer. *PERC Research Study*, RS02-1. Bozeman, MT: PERC.

9

Agriculture and the Environment: A Thirty-Year Retrospective

John K. Hosemann

During the past thirty years, U.S. farm production increased more than 80 percent. On the livestock side, genetic improvements and better animal nutrition have enabled beef, pork, dairy, and poultry producers to achieve higher output levels relative to inputs. On the crop side, similar output results have been achieved through genetics, better management of soils and water, plant nutrition, and crop pest controls. These advancements are in part the result of government subsidies for research and development. Between 1970 and 2000 taxpayer-funded agricultural research at public institutions averaged almost $3 billion a year.

In addition to subsidies for research and development and extension education, there were other important subsidies on the farm output side through direct federal payments and federal price guarantees for major crops (feed grains, soybeans, wheat, rice, peanuts, sugar, tobacco, cotton, and dairy). Price guarantees accrued primarily to large-output producers because subsidies are based on volume of production. The subsidies encouraged purchases of more advanced technologies, larger farm equipment, and more land.

Companies that produce advanced technologies are better able to finance such projects because crops and commodities are less risky due to the role of the federal government. On balance, government-sponsored research, direct government subsidy payments to farmers, and commodity price guarantees have resulted in high-tech, high-yield intensive agriculture.

The story does not end there. The government reduced farm and agribusiness risks in many other ways through subsidized credit programs, crop insurance programs, food purchases, and domestic and export sales. All of these risk-reducing programs had a predictable outcome: more output than would have otherwise been the case.

The flipside of the government subsidy story is regulation. During the past thirty years, federal regulation of the resources used in agriculture has shifted from giving technical and educational support to farmers to make voluntary decisions on conservation practices to imposing criminal penalties on farmers for carrying out what had been routine farm practices. Copeland captures this shift in federal regulatory enforcement actions against farmers:

> The federal environmental criminal enforcement program began in the mid-to-late 1970s when the Department of Justice undertook some well-publicized prosecutions for environmental violations. . . . It was not, however, until the mid-1980s that the federal criminal enforcement program became aggressive. . . . At the request of the Environmental Protection Agency (EPA), Congress added new environmental crimes to existing statutes and significantly increased government criminal provisions already on the books.
>
> Twenty-five years ago, none of the major environmental laws in effect contained significant criminal enforcement provisions. But not today. . . .
>
> Agricultural activities put farmers, ranchers, and agribusinesses at risk as to environmental violations. Raising livestock, plowing, clearing land, draining water off of property, repairing levees, fencing property, clearing drainage ditches, using pesticides and other chemicals, controlling predators, harvesting, storing and processing crops can all potentially expose a farmer, rancher, or agribusiness to criminal prosecution for environmental crimes. (Copeland 1995, 237–38)

Given the long history of government involvement in agriculture, the outcome of more federal environmental regulations was inevitable particularly as the critics of the intensive agriculture model gained political clout.

Even without government subsidies, farm consolidations were inevitable as successful farm firms pursued economies of scale and resources shifted to more efficient producers. Government subsidies simply accelerated the process of technological development and the rate of technological adoption by producers. Without government subsidies, more on-farm trial-and-error research and experimentation would have taken place.

The intensive agriculture outcome has not been without critics. The industrialization of production agriculture and the overall food system has permanently changed the number and structure of farms away from the small-farm Jeffersonian model. Concentration of livestock production (beef feedlots, vertical hog and poultry systems, large dairy production units) has given rise to criticisms by environmentalists, a growing number of consumers, and those within agriculture devoted to small community-based farm production and marketing. Antichemical and antibiotechnology are core beliefs of these political forces. Ironically, the larger concentrated animal units are more likely to adopt more advanced environmental control systems by allocating the high fixed cost investments over greater output. Smaller output, limited resource farms are more likely to run afoul of land and water environmental controls.

The industrialization of agriculture during the past three decades has also been driven by the need for processing firms to control all processes from conception to consumption in light of federal food safety laws and consumer demand for quality and consistency. Drury and Tweeten (1999, 24) explain the basic reasons for this industrialization: "Farm industrialization is driven by needs for precision farm production and marketing, management, technology cost control, capital requirements, and concentration in agribusiness. Concentration in agribusiness as in farming is pushed by economies of size."

To examine the overall relationship between changes in agricultural practices and environmental concerns, it is necessary to explain the major policies that shaped the industrial farm model, assess the positive and negative environmental impacts of these policies, and draw conclusions for policy makers with regard to what to do and what not do if U.S. agriculture and agribusiness are to be internationally competitive.

ASSUMPTIONS IN THIS DISCUSSION

First, production and marketing agriculture is dependent on the right to own, use, and dispose of private property perhaps more so than any other economic sector. Given the variations in weather, pests, and natural biological processes, it is essential that farm and ranch operators maintain the capacity to make production and marketing decisions quickly. These decisions cannot be done without the right to own, use, and dispose of property. Alternative central control systems lead to higher cost output in terms of lost human capital, slower decision making, and missed opportunities. Basic farm inputs (land, air, and water) have become increasingly subject to federal and state rules.

A second important assumption is that if government wants more of a good or service than the market will produce, a subsidy will be provided. This occurred repeatedly during the past thirty years. Producers of major field crops farmed for the federal program, not the market. Production went up, prices went down, and farm groups clamored for even more subsidies. There is no end in sight with regard to how much taxpayer subsidies would be needed to make farmers and their politicians happy. There is no practical way to separate (or totally decouple) government farm subsidies from farmer-level business and household decision making. Farming for government payments essentially replaced farming for the market.

Third, "saving the family farm" is a political myth that farm politicians have perpetuated since the 1930s. After decades of lip service to this myth, there are fewer family farms than ever. Most of the federal farm welfare has gone to large-scale commercial units. The average net worth of these units is four times that of the average taxpayer who provides these transfers. In addition, the economic returns to large-scale commercial farms (farms with annual sales of $250,000 or more) are competitive with similar size nonfarm businesses.

Fourth, U.S. agriculture began its integration into the overall economy when farmers began purchasing essential farm production inputs (tractors, fertilizers, chemicals) after World War II. Events in the general economy became much more important to agriculture as a result.

Fifth, command-and-control inputs are incompatible with free market outputs. Command-and-control inputs are by definition high-cost inputs because they divert producer attention away from important day-to-day farm decision making on how to better produce and market a bushel, bale, pound, or hundredweight to responding to unproductive bureaucratic regulatory directives that now entangle most of agriculture. The alternative lies within the realm of adhering to markets, private property, and common law for solving real environmental problems.

Over the years, farmers as individual decision makers have learned to cope with the vagaries of weather. But few, if any, have learned how to cope with the vagaries and uncertainties of political decisions and bureaucratic regulatory edicts beyond asking for more federal money to offset all or part of the regulatory impacts. With the estimated cost of federal regulations on agriculture at $20 billion per year, one could make the case that welfare transfers to farmers around $20 billion annually are an offset to the regulatory burden. The problem is that these costs are not evenly distributed to all farms. Commodity-based production payments are skewed to large-output farm units that have more political influence.

I presume here that most of what has been cobbled together as farm policy has been done so in short-term political responses to events and policies external to the farm economy: the Russian grain deal, rising inflation, declining inflation, deflation, grain embargos, environmental hysteria, and food safety paranoia. Of special political interest, farmers who receive federal subsidies are in a better financial position to funnel some of the taxpayer subsidies back into political campaigns to reelect those politicians who faithfully protect the farm welfare payment system. This special interest perpetual motion machine gives farmers and their political incumbents (both Democrat and Republican) a big advantage at reelection time. Both parties have become adept in the vote-getting business. This was vividly demonstrated in the political maneuvering during the 2002 farm bill.

RISING INFLATION

Beginning in the late 1960s the Federal Reserve essentially printed more money to finance federal budget deficits to fund the Vietnam War and expanded social programs. Inflation began and reached progressively higher levels during most of the 1970s. When inflation reached double-digit levels in 1979, Chairman Volcker applied the monetary policy brakes. Interest rates also rose to double-digit levels. The high inflation period took its economic toll at the farm level. Inflationary expectations became the rule in farm business decision making. Many farmers shifted much of their decision making to land and machinery speculation, betting that prices would go even higher. Once inflation was viewed as permanent, farm debt loads were increased as the bidding for farmland escalated among the farmers and other speculators. Used farm equipment often sold for as much or more than it cost when purchased new. As farmland prices increased, so did the assessed valuation for property tax as local governments jumped on the inflationary spending bandwagon. Part of the inflationary process was a run-up in farm commodity prices in the early 1970s. Soybeans reached a historical high price of more than $10 per bushel; today soybean prices are in the $4 to $5 per bushel range.

With staying ahead of inflation as the main driver in decision making, most farmers pursued short-term decision making to the detriment of long-term decision making, which is the bedrock of land and water conservation: the environment. Aided by government programs, large tracts of forestland were clearcut and drained in the Delta region particularly, but also in the mid-Atlantic states. These tracts were planted primarily to soybeans. In the American heartland, pastureland was converted to cropland. Historically, pastureland has generally been less productive due to erosion, and rougher terrain soils are not suitable for crops. The inflationary period thus laid the foundation for criticisms of farm resource uses in the years ahead.

The inflationary period also set in motion political forces that remain today as various groups, particularly those on fixed incomes, clamor for government relief. Farmers were no exception.

Cost of living adjustments (COLAs) became a permanent feature of the social security program, and farmers lobbied for and received higher guaranteed government prices. Government target prices and loan rates were repeatedly adjusted for inflation.[1] Inflated government-guaranteed prices coupled with the economic stagnation of the late 1970s produced a buildup of commodity stocks. In 1983 the payment-in-kind (PIK) program was initiated as a less expensive way to reduce government commodity stocks in light of increasing federal budget deficits.[2]

DECLINING INFLATION

During the 1980s and early 1990s, inflation was reduced. Farmers benefited from reduced inflation on the cost of farm inputs, but the long-term economic damage to the farm sector during the inflationary period had already been done. Inflation was down, but based on inflationary expectations many farmers had leveraged inflated land values into debt loads that could not be serviced out of the revenues from crops and livestock.

Heavy debt loads caused problems for many farm operators. The farm credit crisis persisted until the 1986 federal bailout of the Farm Credit System, which owned a substantial share of the speculative bad debt on farms. Debt restructuring became commonplace. Farm consolidations increased as resources shifted to operators with stronger financial positions.

Given the farm debt situation, continuing budget deficits, and escalating farm program costs, the political stage was set for changing the farm law to more market orientation.[3] Congress moved to correct the pricing mistakes in the 1981 law with the 1985 farm law. By the time of the 1985 farm law negotiations, environmental critics of farm policy had built a political argument that farm programs with acreage-reduction programs led to an increase in the use of fertilizers and pesticides on the acres that farmers were allowed to cultivate. The implications for water quality were obvious.

The 1985 farm law contained the Conservation Reserve Program (CRP).[4] The CRP became yet another government program for transferring money to some farmers but also to absentee landowners, retiring farmers, and speculators. Environmental gains in land and water quality improvements have not been scientifically determined relative to the nearly $2 billion annual cost of the CRP program. Much of the CRP land had marginal value in crop and livestock production. Some political support for CRP is based on the simplistic notion that conversion to CRP status will improve water quality. Not taken into account is that other lands may be put into production and that land still farmed is likely to be subject to increased levels of fertilizer and other chemicals. CRP payments are skewed to the marginal wheat-producing region in the Great Plains and to marginal crop lands in the South, where climate and land quality generally favor forestry and grazing.

The CRP distorted land rents upward and limited opportunities for younger farm operators to expand. The CRP did not have a significant impact on commodity supplies and prices. The CRP is a political derivative of the government soil bank programs of the 1950s and 1960s that sought to short the market in order to raise farm prices.

In many areas around larger metropolitan areas, CRP payments are used by some realtors as an enticement to urbanites to purchase rural properties. Thus, another agricultural policy favored by some environmental groups produces contradictory results. Environmental groups also rail against urban expansion but support CRP subsidies that encourage it.

In summary, inflationary monetary policy distorted producer decisions away from long-term conservation decisions toward short-term monetary gains. Farmers used the political process and government programs to try to offset the negative impacts of reducing inflation, lower farmland values, and lower farm prices. Farmers used the political process to try to maintain both their inflated income and inflated net worth positions as deflation set in. Farmers continue to use the argument that farm input cost increases are outstripping commodity prices. Ignored in this view are the contributions of new technologies to farm productivity gains and declining real farm prices.

DEFLATION

Monetary policy has been marked by periods of excessive money supply creation followed by sharp declines once inflation became unacceptable. It was not characterized by a steady increase in the money supply consistent with the liquidity needs of real economic growth. The Federal Reserve began further tightening the money supply in the late 1990s when worldwide supply-driven deflation had already set in. Supply-induced deflation continued to be met by tighter monetary policy to ensure no inflation. Raw material prices, including farm prices, declined on a worldwide basis.

To insulate farmers from the negative effects of restrictive monetary policy, the 1996 farm law provided farmers almost $105 billion in transfers between 1997 and 2002.[5] The commodity price index was at or near historic lows. Some politicians from farm districts continued to blame the 1996 farm law for the price deflation in farm commodities. Policy makers and many economists continue to ignore the role of the deflationary process. Deflated commodity prices put pressure on farmers to farm for the farm program, not for the market. Most farm production and marketing decisions, under the current law, are made to maximize loan deficiency payments (LDPs), but these decisions are not based on what is or is not good for the land and water resources. LDPs are the difference between the lower market price and the higher government-set loan price.

Corn and soybeans are now planted in marginal production areas. With the soybean loan rate higher than the corn loan rate, the government incentive, not the market incentive, is to plant more soybean acres. Minimum-till and no-till technologies coupled with the introduction of genetically modified seeds have enabled producers to produce soybeans, corn, and cotton cheaper, but to do so on some land with erosion and water runoff problems.

Paralleling the deflationary decline in farm prices has been the emergence of large-scale hog production units patterned after the vertically integrated poultry units that have operated without major environmental controversy for more than thirty years. Hogs are different. Wet manure is pungent, so concentrated operations can cause air quality problems. Opposition to factory hog farms has come from small-scale farm operations, environmentalists, and those opposed to corporate agriculture for displacing independent family farms and negatively affecting rural communities.

The environmental concerns are both warranted and unwarranted. They are warranted in that larger volumes of manure do accumulate, which requires larger crop acreage to utilize these nutrients. They are unwarranted in that larger units are more likely to use more scientifically advanced waste-handling systems and water quality testing methods. In special cases, large volumes of manure also allow the use of manure in methane gas production and electricity generation.

Rising inflation, declining inflation, and deflationary monetary policies amplified the normal ups and downs of production agriculture. This added to political pressure from farmers to take action to offset economic impacts. The result has been a hodgepodge of short-term programs to funnel subsidies to farmers. These programs have had positive and negative environmental dimensions.

The one constant over the past thirty years is that the role of the federal government in U.S. agriculture has not diminished. It has simply shifted from micro management of farm production, storage, and marketing to dispensing income transfers from taxpayers to farmers who produce certain crops. The following is a retrospective on these programs.

FARM POLICY AND
ENVIRONMENTAL IMPACTS

Against the backdrop of rising inflation, declining inflation, and deflationary monetary policies, major farm laws were passed in 1973, 1978, 1981, 1985, 1990, and 1996. When each of these laws was passed, they were expected to last four or five years without amendment; however, there were farm program changes passed as part of annual appropriation bills. Each of these laws had direct and indirect environmental implications.

The 1973, 1978, 1981, and 1985 laws maintained acreage reduction programs (ARPs). ARPs, though still on the books between 1990 and 1996, were not used due to stronger prices in the market. ARPs were one of the policy tools used to maintain commodity prices within a range that would minimize the cost of farm programs to the government in light of continuing federal budget deficits. The 1996 farm law abandoned ARPs, allowing farmers to plant whatever mix of crops and acreage they chose in return for a schedule of declining annual fixed payments aimed at moving crop farmers from subsidies into a more market-based system.

The basic economic problem with the ARPs and crop set-asides, was that the opportunity cost to the individual farm was high in terms of foregone crop output. To offset that cost, producers increased their use of inputs (fertilizers, pesticides, and technologies) to maximize yields on the acres they were allowed to plant. Thus the acreage restrictions set the stage for potential environmental impacts, particularly that on surface water from the intensively cropped acres.

In addition, unilateral acreage reduction programs by the United States led to increased production by foreign competitors. Increased foreign output has its own environmental fallout over the longer run, particularly in the Southern Hemisphere where large areas of forestland and pastures were cleared for crop production.

Because farm program payments are based on volume of production, larger farms especially tend to purchase the more advanced technologies with the larger government subsidies. Larger farms, not the mythical small family farm, are more likely to practice superior conservation methods. For example, the 100-horsepower tractor (not common on smaller farms in the early 1970s), which facilitated deep chisel plowing and minimal tillage, did more to reduce soil erosion and water runoff from cropland than other conventional tillage practices, particularly in regions where the cropland terrain is more prone to soil erosion during heavy rainfall. Because larger farm units generally practice better conservation, the transfer of billions of taxpayer dollars to these farms via farm programs should have protected soil and water resources better than would have been the case otherwise.

Intensive agriculture has been credited by Alex Avery and Dennis Avery (2003) and others for improving the overall environment and increasing wildlife habitat through more productive use of existing cropland. But questions remain. Were farm programs responsible, to some extent at least, for this outcome? Could government subsidy incentives produce more conservation and more total output at the same time? The record supports this outcome. Erosion is down, fertilizer use efficiency is up, conservation tillage is up, and wetland losses are down. In addition to farm program subsidies that skew benefits to the large producers, there have been direct cost-sharing subsidies to farmers for carrying out specific conservation practices such as the construction of stock and retention ponds, grass waterways, and contour terraces.

Separating the positive contributions attributable to farm program subsidies from the positive contributions of direct government cost-sharing conservation practice payments is beyond the scope of this paper. It is likely that there has been more soil and water conservation during the past thirty years than would have been the case without taxpayer subsidies. What might have been the structure of farms and the condition of soil, water, and air, without federal interference is unknowable. Scientific measurement would be very difficult for a number of reasons, not the least of which is the large amount of cropland covered by farm programs, which is operated on a tenant basis. Historically, ownership of land has had more influence on farm operator adoption of conservation practices. Ownership tends to give incentives for long-term, low-return conservation investments.

The 1985 farm law ushered in the CRP. Since then, an estimated 35 million acres, an area about the size of Alabama, have been removed from crop production. For the most part, CRP acres are left to return to weed and brush growth with low maintenance and upkeep on the part of contractees. The basic appeal to farmers and their political representatives was that this was another way to funnel taxpayer monies to farmers while also currying favor with environmental and hunting interests. The federal government rents the CRP acreage from landowners under ten-year contracts. Land enrolled can be signed up again on a bid basis or taken out of the program. The environmental appeal was that by idling these cropland acres, soil and water would improve because there would be no pesticides, fertilizers, or soil erosion from the idled acreage. This presumption does not take into account the runoff from remaining acres that are more intensively cropped. Returning CRP acres to production after the contracts expire poses special challenges for crop producers in terms of land preparation. The environmental impact of the CRP also appears in cropping patterns by reducing the availability of cropland and pastureland for remaining farms. The law had the unintended consequence of harming some farms while helping others and subsidizing landowners who do not farm.

In the early stages of the policy debate on the 1985 farm legislation, there was a push by environmental activists to make reductions of up to 50 percent in the use of crop chemicals as a condition for participating in government farm programs. That idea was defeated when research showed higher farm production costs, reduced production and farm income, and higher food prices. Instead of mandated reductions in farm inputs as a condition for farmers getting federal subsidies, activists shifted to demands for farm-level conservation plans as a requirement for receiving federal subsidies. Conservation compliance plans essentially replaced the farm chemical and fertilizer use restrictions advocated early in the 1985 farm bill debate.

Absent throughout the farm policy and environmental debates since 1985 has been scientific research to clearly define, in site-specific terms, the role of U.S. crop and livestock production in soil erosion and water quality for both runoff and underground water supplies. There is little sound evidence of the impact of CRP, which has simply been asserted to be beneficial.

ENVIRONMENTAL POLICY
IMPACT ON AGRICULTURE

Although major environmental laws affecting crop and livestock producers were enacted in the early 1970s, the direct impacts on farms and ranches didn't really materialize until much later. For the most part, regulations promulgated to implement the Clean Water Act and the Endangered Species Act did not single out crop and livestock producers for regulatory compliance and penalties, but the effects have been huge.

The first signs of things to come were the federal regulations governing the use of chemicals in fruits and vegetable production subject to the Federal Insecticide, Fungicide and Rodenticide Act. In the early 1970s, regulations were adopted that governed the amount of time between chemical applications and when hired farmworkers could reenter the treated fields. The Endangered Species Act had its first major impact on farmers when DDT, which has been subsidized by the government, was removed from the market (Meiners and Morriss 2001). The first major conflict between farmers and the Clean Water Act was the arbitrary enforcement of wetland rules by the U.S. Army Corps of Engineers in the 1980s. The definition of "waters of the United States" was expanded by the corps to include, literally, isolated mud puddles in the midst of cropping areas. This expansion of federal land use control got the attention of farmers because most farmers have producing areas that are wet at least twenty-one days during some part of the year. The fear was that federal control over isolated wetlands (not bona fide marshes, bogs, and swamps) would ultimately lead to federal control and restrictions over the land adjacent the isolated wetlands.

Federal environmental involvement in agriculture shifted away from technical support and education to the criminalization of environmental rules governing the Clean Water Act and the Endangered Species Act in particular. This shift was at odds with the tradition in agriculture of having land-grant universities and the Soil Conservation Service define conservation problems, conduct research on alternative solutions, and use the Agricultural Extension Service to educate farmers about scientific practices to solve the problem at hand. Contour farming, grass waterways, retention ponds, stock ponds, and forestry practices are good examples of this effort. Indeed, farm ponds were often man-made wetlands.

Expansion of federal regulatory controls on land and water gave rise to the property rights movement. Those who became active in the movement were often farmers and landowners who experienced a direct confrontation with federal authorities over some regulatory restriction of their land. To the landowners, the restrictions on use seem to be a taking of property without compensation, but the law does not treat it that way.

An economic result of evolving federal enforcement of land and water use rules has been the unintended consequence of increasing farm size beyond what would have happened anyway. Farm units have gotten larger to accommodate the higher scientific, legal, and other costs of federal environmental interventions on farms, ranches, and forests. Today many large poultry, hog, and dairy operations have water quality programs that meet or exceed federal and state standards.

In retrospect, had farm, ranch, and forest owner/operators been shown the scientific evidence of water quality problems, endangered species problems, and farm chemical use problems in site- and farm-specific terms, and then shown economically viable solutions to real problems, the outcomes in terms of ecological gains likely would have been different, but may have been superior in some ways we cannot know.

The approach of first respecting private property would have evolved into a network of different programs and practices that reflect local conditions to achieve environmental gains at lower costs. Instead, federal command-and-control one-size-fits-all rules over land, water, and chemicals, have produced limited benefits at very high costs. There continues to be political controversy over farm and ranch ecology and substantial ill will among many farmers and ranchers toward the federal government. It is ironic that environmentalism should have a bad name to many who are on the front lines of environmental protection.

The possibility of criminal penalties, piled on top of costly and complex regulatory mandates, characterize the evolution of environmental policies for agriculture. This gave impetus to calls from producers for even more federal subsidies to offset these mandated costs. Had the environmental vision for agriculture been one of respecting private property and looking to markets and common law, the outcome would have been to solve real environmental and ecological problems where these did exist (Meiners and Yandle 1998). As it turns out, there are now federal rules for just about everything done on farms and ranches (Copeland 1995).

In spite of the federal regulatory overhead imposed on farm production, environmental gains remain elusive. In short, whatever farmers have done, it is never good enough. The goalposts continue to be moved simply because there have been no scientific standards defining the problems. "Fishable and swimmable" rivers are political, not scientific standards. It is not possible to achieve zero environmental impact from farm and ranching activities, or any other human activity.

At its basic economic impact level, environmental regulations have diverted capital on farms and ranches to a large but undetermined extent away from productive activity on how to produce low-cost bushels, bales, pounds, and hundredweights. This waste of capital is showing up in market share losses to foreign competitors where environmental standards are less stringent. It is beyond the scope of this paper to speculate on the magnitude of these losses, but one is left with the question of what would producers have done with the resources devoted to regulatory compliance? At a minimum, command and control of farm inputs has given political footing to farmers and their organizations to call for and defend increasingly larger subsidies from taxpayers. At the same time, there continues to be rapid development of new technologies that impact agriculture and the environment.

TECHNOLOGY'S IMPACT

During the past thirty years, crop and livestock production has changed dramatically. For major crops (wheat, soybeans, feed grains, and cotton), field practices have shifted from extensive use of moldboard plows to no till. On the livestock side, for example, it is commonplace to wean beef calves at 600 pounds at six months of age compared with 350 to 400 pounds at the same age in the early 1970s. Feed use efficiencies have risen dramatically for all classes of livestock and poultry.

The shift from conventional tillage to no tillage has meant a decrease in erosion but an increase in the use of weed control chemicals and fertilizers. This has produced criticisms from those opposed to such technology even though most chemicals break down in short periods. Substantial increases in wildlife numbers in many classes of game argues against the doomsday scenarios advanced by environmental activists. For example, in Wisconsin there was recently a debate about whether to have a hunting season on doves and sandhill cranes.

Larger field and harvesting equipment and advanced technologies have enabled crop producers to cope more effectively with the vagaries of weather. Planting and harvesting now happen very quickly, allowing the annual production of food and feedstuffs to leave a much smaller footprint on the natural landscape and resource base.

More drought-tolerant crop varieties have ensured some level of production when rainfall has been inadequate. The aggregate effect of improved varieties, larger and faster field equipment, and advanced technologies in fertilizers and pest controls is a lower cost food and feed supply. In effect, advanced equipment and other technologies have had a countervailing effect to government rules and regulations but not without the cost of a permanently altered farm structure.

Advances in technology have given rise to political issues. Biotechnology once touted as a superior alternative to increased chemical use is now considered by some to be an environmental problem (Goklany 2003). The idea of moving genes from one species to another is problematic to some scientists, ethicists, and farmers. Initial enthusiasm for developing plants resistant to pests and crops unaffected by certain weed-control chemicals has been dampened.

Opposition to rapidly changing technologies in agriculture has come from activists who believe that the structure of agriculture should be one of a large number of small to medium-size farms, not a small number of industrial-size farm units. The changed structure and number of farms were probably inevitable as farmers sought to improve their living standards through expanding output. Nevertheless, the federal government has subsidized the industrialized farm model to the detriment of mid-size units (units with less than $250,000 in annual sales). Environmental gains in crop production can be traced to a large extent to federal subsidies to larger farm units, which practice better conservation because these farms can spread the high-cost, low-return regulations over more output. The effects are often not easy to foresee.

There are no direct federal subsidies for beef, pork, poultry, and dairy producers; however, direct subsidies to feed grains and soybeans constitute indirect input subsidies to livestock, poultry, and dairy. Further, in the case of dairy, consumers provide subsidies via government-administered price floors for milk. On beef, pork, poultry, and dairy farms, manure is an important economic output. It can be an environmental problem with industrialized livestock operations where there are not enough available crop acres nearby to utilize the manure nutrients. Historically, small to mid-size livestock and poultry farms have maintained reasonable environmental balances between manure produced and manure utilized on crops. These practices occurred without direct government subsidies.

Scientific handling of waste is still in its infancy in terms of testing the waste for nutrients and testing the soils for nutrient loadings. Problems have arisen in areas where phosphorus and nitrate loadings exceed that which can be efficiently utilized by crops. These problems are being highly scrutinized in light of pending federal nonpoint source water quality regulations as Yandle and Blacklocke (2003) discuss in this volume.

INTERNATIONAL TRADE

On the international trade front, the links are less obvious between the environment and agriculture. Two major embargos stand out as having significant short- and long-run environmental implications. The first embargo in the early 1970s was justified by the government on the basis of a short supply of soybeans, soy oil, and meal. This came on the heels of inflated food prices and the need for government to take action to appease consumers. The second embargo, in 1980, was against the Soviet Union for its invasion of Afghanistan. Both of these major trade interventions set in motion events at home and abroad that had environmental repercussions.

At the farm level, both embargos caused a drop in prices, which became the basis for calls by U.S. farmers and their organizations to do something to offset the negative price impact. The federal government reacted with combinations of acreage-reduction programs and farmer-held but government-run storage programs. As noted, acreage-reduction programs generally caused crop producers to use more inputs on remaining cropland in order to maximize yields to offset the high opportunity cost of the ARPs in subsequent crop years. The ARPs were not usually one-year events. Storage programs allowed the federal government to determine the acceptable range of commodity prices in which it would allow grain to enter or exit the grain storage programs. Thus, upside profit opportunities for producers were essentially eliminated. Government-managed grain storage and acreage-reduction programs were the principal policy instruments with which government tried to control the cost of the farm program in light of continued budget deficits.

Reducing the acres planted in theory had potential environmental benefits via resting the soil and reducing erosion and runoff. It should be noted, however, that when ARPs, set-asides, soil banks, and CRP acres are returned to production, substantially more soil preparation and weed and pest control are required before planting.

An important environmental aspect of the trade embargos was the long-term increase in risk and uncertainty at the producer level. Producers probably placed a much lower priority on land and water conservation and much higher priority on economic survival in the face of political risk and uncertainty.

Aside from the economic disruption in the United States from embargos, there was the international reaction, which also had environmental and ecological ramifications. In response to the embargo of soybeans, the Japanese made substantial investments in South American soybean production. Vast areas were cleared and put into production, especially in Brazil, which obviously had environmental impacts.

Over time, farm exports recovered from the adverse impacts of embargos, but the longer-term environmental picture is still unfolding as production continues to increase in Southern Hemisphere countries. Within the United States, there remains the long-term land retirement program (the CRP). The fact that the nation has retired almost 35 million acres annually for the past several years, and has conducted other acreage-reduction programs from time to time has not been without economic costs. The United States has lost some of its competitive position in the world marketplace by trying to hold domestic prices above world price levels; foreign producers exploit the consequences of these domestic policies.

CONCLUSION

Public policy decisions, particularly those with regard to agriculture are all about responding to the short run, rarely the long run, contrary to political rhetoric. My career spanned a long run by economists' standards, but I worked in a series of short runs. This chapter is an effort to describe the underlying economic forces that gave rise to a variety of short-term policy decisions that impacted farming and the environment.

Over the past thirty years, about $275 billion was transferred from taxpayers to farmers. In addition, there have been substantial subsidies from federal and state taxpayers to the land-grant universities. The combination of these direct and indirect subsidies has produced more of everything: commodity, livestock, technical innovation and implementation, and conservation and environmental gains.

Government intervened in numerous ways to reduce the risk in farming, much of which was government induced in the first place: rising inflation, declining inflation, deflation, embargos, food safety rules, the risk and uncertainty of the right to own, use, and dispose of private property, and ever stronger environmental rules.

The taxpayer money transferred to farmers simply fanned the fires of the technological revolution in agriculture that was already under way. Although most of the short-term policy responses to the government-induced risk had some negative environmental implications as the short-term programs were implemented, the key impact on farms was that the taxpayer and consumer transfers to the larger operations were being used to purchase or rent more land and to purchase the more advanced technologies. Advanced technologies, combined with economies of scale, have produced an intensive agriculture that, on balance, is more environmentally benign.

The farm and agribusiness support structure that has emerged is not without its critics. The criticism is based on the decline in rural communities due to the decline in small and mid-size family farm units. Another criticism is that larger farms use more fertilizers and chemicals and therefore contribute to environmental degradation. These criticisms are not well founded. Larger and more technologically sophisticated farm operations are able to plant and harvest crops quicker and more in harmony with natural conditions. Livestock productivity has made similar progress in that larger units are more likely to comply or exceed a multiplicity of environmental standards.

An important question for further research remains: What would have been the relationship between agriculture and the environment had not the farm sector had so much federal intervention and subsequent federal subsidies during the past three decades? One can only speculate on what might have happened without federal subsidies. The rate of technological development and adoption would have likely been much slower, and therefore the environmental gains would have likely occurred at a slower rate.

Having said this, the present farm program and other risk-reducing programs such as federally subsidized crop insurance, which transfers billions of taxpayer monies to large farm operations, is, in many instances, at cross purposes with the environment because crops are planted on acres that would likely be in timber or pasture. But with the high level of federal subsidies to agriculture over the years, there has been an increasing level of inefficient and counterproductive environmental regulations.

In summary, taxpayers heavily subsidized the farm sector on both the farm input side (via the land-grant research system) and on the output side (via price and income guarantees). The output-side subsidies were largely in response to various macro government-induced risks and uncertainties. In the process of short-term policy actions and reactions, subsidies have produced a permanently altered farm structure that has produced cheaper food and released human resources to other productive activities. It is now time for policy makers to revisit farm policy, eliminate the welfare transfers, and treat farming as the business that it is.

Those who worry about the link between agriculture and the environment should consider the impact of monetary policy stability. Consistent monetary policy would shift farm policy decisions back to real farming, conservation, and resource allocations for the longer run. Removing inflationary and deflationary expectations is essential to the long-term husbandry of resources:

> An important institutional challenge during the twenty-first century will be to manage our system of money and credit so as to achieve a reasonably stable price level, a matter of immense importance to agriculture, especially in a global economy. We are only recently free of a long period of sustained inflation. Will that stability continue? Will it deflate? Or will inflation return? (Paarlberg and Paarlberg 2000, 142)

POLICY RECOMMENDATIONS SPECIFIC TO
AGRICULTURE AND THE ENVIRONMENT

For good or ill, the structure of agriculture has been permanently altered by federal interventions, subsidies, and regulations of land, water, and air resources. Because the structure has changed, antiquated federal programs should be changed to reflect the changed farm structure. The "family farm" is political rhetoric that continues to serve, along with environmental rhetoric, to justify a grab bag of agricultural programs, such as the ethanol subsidy discussed by Gary Libecap (2003). Rational policy can address economic, environmental, and ethical concerns, but only by reducing pandering to special interests.

First, for the large-output farms there should be no direct subsidy payments. These farms should only be eligible for a loan rate based on or near the variable cost of production, e.g., $1.20 per bushel for corn. These farms can compete on the world market and can manage their risks, and would be more inclined to do so, if government bailouts were the exception, not the rule. It is now time for these sophisticated business operations that happen to be in agriculture to behave the way other businesses operate in a free market economy.

Second, for farmers without sufficient volume of output to provide the living standards to which they aspire, the following is a potential solution. If a farmer cannot be retrained and is nearing retirement, give him or her a one-time golden government parachute equal to the discounted present value of what he or she expects to receive from social security at age sixty-two. This farmer could invest the money as desired but the farm would only be eligible for the low loan rate "safety" net applied to the large-scale units. There would be no return trips to the federal treasury.

If a farmer is young enough to be retrained for a more productive activity than farming, then the taxpayers would pay for the training with a onetime grant. This plays off the welfare to workforce program that has been successful in the nonfarm sector in some states in reducing the welfare burden. Block grants to the states would be a good approach for conducting this program. The University of Minnesota already has an extension service program to evaluate a farm for long-term real economic viability. If the farmer wishes to continue farming after being retrained, he or she would do so only with a low loan rate "safety net" equal to the rate set for the large-output producer.

Third, for the small-output part-time farmer there would be no federal assistance. This is a lifestyle choice for most of these operators, and they can continue to subsidize their part-time farming with off-farm employment.

For the environment, existing extension service resources can be redirected to gather scientific site-specific water and soil quality data over time. Such analysis could contribute to the public debate on agriculture and the environment. If water quality problems are traced directly to farm activity, they will have to be dealt with by the farmers in that watershed. As Avery and Avery (2003) discuss, major policies for land use are being discussed without benefit of good science about the immediate and secondary environmental impacts.

Lawmakers and regulators at the federal and state levels have passed laws and enacted land, water, and air controls that have ignored the basics of food and fiber production and distribution in the United States: wide variations in rainfall and overall climatic conditions and soil types, crop and livestock patterns, length of growing seasons, and political constraints on biotechnology and farmer/rancher management skills. Lawmakers have generally ignored the fact that farming, ranching, and livestock production depend on the rights to own, use, and dispose of private property. By ignoring such fundamentals, farmers and livestock producers must now confront and spend an inordinate amount of time dealing with a plethora of costly, inefficient, and overlapping rules that have very little if anything to do with improving the overall quality of resources but have a lot to do with expanding government controls over productive resources.

Prior to the past thirty years, government involvement in farm level decision making on land, water, and air resource uses was largely confined to research, education, technical support, and cost sharing to reduce wind and water erosion problems on farms and ranches. Producers responded to these initiatives because it was in their self-interest to do so and because they were involved in soil and water conservation decisions on their land.

Future policy makers and agency rule makers who ignore conservation history and farm and ranch economic fundamentals and who try to impose top-down one-size-fits-all rules for dealing with real environmental problems are destined to failure. Penalizing all farms to get at the few bad actors or a problem peculiar to a certain area is costly, inefficient, and ineffective.

A more enlightened approach would be to spend limited taxpayer monies on watershed level research to first define water- and land-quality problems. A similar approach could be done for airsheds. Once the real problems have been identified, then private interests working via an updated watershed conservation district model can evolve the educational and technical support to develop bottom-up solutions that respect private property, market-driven incentives, common law, and taxpayer resources.

The role of the federal government should be substantially diminished in favor of local and state governments, those units closest to natural resource problems and those units to which the farmer and rancher have more ready access and recourse. Failure to move environmental policies for agriculture in this direction will mean a continued erosion of the economic foundation of agriculture and basic rights to own, use, and dispose of private property. With such erosion there will be a parallel decline in the competitiveness of the farm and ranch sector. That would be a loss of economic opportunity and freedom for all.

NOTES

1. Target prices are the politically determined level of prices against which the government determines payments to farmers. If market prices fall below government-set target prices, the federal government makes up the difference between the market price and the target price through cash payments based on the production level at the farm. Government loan rates are also set by politicians. The loan rate is the price a farmer receives for the cotton, rice, corn, soybeans, wheat, other feed grains, and sugar. When the market price is below the loan rate at the end of the contract period (usually nine or ten months) the government is stuck with the commodity, and stockpiles generally accumulate.

2. Federal budget deficits forced Congress to limit the amount of cash available for farmers. The commodities forfeited to the government under the loan program were

given back to farmers via PIK certificates. Farmers then sold the certificates to grain handlers or other farmers. They then used the certificates to redeem grain from government stockpiles.

3. "More market orientation" has been the political slogan for all recent farm bills. The actual economic outcome has been more, not less, dependence on government payments as a share of net farm income.

4. The CRP was a response to the environmental critics and farmers who were looking for another legitimate way to receive government payments. Up to 35 million acres could be enrolled in the program under ten-year contracts. Farmers submitted bids to their county USDA farm service agency office as to the price per acre they would accept to put all or part of their land in the CRP. In addition to environmental and farmer support for the CRP, the hunting lobby also threw its political weight behind the CRP as an expansion of habitat for hunting.

5. Taxpayer support for farmers takes a variety of forms. These include the loan deficiency payments, when market prices fall below government-set loan prices, market transition payments, market loss assistance payments for loss of export markets due to foreign trade restrictions on U.S. imports, supplemental market transition payments for persistent low farm prices, disaster assistance payments for natural and or economic disasters, an environmental quality insurance program, a wetland reserve program, and a conservation reserve program. Transfers other than those for conservation and water quality are based on historical production. Therefore, large-output farms receive larger government payments that enable larger farm units to outbid other farms for available land and more advanced technologies.

REFERENCES

Avery, Alex, and Dennis Avery. 2003. High-Yield Conservation: More Food and Environmental Quality through Intensive Agriculture. This volume.

Copeland, John D. 1995. The Criminalization of Environmental Law: Implications for Agriculture. *Oklahoma Law Review* 48: 237–38.

Drury, Renee, and Luther Tweeten. 1999. Trends in Farm Structure into the 21st Century. A report submitted to the American Farm Bureau Federation. Ohio State University, Columbus.

Goklany, Indur M. 2003. Agricultural Technology and the Precautionary Principle. This volume.

Libecap, Gary D. 2003. Agricultural Programs with Dubious Environmental Benefits: The Political Economy of Ethanol. This volume.

Meiners, Roger E., and Andrew P. Morriss. 2001. Pesticides and Property Rights. *PERC Policy Series*, PS-22. Bozeman, MT: PERC, May.

Meiners, Roger E., and Bruce Yandle. 1998. The Common Law: How It Protects the Environment. *PERC Policy Series*, PS-13. Bozeman, MT: PERC, May.

Paarlberg, Don, and Philip Paarlberg. 2000. *The Agricultural Revolution of the 20th Century*. Ames: Iowa State University Press.

Yandle, Bruce, and Sean Blacklocke. 2003. Regulating Concentrated Animal Feeding Operations: Internalization or Cartelization? This volume.

Index

acreage reduction programs (ARPs), 180–81
adaptation criterion, 110; GM crops and, 126
agrarianism, 3–4, 6–7, 14n4
Agricultural Adjustment Act, 11
agricultural fundamentalism, 3–4, 6–7, 14n4
air quality: carbon emissions and, 151–53; concentrated animal feeding operations and, 47–48, 62n4; ethanol and, 89–99, 98–99, 101; precautionary principle and, 108–9; technology and, 111
antitrust law, 33–34
Archer Daniels Midland, 90

Baird v. Upper Canal Irrigation Co., 82
biodiversity, 135–37, 140, 141
biotechnology. *See* genetically modified crops
bison, 21
bootleggers and Baptists model, 2–3
Brown v. Maryland, 8
brucellosis, 19, 20
Bureau of Reclamation, 10, 14n9

Campaign for Sustainable Agriculture, 13
carbon emissions, xv, 151–52; greenhouse effect and, 153–54, 164; income and, 152–53, 164–66, 169; land conversion and, 160; natural sources of, 156–57; transfers of, 155–56
carbon sequestration, 152, 154; exports and, 162; fire suppression and, 158; forest harvest and, 158–59; livestock and, 166–68; oceanic, 154–55; silviculture and, 158; soil organic carbon (SOC) and, 160; terrestrial, 155–56; U.S. and, 169
carbon sinks, 151–52, 154; anthropogenic, 161–62; atmospheric carbon levels and, 157–58; livestock and, 166–68; oceanic, 154–55; savanna ecosystems and, 159; U.S. and, 169
cartels: concentrated animal feeding operations and, 45, 46; environmental legislation and, 60–62, 62–63n8; pollution and, 56–59
Clean Air Act, 92, 94–97
Clean Water Act, 57, 61–62, 183

About the Political Economy
Forum Series

PERC is the nation's oldest and largest institute dedicated to original research that brings market principles to resolving environmental problems. PERC, located in Bozeman, Montana, pioneered the approach known as free market environmentalism. It is based on the following tenets: (1) private property rights encourage stewardship of resources; (2) some government policies degrade the environment; (3) market incentives spur individuals to conserve resources and protect environmental quality; and (4) polluters should be liable for the harm they cause others. PERC associates have applied the free market environmentalism approach to a variety of issues, including national parks, resource development, water marketing, integrity of fisheries, private provision of wildlife habitat, public land management, and endangered species protection.

PERC's activities encompass three areas: research and policy analysis, outreach, and environmental education. Its associates conduct research, write books and articles, and lecture on the role of markets and property rights in environmental protection. PERC holds conferences and seminars for journalists, congressional staff members, business executives, and scholars. PERC also holds an annual free market environmentalism seminar for college students and sponsors a fellowship program that brings graduate students to its facilities for three months of research and study on an environmental topic. PERC develops and disseminates environmental education materials for classroom use and provides training for kindergarten through twelfth-grade teachers.

In 1989, PERC organized the first of an annual conference series called the Political Economy Forum aimed at applying the principles of political economy to important policy issues. Each forum brings together scholars in economics, political science, law, history, and other disciplines to discuss and refine academic papers that explore new applications of political economy to policy analysis. The forum papers are then edited and published as a book in PERC's Political Economy Forum Series. PERC believes that forums of this type can integrate "cutting edge" research with crucial policy issues.

The papers that form the chapters in this volume were prepared for a December 2001 Political Economy Forum, "Environmental Policy and Agriculture: Conflicts, Prospects, and Implications," which was held at Chico Hot Springs, Montana. Organized and directed by PERC senior associates Roger E. Meiners and Bruce Yandle, the forum focused on the environmental record and challenges faced by U.S. production agriculture. The papers span topics as broad as why farming receives special treatment by government and as narrow as environmental policies related to confined animal feeding operations. Throughout the papers, the authors focus on economic incentives and market forces that affect environmental outcomes.

PERC hopes that scholarship such as this will help advance the environmental policy debate and looks forward to future volumes in this series.

The forum participants were as follows: Terry L. Anderson, PERC and Hoover Institution; Bruce Beattie, University of Arizona; Thomas R. DeGregori, University of Houston; Susan Dudley, Mercatus Center; Molly Espey, Clemson University; Holly Lippke Fretwell, PERC; Robert Innes, University of Arizona; Russell Lamb, North Carolina State University; Clay Landry, PERC; Hertha Lund, Washington State Farm Bureau; Brian Mannix, Mercatus Center; and Richard L. Stroup, PERC and Montana State University.

About the Contributors

Alex Avery is director of research and education at the Center for Global Food Issues at the Hudson Institute. He received his bachelor's degree in biology and chemistry from Old Dominion University. Previous to joining the Center in 1994, Avery was a McKnight research fellow at Purdue University conducting basic plant research with the goal of improving grain production in the African Sudan. He also represented the center at the United Nations World Food Summit in Rome in 1996.

Dennis T. Avery is director of the Center for Global Food Issues at the Hudson Institute, a nonprofit public policy think tank headquartered in Indianapolis, Indiana. He was raised on a U.S. dairy farm and studied agricultural economics at Michigan State and Wisconsin. He has done agricultural policy analysis for the U.S. Department of Agriculture and President Johnson's National Advisory Commission on Food and Fiber. He also served for nearly a decade as the senior agricultural analyst for the U.S. State Department, where he won the National Intelligence Medal of Achievement in 1983.

Sean Blacklocke specializes in research on the use of markets for managing water quality. He was employed in water quality management with the South Carolina Department of Health and Environmental Control, worked as a research assistant with the Clemson University Department of Agricultural and Applied Economics and was a KCI fellow at PERC when this research was completed. Blacklocke holds an M.S. degree in environmental science from the South Carolina Medical University and an M.S. in agricultural economics from Clemson University.

B. Delworth Gardner is professor emeritus of economics at Brigham Young University and professor emeritus of agricultural economics at the University of California–Davis. He was educated at the University of Wyoming and at the University of Chicago. He has held professorial appointments at Colorado State University, Utah State University, the University of California–Davis, Brigham Young University, and the Foreign Affairs College in Beijing, China. Gardner was director of the Giannini Foundation of Agricultural Economics at the University of California from 1976 to 1984, and he is a fellow of the American Agricultural Economics Association. Research interests lie mainly in the fields of water economics, public land policies, agricultural and resources policy, and international development.

Indur M. Goklany has worked with federal and state government and the private sector on food security, agriculture, land use, biotechnology, biodiversity, and other natural resource and environmental issues for more than twenty-five years. He has written extensively in the peer-reviewed literature and elsewhere on the impacts of agricultural technology on public health and the environment, and was probably the first to note that greater productivity means lower land conversion to agricultural uses. In 2000 he was selected as the first D&D Foundation Julian Simon Fellow at PERC, Bozeman, Montana. He is the author of *Clearing the Air: The True Story of the War on Air Pollution* and *The Precautionary Principle: A Critical Assessment of Environmental Risk Assessment.*

Peter J. Hill is professor of economics at Wheaton College, where he holds the George F. Bennett chair. He is a senior associate of PERC. His research and articles, especially on the evolution of property rights in the American West, helped found the new resource economics that is the basis for free market environmentalism. He is coauthor, with Terry L. Anderson, of *The Birth of a Transfer Society* and, with Joseph L. Bast and Richard C. Rue, of *Eco-Sanity: A Common Sense Guide to Environmentalism.* As an economic consultant he has worked with the Bulgarian government in its attempts to privatize agricultural lands. Hill has a B.S. from Montana State University and a Ph.D. from the University of Chicago.

John K. Hosemann had a twenty-seven-year career at the American Farm Bureau Federation at its Chicago headquarters. He worked as a commodity policy analyst and as a research economist before spending twenty years as chief economist and director of the Public Policy Division. His duties included advising the president, board of directors, and other leaders with regard to the economic impact of policies affecting farmers and ranchers. He spoke to a wide range of farm and nonfarm audiences on the importance of federal monetary and fiscal policies on agriculture in addition to his work on farm and environmental policies. He holds B.S. and M.S. degrees from Mississippi State University in agricultural economics and did doctoral work in the same field at Virginia Polytechnic Institute. Hosemann retired to his farm in Wisconsin in June 2000 where he continues to write and speak on policies affecting agriculture.

W. Walker Hunter III is a graduate student at Clemson University in South Carolina. His research interests are currently free market environmentalism and financial economics. Hunter's research experience includes being a Julian Simon research assistant at PERC during the summer of 2001, and presently a graduate research assistant at Clemson.

Gary D. Libecap is Anheuser Busch Professor and professor of economics and law, the University of Arizona; director, Karl Eller Center, Eller College of Business & Public Administration; and research associate, National Bureau of Economic Research. He is former editor of the *Journal of Economic History* and member of the National Science Foundation Economics Panel. His research has focused on the development of property rights and regulatory institutions and their impact on economic behavior. Subject areas include natural resources, environment, and legislative and bureaucratic actions.

Robert E. McCormick is professor and BB&T scholar in the John E. Walker Department of Economics at Clemson University. He is director of the Center for Legal Studies and Policy Analysis in the College of Business at Clemson and codirector of the Kinship Conservation Institute, an educational enterprise collaboration between PERC and the Kinship Foundation. McCormick's research spans industrial organization and the theory of the firm and public choice economics. He is currently an associate editor of the *Journal of Corporate Finance.*

Roger E. Meiners is professor of law and economics at the University of Texas at Arlington and a PERC senior associate. He received his Ph.D. in economics from Virginia Tech and his law degree from the University of Miami where he was an Olin fellow at the Law and Economics Center. He has taught at Texas A&M University, Emory University, Clemson University, and the University of Miami, and he was director of the Atlanta office of the Federal Trade Commission. Meiners is coeditor with Peter J. Hill of *Who Owns the Environment* (1998), with Andrew Morriss of *The Common Law and the Environment* (2000), and has written other books and articles on law and economics.

Andrew P. Morriss is a senior associate at PERC and Galen J. Roush Professor of Business Law and Regulation at Case Western Reserve University

School of Law, Cleveland, Ohio. He has an A.B. from Princeton, a J.D. and master's of public affairs from the University of Texas at Austin, and a Ph.D. in economics from Massachusetts Institute of Technology. He has written numerous articles and book chapters on environmental issues, including work published in the *Ecology Law Quarterly*, *Environmental Law*, the *Tulane Environmental Law Journal*, and the *Oregon Law Review*.

Joshua A. Utt is completing a Ph.D. in economics from Washington State University. His dissertation will explore further the field of carbon sequestration. During 2001 Utt was a PERC graduate fellow and a research assistant with the Center for Policy and Legal Studies at Clemson University. Former employment includes the Cato Institute and the U.S. Senate Committee on Energy and Natural Resources. His interests include the application of market incentives to environmental policy, the economics of corruption, and sports economics.

Bruce Yandle is a PERC senior associate and alumni distinguished professor of economics emeritus at Clemson University. He is a faculty member with George Mason University's Capitol Hill Campus. Yandle received an A.B. from Mercer University and a Ph.D. from Georgia State University. He served as senior economist on the President's Council on Wage and Price Stability and as executive director of the Federal Trade Commission. Yandle is author or editor of many books, including *The Political Limits of Environmental Regulation*, *Common Sense and Common Law for the Environment*, and *Land Rights: The 1990s' Property Rights Rebellion*. He is a member of the editorial board of the *European Journal of Law & Economics*.

Date Due

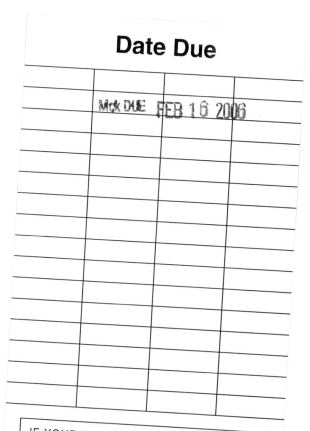

McK DUE FEB 16 2006